Rachel Lumsden
Return of the Huntress

[English]

Verlag für moderne Kunst

This publication and the accompanying exhibition bring together Rachel Lumsden's latest paintings with works from recent years. They offer a view of a work that is characterised by an intensive contemporaneity, a diversity of pictorial language and unconventionality.

Lumsden is image-hungry, even more: she seems to be able to feed herself from today's flood of media images. She takes everything: newspaper photos, art historical images, dream pictures, circuit diagrams, advertising material ... Insatiable and curious, she guzzles enormous amounts of source material which she collects from the length and breadth of both the physical and digital world in order to feed her own visual process.

The fact that the process does not stop as a mere sampling or collage, but in the end generates imagery as unexpected as it is matter of course, is actually the significance of this visual fusion process. It is Lumsden's use of paint as material which enables a seamlessness and burgeoning in her painting. In her hands, paint is not subordinated, but stands with integrity in its own right and can thus act as a substance according to its own nature.

This, and Lumsden's insight that every painting obeys only its own rules, leads to an astonishing variety of visual language. She is not interested in style as a business card; but seeks out the "painterly risk", there where content and paint cross paths "off-piste", perhaps to trigger a visual avalanche. But neither is this breaking new ground an end in itself, but rather an attempt to move closer to the mysterious inner life of the painting, the true pulse, that Lumsden, time and again touches upon in her work without needing to explain.

Showing the world over and again in a new light, century by century, is the miracle of painting. With regards both to this great historic tradition as well as to the here and now of contemporaneity, Lumsden's work meets us head on as a reality. To explore this reality in depth is the purpose of this publication and the exhibition.

The solo exhibition of Rachel Lumsden's work from the last ten years is the most comprehensive presentation of her paintings to date. It is also the result of a fruitful collaboration between three institutions: the Fondation Fernet-Branca in Saint-Louis, France, the Kunsthaus Pasquart in Biel, Switzerland and the Kunst(Zeug)Haus in Rapperswil-Jona, Switzerland. We are extremely grateful to Rachel Lumsden for the generosity and commitment she has given to the exhibition and publication. We would also like to thank Bernard Jordan, as well as the funding bodies – Kulturförderung Kanton St. Gallen, Lotteriefonds Kanton Thurgau, RHW Stiftung, Stadt St. Gallen Fachstelle Kultur, the Stanley Thomas Johnson Foundation and the Swiss Arts Council Pro Helvetia – who have given invaluable support. Not least we would like to thank Charlotte Mullins and André Rogger for their insightful texts and Thomas Bizzarri and Alain Rodriguez for their innovative and elegant design for this publication.

Pierre-Jean Sugier
Fondation Fernet-Branca

Felicity Lunn
Kunsthaus Pasquart

Peter Stohler
Kunst(Zeug)Haus Rapperswil-Jona

2

As the twentieth century dawned, Dutch writer and psychiatrist Frederik van Eeden was busy recording hundreds of his lucid dreams. In his subsequent novel, *The Bride of Dreams* (1913), he wrote, 'He who dreams is more awake than he who sleeps,' concluding, 'The solution of the secret of our lives lies in our dreams'.[1] Rachel Lumsden's paintings seem directly connected to the potency of dreams and their intangible promises. With their spectral figures, rich spectrums of colour, unruly patterns and claustrophobic interiors her paintings impact on the mind with a similar intensity to memorable dreams, offering an emotive network of connections whose overall meaning nevertheless remains tantalisingly out of reach. Each painting fills the viewer's field of vision and overwhelms the senses, transporting us elsewhere, to places with their own internal logic, places that feel strangely believable despite often including fantastical elements.

Haruki Murakami – a novelist Lumsden admires and whose novels have a shared hallucinogenic intensity – encapsulated the emotive power of dreams in his short story 'Sleep'. The narrator describes a 'dark, slimy dream', explaining: 'I don't remember what it was about, but I do remember how it felt: ominous and terrifying.'[2] In a similar way, Lumsden's paintings appear not as clear-cut narratives but as states of mind, as affecting experiences.

Lumsden moved to Switzerland from England fifteen years ago. An occasional motif reflects her Swiss surroundings – the snow poles in *Rope Walk* (2015, p. 46), for example – but Lumsden's landscape is overwhelmingly an internal one. Childhood experiences, fairy tales, dreams, paintings and photographs all impact on her work as she draws on memories and asks them to coalesce on the canvas. Her deep knowledge of painting, both historic and contemporary, is much in evidence in her recent paintings. In *Return of the Huntress* (2016, p.28) the echo of Pieter Bruegel the Elder's *Hunters in the Snow* (1565) is self-evident, but now the hunter (the artist) has become female and hunts alone. She walks away from the viewer towards a vertiginous snowy bank that overlooks a contemporary urban landscape under a viridian and magenta sky. Paint leaches between the branches of the skeletal trees, pinning the image to the surface of the canvas, forcing the eye to oscillate between following the huntress down the bank and tracking the aurora of paint across the surface.

In several recent interiors, such as *Antechamber* (2015, p. 13), *Here we go Again* (2014, p. 89) and *Red Room* (2016, p. 91), Lumsden's repeated use of mirrors and frames questions where the viewing experience begins and ends. In *Here we go Again* a gilt-edged mirror dominates the picture plane, creating doubles of the ornaments on the mantelpiece, bringing into view a woman's head, a partridge on a perch, a lively blue shadow that threatens to break free from its domestic source. The ambiguity of Édouard Manet's *A Bar At The Folies-Bergère* (1882) collides with the cluttered interior of Walter Sickert's *The Mantelpiece* (c. 1906–07), as mementoes from Lumsden's life – a ceramic dog, porcelain pugilists, a statue of a Storm Trooper – crowd into the frame. In *Red Room* a similar mirror reflects a room we cannot see for ourselves. The parrot on a stand morphs into a hook-beaked crow, its ominous shadow reminding the viewer that all is not as it seems. Perhaps the conjured crow alludes to Plato's shadows on the cave wall; is the domestic world not to be trusted? The flame-red and charcoal-black room seems charged with possibility, with latent change, as if it could spontaneously combust or dissolve when the dream ends.

At the epicentre of Lumsden's work lies the figure, whether as an amorphous form, as in *Sailing to Byzantium* (2016, p. 73), or more clearly delineated, as in *Lightning Rod (Mr and Mrs Andrews)* (2016, p. 80). (In *Red Room* the figure is absent but an empty chair suggests the possibility of presence.) The figure is never a direct portrait but is put to work to serve the painting as a whole, at times reduced to a suggestive shape or presence, at other times obliterated by a bold surface gesture (as in *Lightning Rod*) to ensure tautness between three-dimensional subject and two-dimensional painting. For while many of Lumsden's large paintings have discernible subjects – figures, interiors, city skylines – there is always a sense that the paint on the surface has the upper hand.

Often Lumsden is drawn to unusual motifs, such as the doppelgänger in *Leap Minute* (2015, p. 31), the goggled figures in *Crow Tribe* (2016, p. 101) or the anthropomorphic bear in *Highway Gamblers* (2008, Fig. H, p. 128). There's more than a hint of what Sigmund Freud called the *unheimlich* or the uncanny at play, but ultimately it is the paint that encodes this reading. As Lumsden says, 'You go on an adventure when you paint. In one sense you think, don't do too much, leave some areas open, but then there's a sense that if the subject is known, what is beyond that?'[3] In *Leap Minute* Lumsden ended up painting out the girls' faces, renouncing their identity for a more unsettling experience where their heads swivel untethered and the wallpaper behind them becomes surface pattern and slides over the couch. Lumsden wants to retain slippage in each work, space for the viewer to enter and form their own opinions. She doesn't want to pin things down too much and allows paint to have its head, trusting decisions made while working rather than adhering to a rigid plan.

This approach has been pushed to the limits in her recent paintings, particularly in the interiors that threaten to disassemble into a flurry of abstract marks. In *The Elder Flower* (2015, p.51) a woman in a dark dress stands up from a chair, slats of sunlight illuminating her face. However only in reproduction is such a clear reading possible. When you stand before the painting the surface almost entirely breaks down: the sunlight becomes a creamy white fluorescence; the shadows of pale blue, cobalt and aubergine run like railway sleepers across the surface and the face – if we can even call it that – comprises white and taupe patches over a scumbled blue ground. A solitary circle of white tethers the facial marks so we intuit an eye, a brow, a chin. This symbiotic relationship between subject and surface is something Lumsden calls 'splitting the atom', asking the paint to 'moonlight' as subject while the subject itself explodes into loops and whorls, patterns of colour and form.[4] The point at which both are possible and simultaneously present charges the work with a crackling energy.

Ultimately the paint drives Lumsden on, whether to create the sherberty-orange glow in *End of a Short Day* (2015, p.49) or the bold borealis in *Return of the Huntress*. It is sparse and dry in *Think Tank* (2015, p.21), scratchy and highly-strung in *Leap Minute*, fiery and wraithlike in *Red Room*. Paint, in her hands, catches in the throat of the viewer, its myriad colours infusing our minds and connecting directly with our hearts. These are not paintings to be read from afar, or in reproduction, but to be physically experienced, to be felt – and to be dreamt.

Endnotes

1   Frederik van Eeden, *The Bride of Dreams*, 1913, extract in *States of Mind: Experiences at the Edge of Consciousness*, ed. by Anna Faherty, ex. cat. (London: Wellcome Collection 2016) pp. 112–114.
2   Haruki Murakami, 'Sleep', in *The Elephant Vanishes* (London: Vintage, 1994), pp.105–106.
3   The artist in conversation with the author, 29 November 2016.
4   ibid.

It's a late winter afternoon, the sky mauve and emerald, the light subdued. The huntress returns over the brow of the hill towards a cityscape of office buildings, factories and rooftop car parks, a dog trotting at her heels. It is very still.

We are some distance behind the huntress, almost at the very border of the canvas where slushy white brushstrokes sit between black vertical bands that, under the spell of the huntress, become trees.

We are aware of how *Return of the Huntress* (2016, p. 28), a new painting by Rachel Lumsden, is constructed; aware of the materiality of the paint with thick impastos over thin bleeding washes; aware of the celebration of the way paint can be pushed and shoved over a surface, how it can be coaxed and manipulated to evoke texture and depth and, yes, touch and sound … and yet we are the huntress too, she walks with us, we walk with her.

All of these qualities were inherent in Rachel Lumsden's work fifteen years ago but as this publication and the exhibition it accompanies demonstrate, her paintings have moved through many changes in that time, both in terms of subject matter and the handling of paint.

When Lumsden arrived in St. Gallen from London in 2002 it was only four years after she had graduated with an MA in painting from The Royal Academy Schools. The legacy of Francis Bacon, Lucian Freud, Frank Auerbach and other painters of the London School, as well as the more recent influence of artists such as Peter Doig, Elizabeth Peyton or Dexter Dalwood, have kept figurative painting in Britain very much in the spotlight. It is no coincidence, then, that Lumsden's approach to her medium has much in common with these precedents, and that her style stands out in the Swiss art scene as being palpably different. Her surprisingly large paintings are at least as big as Lumsden herself, ensuring both her own physical relationship with the work and a direct engagement of the viewer. They communicate a strong sense of how they were created, of an artist sensitive to the character of her material and how it operates. Lumsden's work cannot be described as narrative as the paintings are too open-ended and ambiguous to be clearly read; instead they depict charged atmospheric environments, bristling with energy. Her chosen themes combine the overlooked paraphernalia of the everyday with the fantastical, autobiographical fragments with those from the collective unconscious and often coincide with the Zeitgeist in painting as well as with current social and political issues. They nevertheless remain remarkably individual. Lumsden creates images that exude a mysterious energy, oscillating between surface matter and the imaginary dimension.

Work Groups

Until 2010 Rachel Lumsden chose to paint in series. This process allowed the gradual unfolding of different aspects of a subject, employing the repetition of imagery and ideas to chart her exploration over a period of several months and reinforce their impact on the observer. The result was impressive: whilst the series structure created a staggered dialogue with the theme, the individual works are so dense that they function like a film whose temporal sequence has been collapsed into a single powerful image.

The earliest series examined here focuses on one clearly defined object that represents aspects of Lumsden's past. In *Ancestral Inheritance* (1998, Fig. A p. 127) each painting depicts an item of furniture that once belonged to her grandmother. If the larger-than-life character of everything recalls the shrunken Alice's sensations in the environment of Wonderland, the looming presence of the darkness underneath the furniture – both thrilling and frightening – has echoes of Roald Dahl or Edgar Allan Poe.

The series which Lumsden subsequently embarked on, *Arc Light* (2001, Fig. K p. 129), also concentrates on a single item of furniture, an old-fashioned lampshade. The brooding dark background to each painting acts as a foil for the whimsiness of the object but it is the exaggeratedly long drips of colour that transform the image from being a simple figure/ground relationship into a sinister interpretation of the accoutrements of everyday life. Lumsden was interested in how these banal objects assume psychological dimensions as powerful as a human portrait. Indeed, it is significant that Lumsden has almost never depicted the faces of her figures in detail, preferring to convey character and mood, as well as relationships, through posture or movement rather than facial expression.

The other aspect of Lumsden's work already apparent in *Arc Light* is her interest in the contrasts of light and dark. Symbolised in this series by a source of artificial light, in subsequent paintings daylight is often seen through a window of a gloomy interior, while sunlight exaggerates the shadows of things or enhances the drama of windswept or darkening skies. Several aspects of Lumsden's practice emerged in these works and have been re-assessed and developed by the artist in a number of ways since.

The series *Homeland Security* (2003, Fig. B,C, p. 127) continued Lumsden's investigation of the trivial underbelly of domestic life, particularly in connection with the culture and traditions of her own country, Great Britain. Her choice of the ubiquitous tea cosy as subject matter was directly connected to the artist's recent arrival in Switzerland, concurrent with 9/11 and the war in Afganistan. Disturbed by the negative propaganda directed at the UK for its part in the latter and conscious of her displacement in a new country, Lumsden chose the tea cosy as an archetypally British symbol of bad taste that, when grouped together and painted to fill the canvas, hint at the shapes of manoeuvring tanks.

She went one step further in playing with the ambivalence created by elevating something small and insignificant to the status of a monumental painterly subject in the following series, *Dashboard Talisman* (2005, Fig. M p. 129). There was a doggedly eccentric quality to her choice of the furry, animal-imitation mascots that people hang from the rear-view mirror of their cars as the theme of large-scale paintings. However, her voyeurism in leaning over the bonnet of each car to record the garish creature resulted in a perspective that was concerned more with spatial relationships as well as the breaking of established taboos about personal territory than in loyally reproducing drivers' fetishes.

Lumsden's interest in both natural and mechanical structures is evident as a thread running through her practice, most recently in the large-scale permanent work she produced for the BZA, School for robotics and mechatronics in Kanton Thurgau. The black grid-like structure suggesting circuits and nodes overlays a richly coloured diamond pattern which recalls the series *Silent Inhabitants* (2006, Fig. D,E, p.127). In these paintings, microcells and motherboards are juxtaposed with flowers, birds and insects that have become parasites in order to survive in a new environment. The series introduced a major feature of Lumsden's practice which recurs in later paintings: her ability to create atmosphere without resorting to narrative. In the work *Kriechstrom* (2006), for example, she dragged a nailbrush across the canvas to produce irregular, spidery lines that resemble an electrical pathway diagram and imbue the painting with both a sense of urgent movement and a visual equivalent to white noise.

Uneasiness continued as the general tone in the group of paintings entitled *Bird Wars* (2007-2008, Fig. F,G, p. 128) which, once again, employ birds and animals as a stand-in for the human figure and their emotions. In spite of their more conventional composition based on the combination of trees, figures and birds, these works evade a straight reading. They rely rather on disparate recollections, from the disturbing characters of children's storybooks and 17th century book illustrations and prints to the sociocritical satires and caricatures of Hogarth and Goya, as well as computer games.

The encroachment of the past

There has always been an art historical context for Lumsden's work and she has no reservations about appropriating subject matter or ways of handling paint: "I love Corot's autumnal landscapes, loaded with atmosphere, but am also fascinated by Malcolm Morley's painting, which is quite the opposite of my own approach".[1] She expressed her homage to the British artist's depictions of figures in familiar settings in the small format work *Morley's Deckchair* (2015, p. 85). Lumsden's references to historical imagery such as baroque costumes or one of Otto Lilienthal's flying machines in *Bird Wars* or public monuments in *12 O'clock High* (2012, Fig. J, p. 129) and *Mr Wolf* (2012, p. 52) have the effect of condensing past and present, whilst synthesising the historical, political and social. British history is a recurring backdrop to the work, for example in the World War II control room of *When Push Comes to Shove* (2012, Fig. L, p. 129), casually juxtaposed with amusement arcade motifs.

The encroachment of the past on the present is expressed primarily in the atmosphere of Lumsden's interiors. The out-of-date furnishings that appear in many of her interiors – notably an occasional table, lamp and ornaments – root the paintings in the mustiness of old-fashioned sitting rooms that remain, in Britain at least, part of a particular strata in contemporary society. Lumsden's continuing interest in the genre, which has a strong tradition in British painting, has perhaps been reinforced by living outside the country for so long: "One of the strongest and abiding influences on my work are the late 19th century paintings of Walter Sickert. His slightly gloomy bourgeois sitting rooms, as well as depictions of the grimier side of London life feed into my own interiors."[2] A depiction of a room can express so much, with objects, particularly lamps and furniture, standing in for the figure and the ambiguity of space used to heighten the atmosphere. In *Here we go Again* (2014, p. 89), for example, it's not immediately obvious that one's looking at a mantelpiece reflected in a mirror. The interiors are usually cropped close, presenting a fractured view and simultaneously enclosing the observer in their introspection. The uncomfortable sense that there is always more to things than meets the eye is reflected throughout Lumsden's work by the presence of doors - intimating that other worlds might lie behind them - and windows, providing a theatrical framing device to form pictures within pictures.

Bending the paint

This ambiguity of reading extends to the way the paintings are made. Lumsden's handling of paint – both as colour and as physical material - is radical. Colour is simultaneously lurid and grimy, rich and off-key. The melancholy rooted deep in bourgeois life is reflected in the grime and toxicity of fusty interiors from the *Ancestral Inheritance* series to the claustrophobia of more recent paintings such as *Leap Minute* (2015, p. 31). Until works such as *End of a Short Day* (2015, p. 49), with its fields of luminous orange, it has been rare that any one colour has fully come into its own. This has occurred most often in oily outcrops that are more pure painting than description, or puddles of turpentine that appear in the image like deep holes. Black plays a surprisingly important role. It shimmers through the layering of other colours or soils these directly, while black particles cling to objects or hang in the atmosphere. Its presence is also felt, however, as the contrast to the light, which illuminates Lumsden's work, radiating seemingly from within.

However, even dark shadows thrown by strong sunlight dissolve when viewed close to, the paint-surface giving little clue as to the represented subject, which only becomes legible when viewed from further away. Forms are especially blurred in areas where the paint has coagulated. For this reason, the content of the work is encapsulated in the relationship between colour and the materiality of paint-substance, with the latter often co-existing as a form of autonomous abstraction. Using oil paint repeatedly reworked with brushes and other implements, Lumsden employs soft, gestural brushwork for large areas, contrasted with energetic brushstrokes. It is significant that Lumsden hardly works with medium format but regularly produces small paintings on Formica plates, paper or canvas. These can function as working drawings for larger paintings but are also regarded as works in their own right and on their own terms.

Although Lumsden's painting is clearly representational, the role of the human figure is ambiguous, not least because the artist rarely depicts facial features, thereby avoiding references to narrative or character. Figures are part of the recurring wry humour that is a crucial characteristic of Lumsden's work, lightening the sometimes gloomy atmosphere and oppressive subject matter and at other times emphasising irony, from the hybrid creatures in *Bird Wars* to the triangular relationship of man, woman and puma in *On a Sticky Wicket* (2012, Fig. I, p.128). The artist often obliterates an element of the work in order to activate something else, so that contrast can be built up again: "Painting for me is about these acts of destruction which allow a work to enter a second or even third life. An example is the painting of two girls, *Leap Minute*. I obliterated their faces because even though they were convincing, the work became a clearly defined portrait rather than a movement between different visual layers. I wanted the concrete world to dissolve into more ambiguous forms." [3]

Lumsden's relationship with her material has changed in the last two or three years, largely because she has become more daring, relying on fewer safe strategies than in the past. She works with dry impasto marks and uses thin layers of fluid paint to tone down an area but also pours paint, covering the surface "until it's really soupy, until I feel as though I'm swimming in paint". [4] By dragging and pouring the paint in a way that can be partially but not completely controlled the artist can create both dry and tackier areas. It's through this struggle – a dialogue with the materiality of the painting - that she gives space for something to happen, so that she can reach new territory. As Lumsden formulates it, "Painting is a sexy form of quantum physics where every mark on the canvas is not just a blob of paint but also simultaneously the representation of a form. It is this inherent duality that makes painting so exciting. I often have the sense of being on a muddy building site, negotiating between the plan and the materials until a molten slick of paint is steered into figurative content, malleable enough to represent both itself and something else." [5]

The impetus for a new work is usually triggered by something Lumsden has seen. She works intuitively but sees intuition as the knowledge accumulated over many years, thus using intuition as a vital component of the tightrope walk between making imagery and negotiating with the paint. The unpredictability of the medium also gives Lumsden the freedom to court mistakes or accidents – albeit "with a certain anticipation of the outcome" [6], to focus on the process rather than on a clearly defined result. "All my work is about materiality, to the extent that I let go of many of my ideas in order to allow the paint itself to develop. Every canvas is its own universe, each with a different set of rules, to which I have to be able to respond. More and more I understand that painting only occurs on the canvas, in the very moment of painting. I can research themes, look for source material, experiment with compositions in Photoshop, make sketches. But all that is just preparation for the moment in which paint is applied to the canvas." [7]

The huntress returns with a light step as if she were dancing. The dog nudges against her legs, sniffing the booty slung over her shoulder.

At the edge of the forest she pauses briefly, her eyes scanning the evening city. It is very still. It is there that she will spread her images for others to collect, to be seen and pondered, until sated they go on their way.

Endnotes

1   From a conversation between the author and Rachel Lumsden on 15 August 2015.

2–7   ibid.

An aeroplane stands on a runway in the bright midday sun, the paintwork on the tailfin too blurred for it to be assigned to a particular nation. Perhaps it's a scene in the Tropics, for in the foreground, next to the heat-shimmering tail of the aircraft, is a palm tree and the silhouette of a curly-headed figure seen from behind. A boarding stair is docked on to the aircraft enabling passengers to disembark or board, but no one seems to want to use it. It's a scene that is strangely shrouded in silence with the slightly troubling associations of images of hijackings seen in the past. Or there is an alleyway alongside the perimeter wall of the Forbidden City in Beijing: shadows of trees cast in a dense rhythm on the chalk-white pavement, on the pedestal zone along the wall, likewise whitewashed, and on the wall above, gleaming in Chinese red. Our eye is drawn into some indefinite depth that you somehow feel you don't really want to explore any further on foot. And what about that car park, abandoned in the night, where the security lighting set up high on a pole creates a sense of unreal clarity? Does this dazzlingly sharp light, surrounded by a milky aura, actually protect the few cars present, or is it not itself more of a threat?

These are but three atmospheres from the sketch-like pieces that Rachel Lumsden paints 'in-between'. She has entitled them *Here and there* (2016) and numbered them sequentially as a series. They are writing paper-sized, spontaneously painted works that are mainly based on photographs of everyday scenes. 'Here and there', leisurely done "in-between" the major works, they offer her free scope to develop ideas for her large-format paintings in which she creates complexly interwoven pictorial worlds. That each large canvas adheres to its own set of rules, where the paint-substance attains such a heightened presence that it co-determines the subject matter, is for Lumsden an integral part of the pictorial equation: the paint-matter sinks away into the canvas, merges and re-emerges in changed consistencies, gets superimposed. It is a creative process that allows the pictorial theme to follow the course of the painted matter.

Since they are smaller in size and swiftly painted, the pieces that arise in-between feature a drier brushwork; the surfaces are placed homogeneously next to or on top of one another. Fresh and exhibiting a slight brittleness, the theme lies before our eyes, and at times only a few streaks of paint attest to the preceding mechanics of painting. It is almost certainly the expressive and radiant colour palette that distinguishes this newer series of studies by Rachel Lumsden, setting them apart from the darker tones of her large formats – with what Lumsden calls their "murkiness", a deliberate dimming of the theme and obscuring of the context. The "murkiness" has given way here to a more rigorous light and thus to a stronger sense of immediacy, achieving in their thematic openness the same aforementioned freedom for the painting process itself. Similarly, the sources of light the artist focuses on have also changed. Instead of the indirect gleam through a wildly patterned lampshade in a London interior, for example, we now see the unabashedly harsh lighting in public outdoor spaces.

At the thematic level, we can discern a shift from the personal, domestic 'interior' toward a more distanced and neutral 'exterior'. The latter notion of 'exterior' as a genre of art is foreign to the classical divisions of the discipline, but was recently put forward as typifying her work in the translation of an interview with the artist. In fact, a very important property of her painting is that her works arise from two cultures, namely Great Britain and Switzerland. The interior has a long-standing lineage in British art, one that reaches back well into the 20th century, whereas painting in Germany, Austria and Switzerland is rich in expressive landscapes. Lumsden draws fruitfully on both worlds, and there would be some justification in saying that the two approaches combine best in the works that arise intuitively in-between, between here and there. If defined in this way as 'exteriors', they do not reflect the artist's personal sensibilities, such as painting in the vein of classic German (or Swiss) Expressionism would do. Just as in Lumsden's large 'interiors', the murkiness of which was developed out of a critical interpretation of the frugal interior paintings by early English Modernist Walter Sickert, whom Lumsden admires, so too the focus here is on a painterly analysis of the inner nature of these image-worlds themselves. How do they generate their materiality, what are their primal elements, how do they respond to one another? And also, of course, how can the paint become an equivalent to this internal image-mechanism?

As in earlier representations of archetypal London bedsits (compact interiors where every object can be attributed to the very personal everyday world of a living room and bedroom rolled into one), equally, in Lumsden's 'exteriors' we do not see an outdoors untouched or untainted by humans. We can most definitely discern the traces of inhabitants in these spaces too, although the only people we actually encounter are, at best, foreground figures. Nor do they help define the space by being obviously absent, as is often the case in Lumsden's large 'interiors'. Indeed, it is this at times abrupt refusal to narrate that perhaps surprises us most when surveying these everyday scenes painted in-between. For however self-evidently they present their themes in seemingly absolutely straight-laced compositions, they nevertheless remain subject only to their own rules when it comes to interpretation. It is the gift of painting that ebulliently draws from countless sources, and in this joyful merger of themes, finds a specific final form of painterly appropriation.

Rachel Lumsden was born 1968 in Newcastle-upon-Tyne (GB). She lives and works in St. Gallen and Arbon (CH), and in London (GB).

1995–1998
The Royal Academy Schools, London, Post Graduate Studies in Painting (MA)

1987–1991
Nottingham Trent University, Bachelor of Arts (Honours) Fine Art

Prizes and Awards

2016
Förderbeitrag Kanton Thurgau (CH)

2014
Werkbeitrag Kanton St. Gallen (CH)

2012
VisarteOst Artist-in-Residence, Cité International des Arts, Paris (FR)

2011
International Art Prize, Vorarlberg (AT)

2009
Förderpreis Stadt St. Gallen (CH)

2008
Artist-in-Residence der Stadt St. Gallen, La Fabrik, Berlin (DE)

2005
Werkbeitrag Stadt St. Gallen (CH)

2001
Art Award, The Pollock-Krasner Foundation, New York (USA)

1998
CrestCo Art Prize, The Bank of England (GB), David Murray Prize (GB), Landseer Prize (GB)

Solo Shows

2018
Kunst(Zeug)Haus Rapperswil-Jona (CH)

2017
Fondation Fernet-Branca Saint-Louis (FR)

Kunsthaus Centre d'art Pasquart Biel / Bienne (CH)

2015
The Other Island, Galerie Bernard Jordan, Zurich (CH)

Straight Flush, Galerie Bleisch, Arbon (CH)

2013
Drunk in Charge of a Bicycle, Kunstraum Kreuzlingen (CH)

Six Impossible Things Before Breakfast, Kunstplattform Akku, Lucerne (CH)

2012
What's the Time, Mr. Wolf?, Galerie Schönenberger (CH)

2009
Man & Beast, Kunstraum Engländerbau, Vaduz (FL)

2008
Bird Wars, Katharinen, St. Gallen (CH)

2006
Silent Inhabitants, Kunsthalle Arbon (CH) (2-person show)

Dashboard Talisman, Galerie Christian Röllin, St. Gallen (CH)

2004
Misplaced, Vertigo Gallery, London (GB) (2-person show)

2001
Arc-light, Bridlesmith Gallery, Nottingham (GB)

Arc-light, The Spitz Gallery, London (GB)

1999
Foreign Body, Rivington Gallery, London (GB)

Group Shows

2017
London meets Altdorf, Haus für Kunst Uri (CH)

2016
Im Rausch – zwischen Höhenflug und Absturz, Kunstmuseum Thurgau (CH)

Werkschau Thurgau, Kunstraum Kreuzlingen (CH)

Ausgezeichnet!, Museum Bickel, Walenstadt (CH)

London Art Fair, Long & Ryle Gallery, London (GB)

2015
20/21 Art Fair, Long & Ryle Gallery, London (GB)

London Art Fair, Long & Ryle Gallery, London (GB)

Twopack, Erfrischungsraum, Lucerne (CH)

Grosse Regional, Kunst(Zeug)Haus Rapperswil-Jona (CH)

2013
Werkschau Thurgau, Bleisch Galerie, Arbon (CH)

Die zweite Dekade, Kunsthalle Arbon (CH)

2012
Central Booking in Berlin, K-Salon, Berlin (DE)

La Suisse est une ville, Salles d'exposition de la Cité internationale des arts, Paris (FR)

2011
The Open West, Cheltenham (GB)

2010
Arthur#5, Kunsthalle, Toggenburg (CH)

Narrative Sequencing, CBA Gallery, New York (USA)

Let the Yangzte Flow, Hubei Institute of Fine Art, Wuhan (CN)

2009
Heimspiel, Kunstmuseum St. Gallen (CH)

12/132 Biennial, Alte Fabrik, Rapperswil-Jona (CH)

Works on Paper, Raab Gallery, Berlin (DE)

AIR 2 Artists in Residence, Substitut, Raum für Aktuelle Kunst aus der Schweiz, Berlin (DE)

2008
Memory Happens, Christies auction, Kaiser Wilhelm Memorial, Berlin (DE)

Fünf Frauen für den Kaiser, Galerie Siguaraya, Berlin (DE)

2005
Berliner Liste, Messe für aktuelle Kunst, Berlin (DE)

2003
Reduced, Century Gallery, London (GB)

2000
Paint!, Vertigo Gallery, London (GB)

Publications

2016
Im Rausch–zwischen Höhenflug und Absturz, Kunstmuseum Thurgau, Verlag für moderne Kunst

2013
Drunk in Charge of a Bicycle, Paintings and Everything in Between, Texts: Axel Jablonski, Robert Guy Wilson, Schwabe Verlag, Basel

2012
Eine Begegnung mit der Sammlung, VP Bank-Kunststiftung Text: Brigitte Ulmer

2011
Sammlung Credit Suisse, Scheidegger & Spiess, Zurich

2010
Let the Yangzte Flow, Katalog FH Zentralschweiz, Hochschule Luzern

2008
Rachel Lumsden,

Paintings 1998–2008, Texts: Felicity Lunn, Uwe Wieczorek, Bucher Verlag (AT)

Collections

Regierungsgebäude Kanton Thurgau (CH), Crédit Suisse Kunstsammlung, Zurich (CH) UBS Art Collection, Zurich (CH) VP Bank Kunstsammlung, Vaduz (FL), Kanton St. Gallen Kunstsammlung, St. Gallen (CH), Stadt St. Gallen Kunstsammlung St. Gallen (CH), Private collections (GB), (CH), (FL), (USA), Asia

Lecturing

Since 2007 Hochschule Luzern Design und Kunst / University of Lucerne for applied Arts and Sciences (CH)

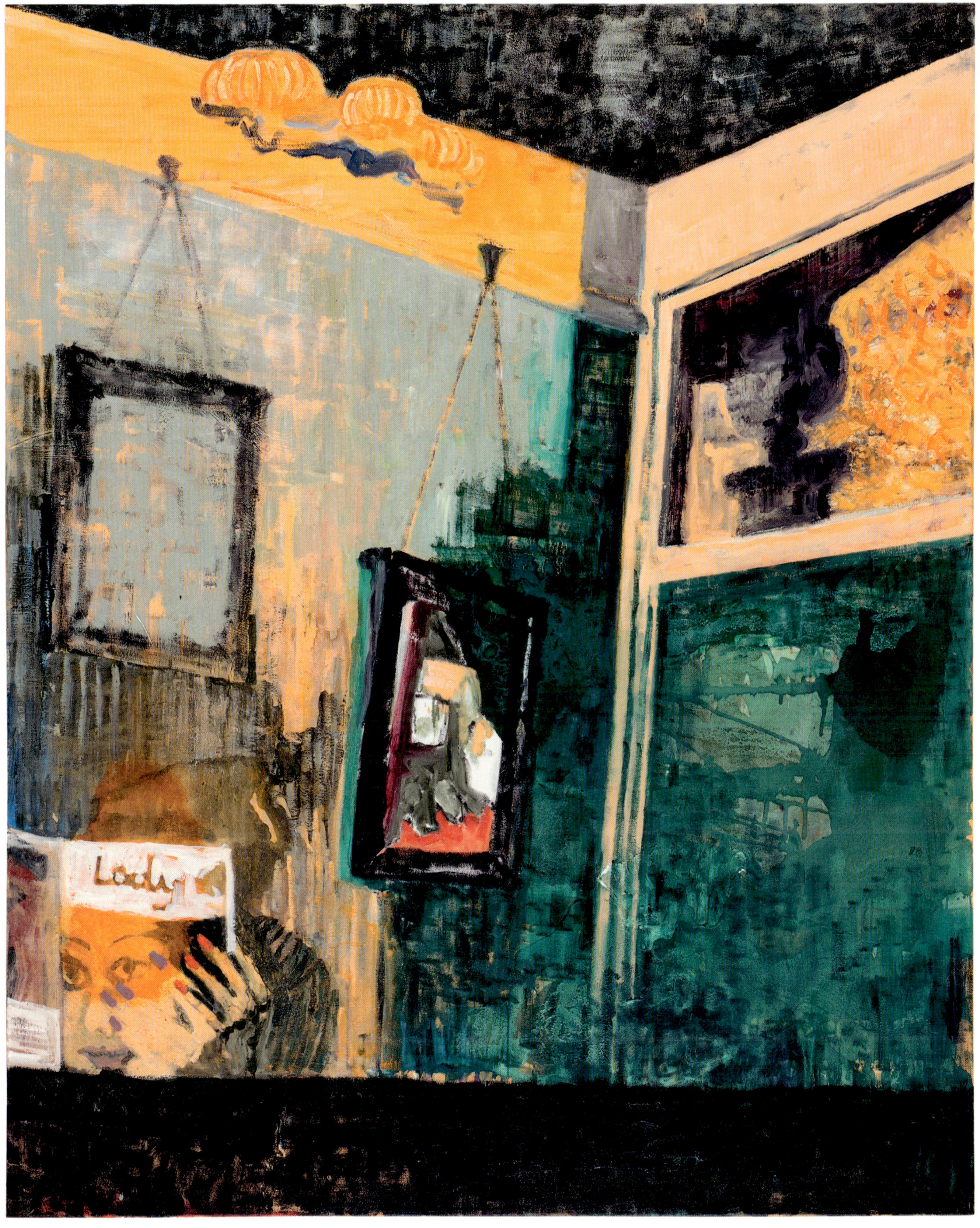

Antechamber 2015 210 × 170 cm

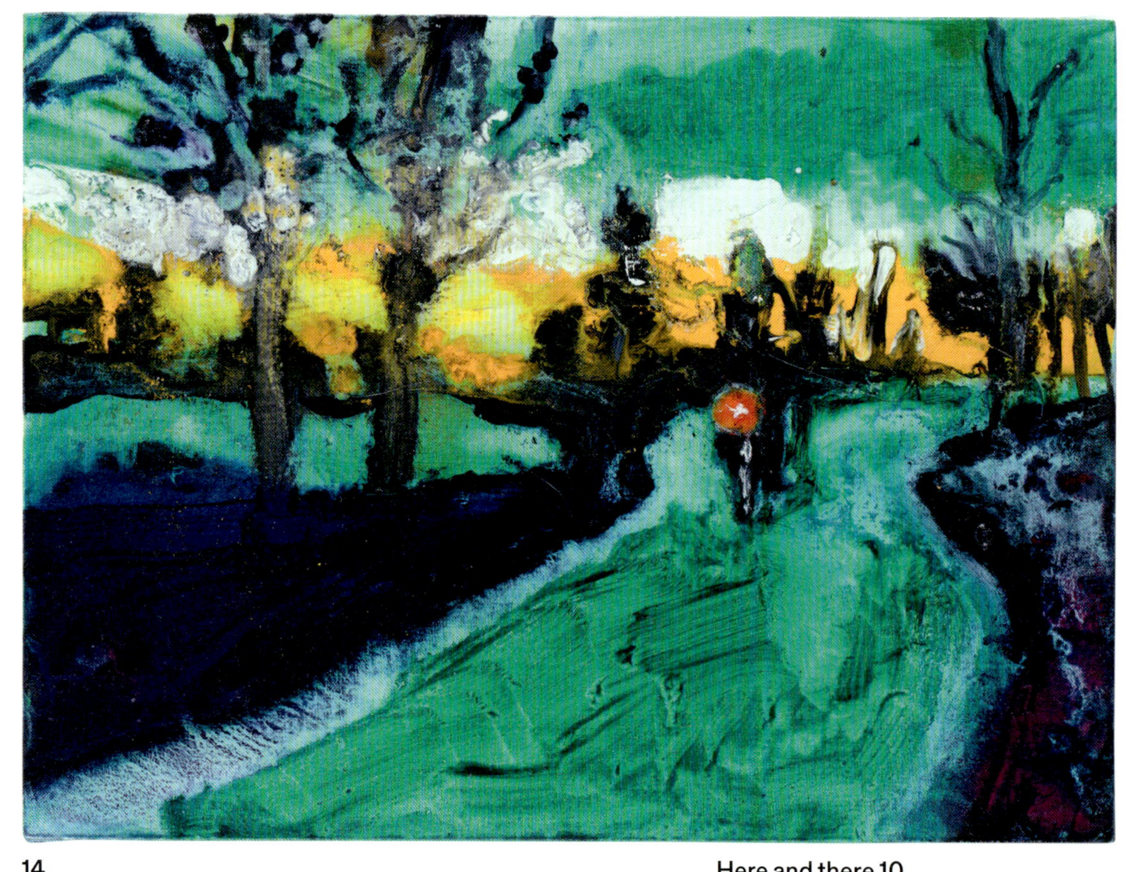

    Here and there 10   2016   21.5×29.7 cm

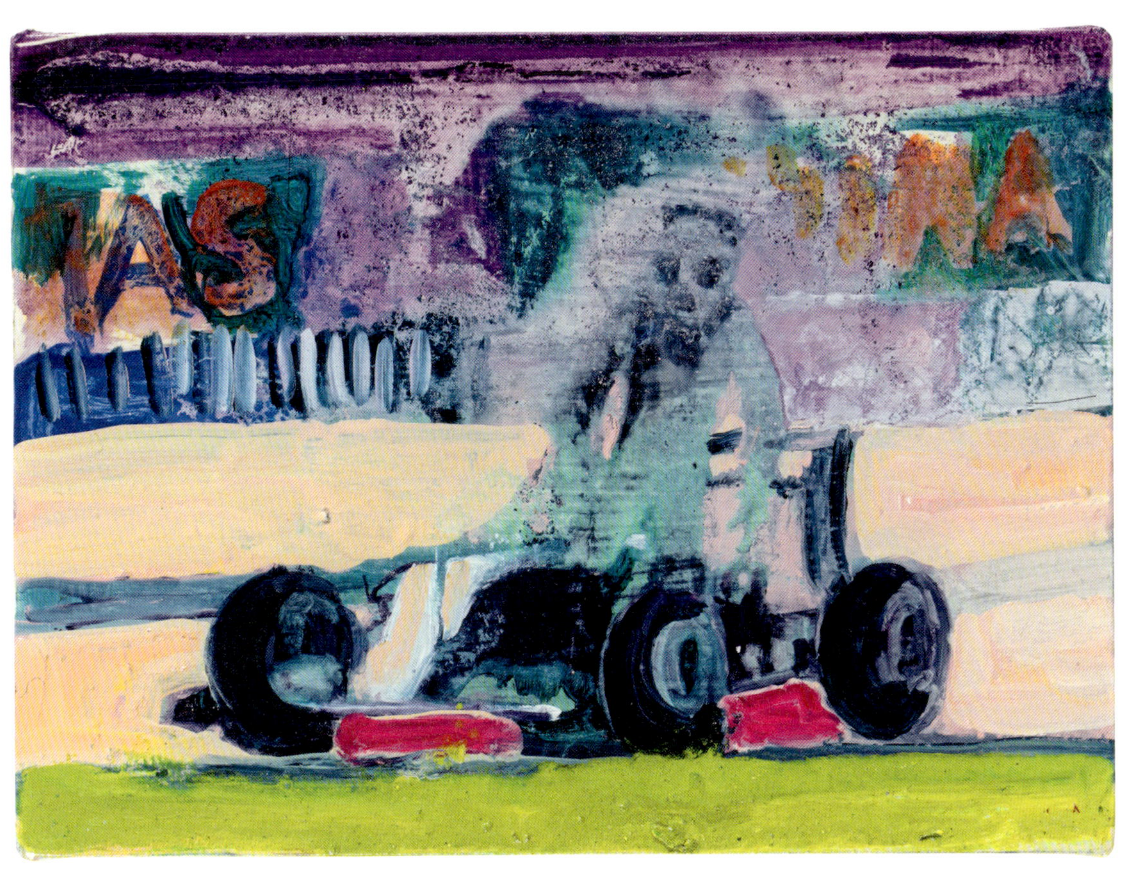

    Here and there 11   2016   21.5×29.7 cm

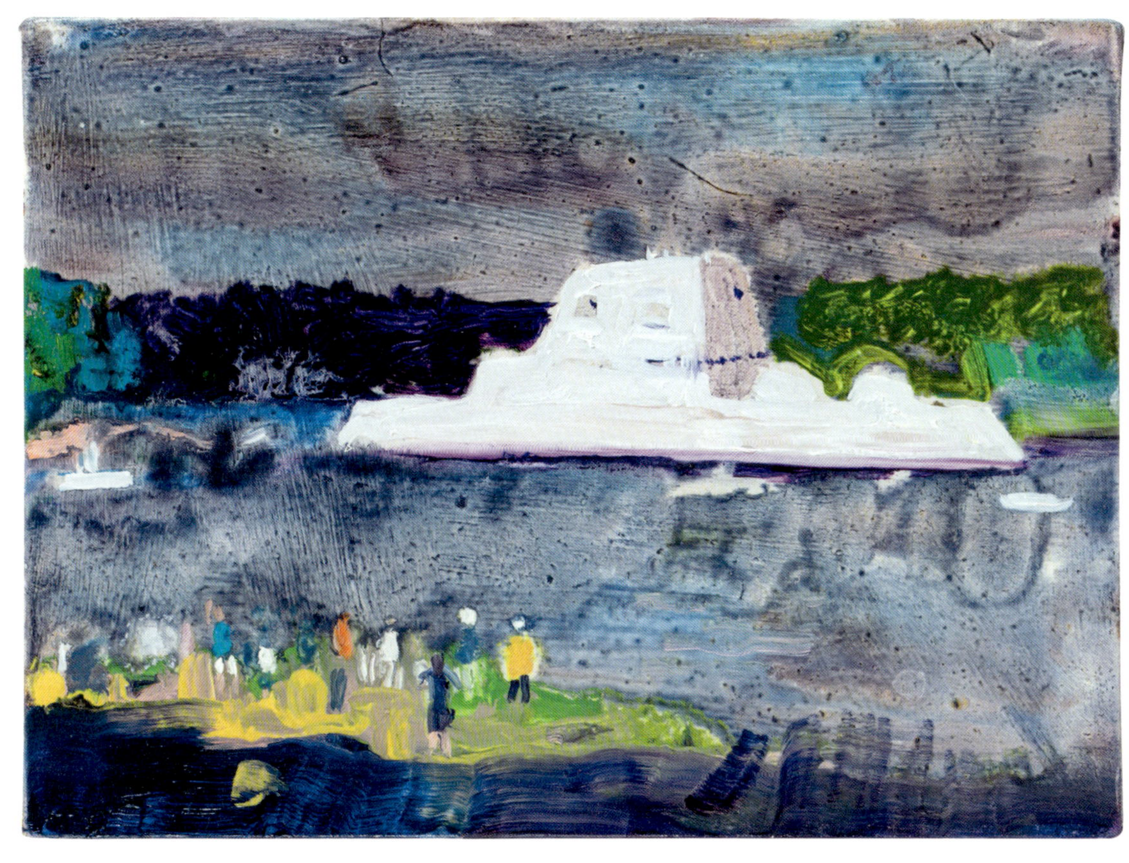

Here and there 7

2016   21.5×29.7 cm

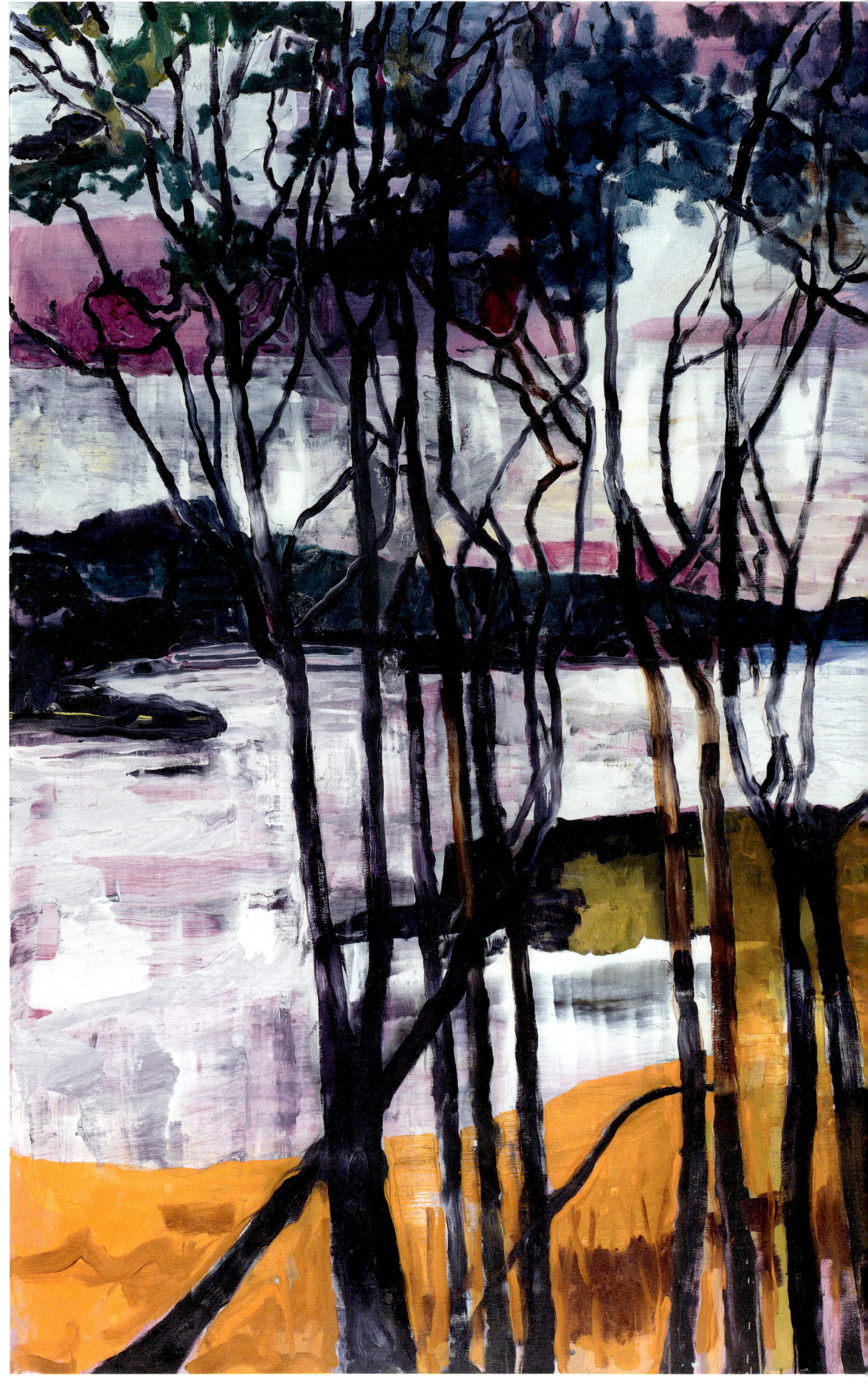

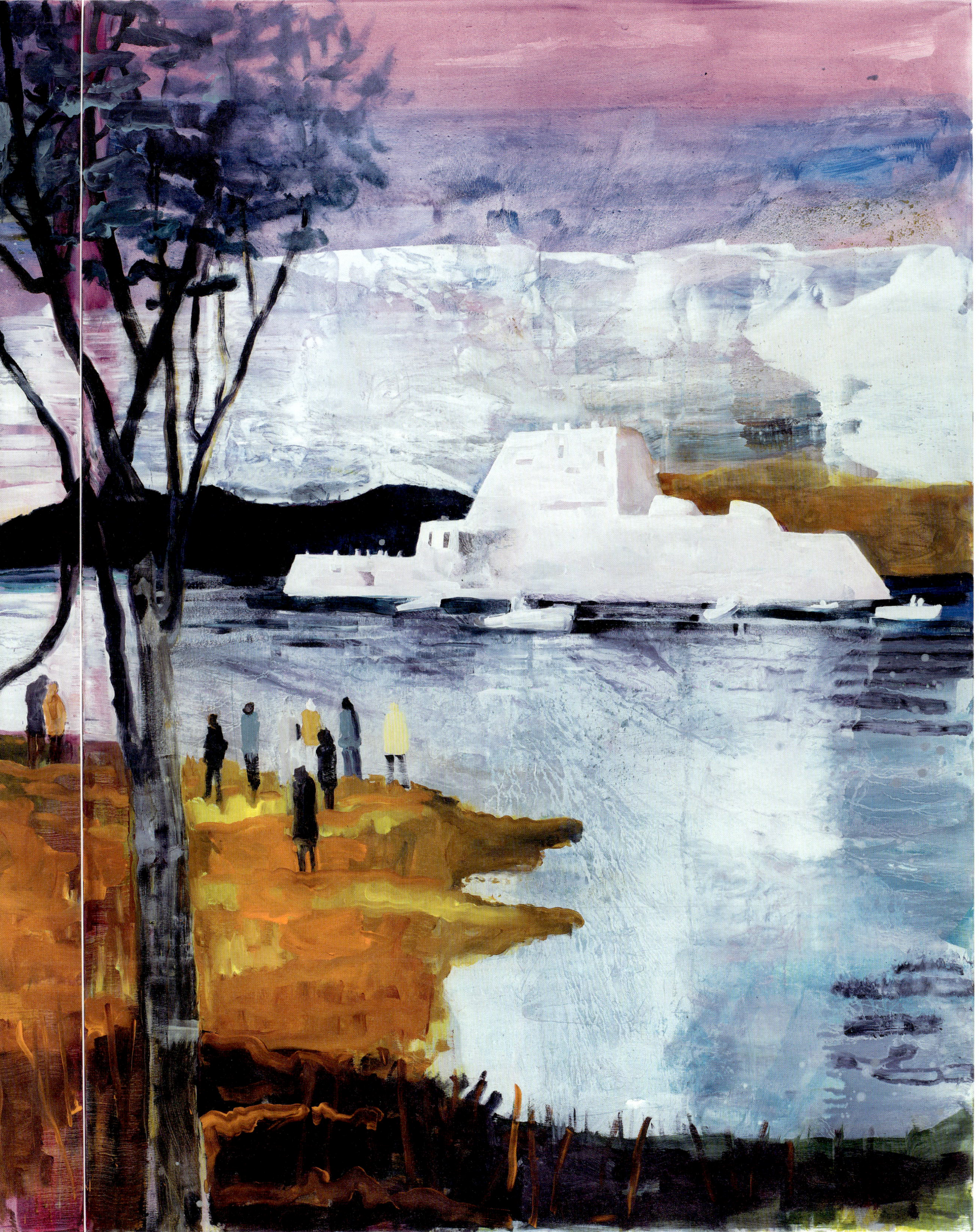

Titanium 2017 230 × 340 cm

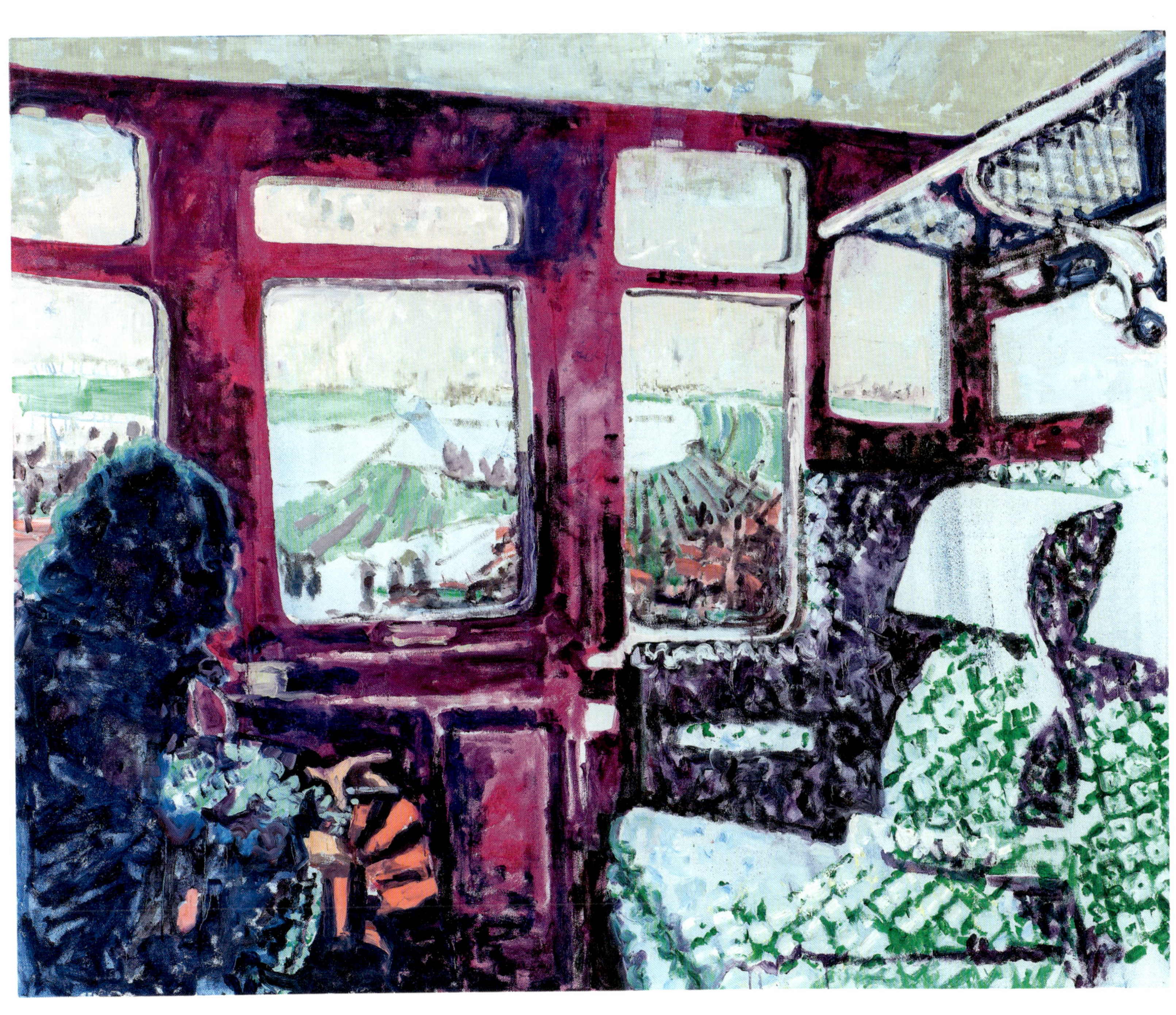

Think Tank   2015   170 × 210 cm

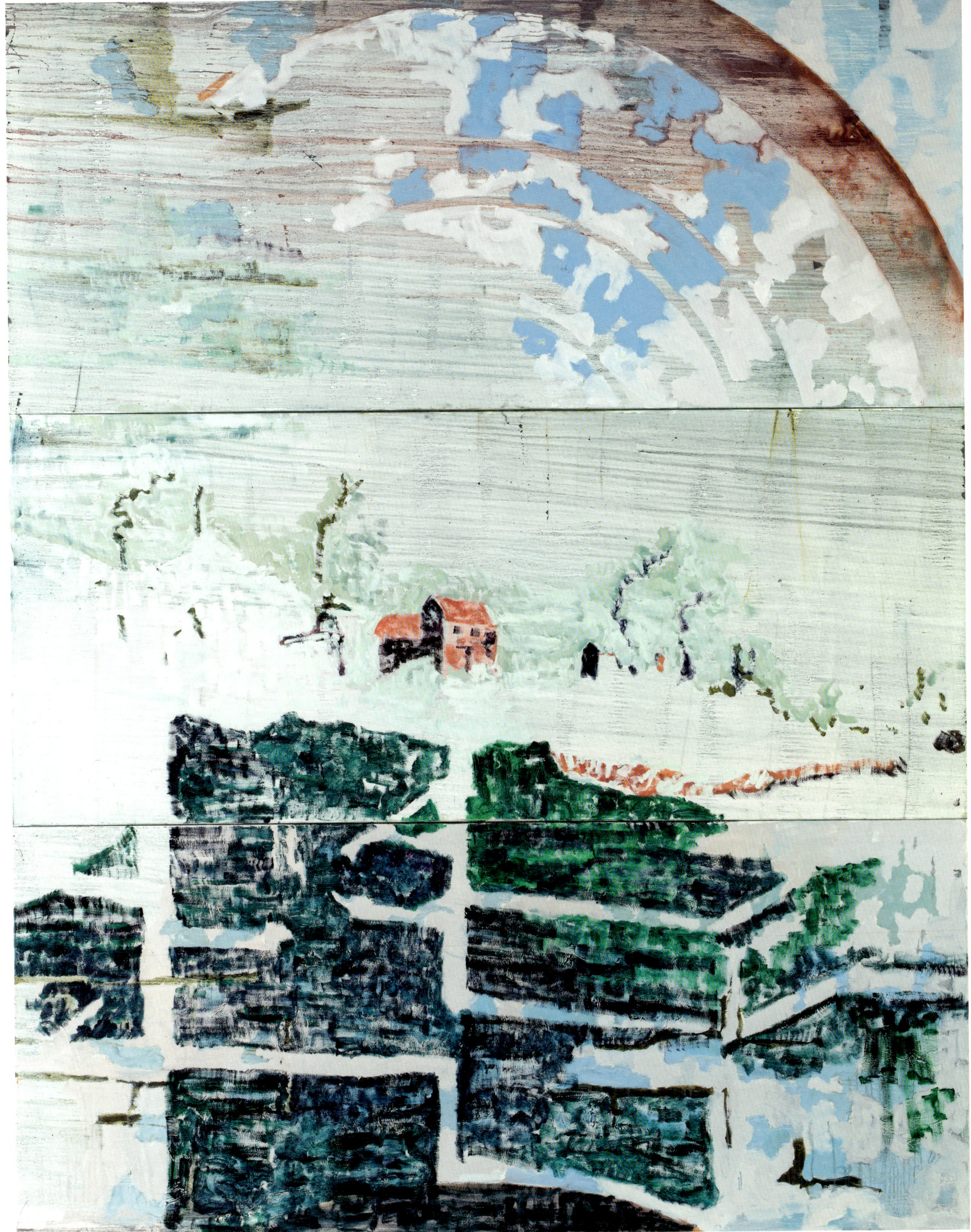

Mansion 2015 300 × 240 cm

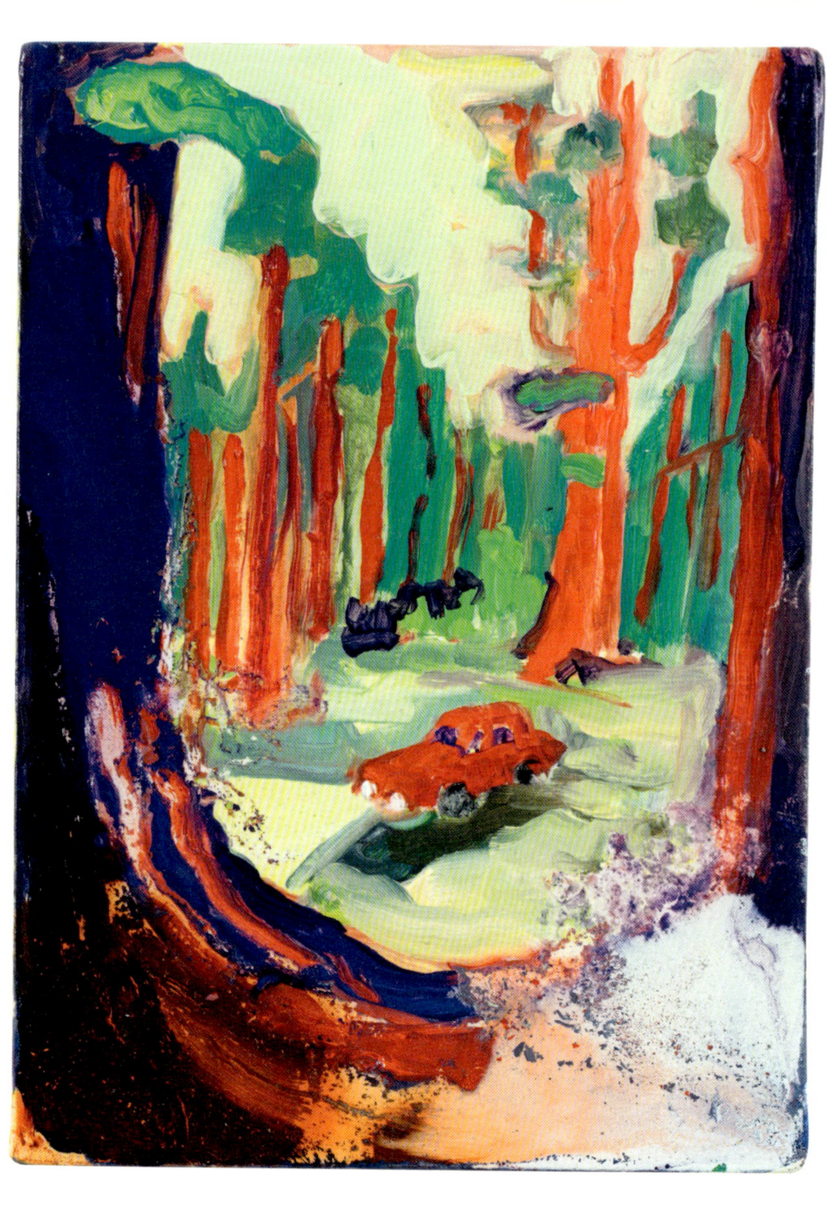

Here and there 8   2016   29.7 × 21.5 cm

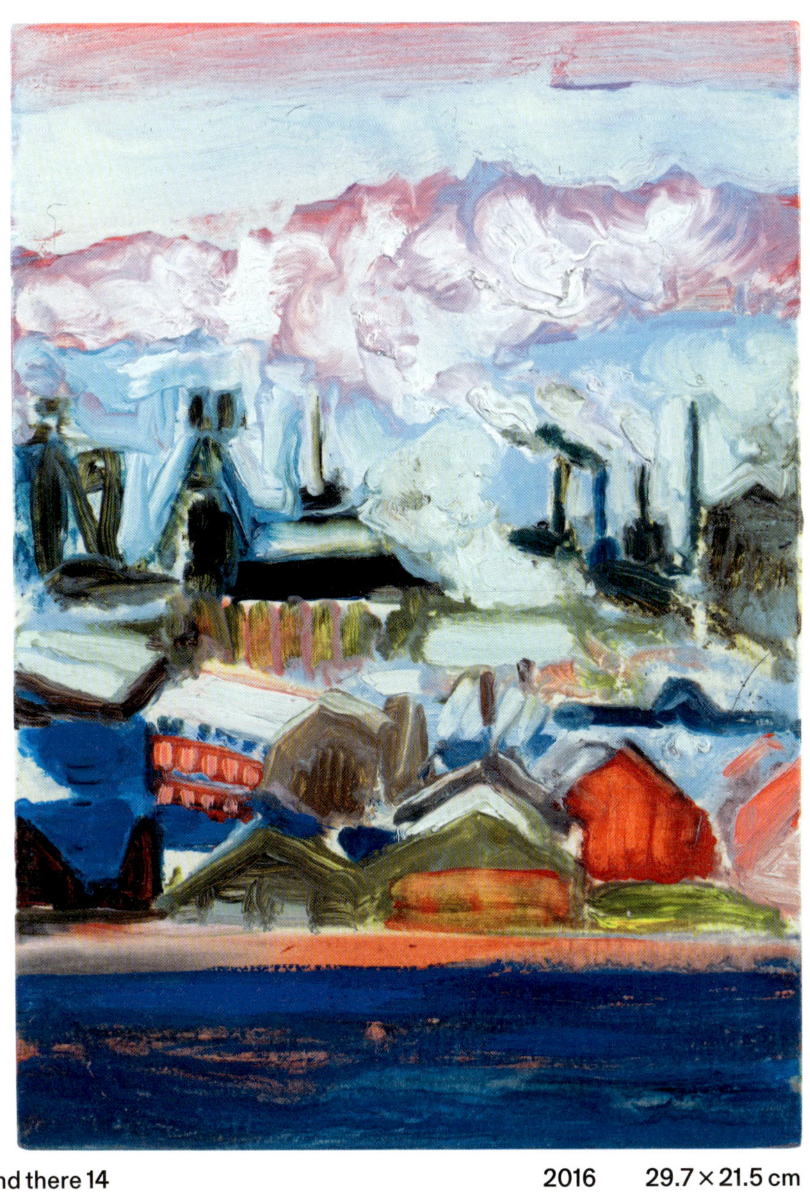

Here and there 14   2016   29.7 × 21.5 cm

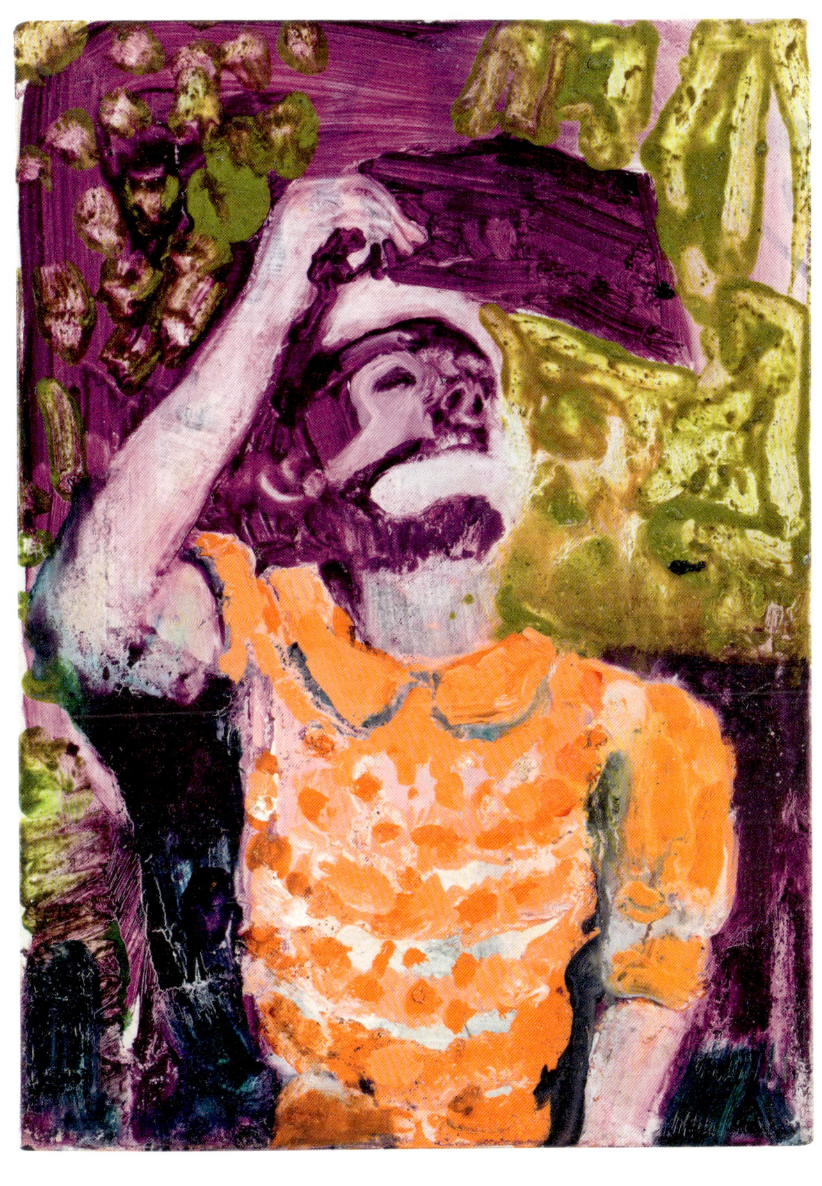

Here and there 19

2016   29.7 × 21.5 cm

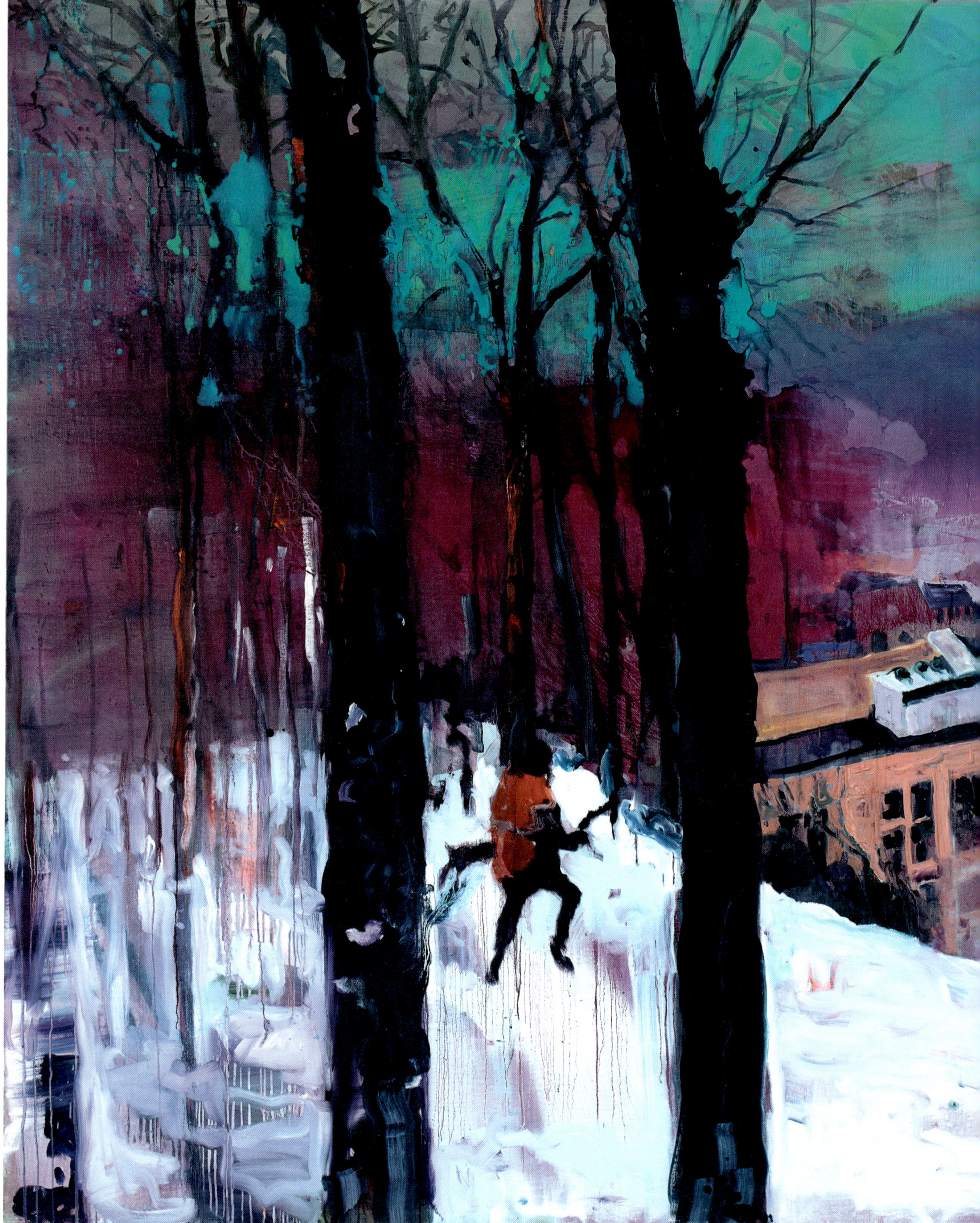

Return of the Huntress   2016   200 × 250 cm

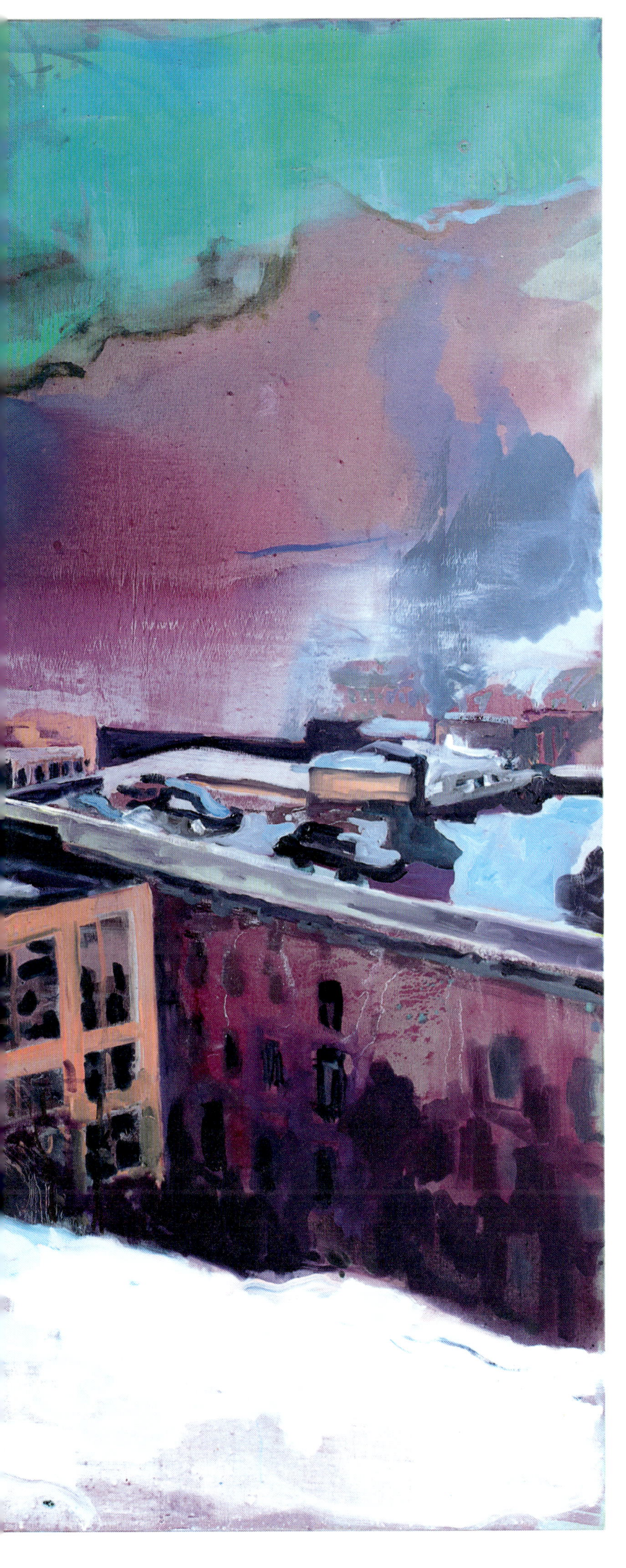

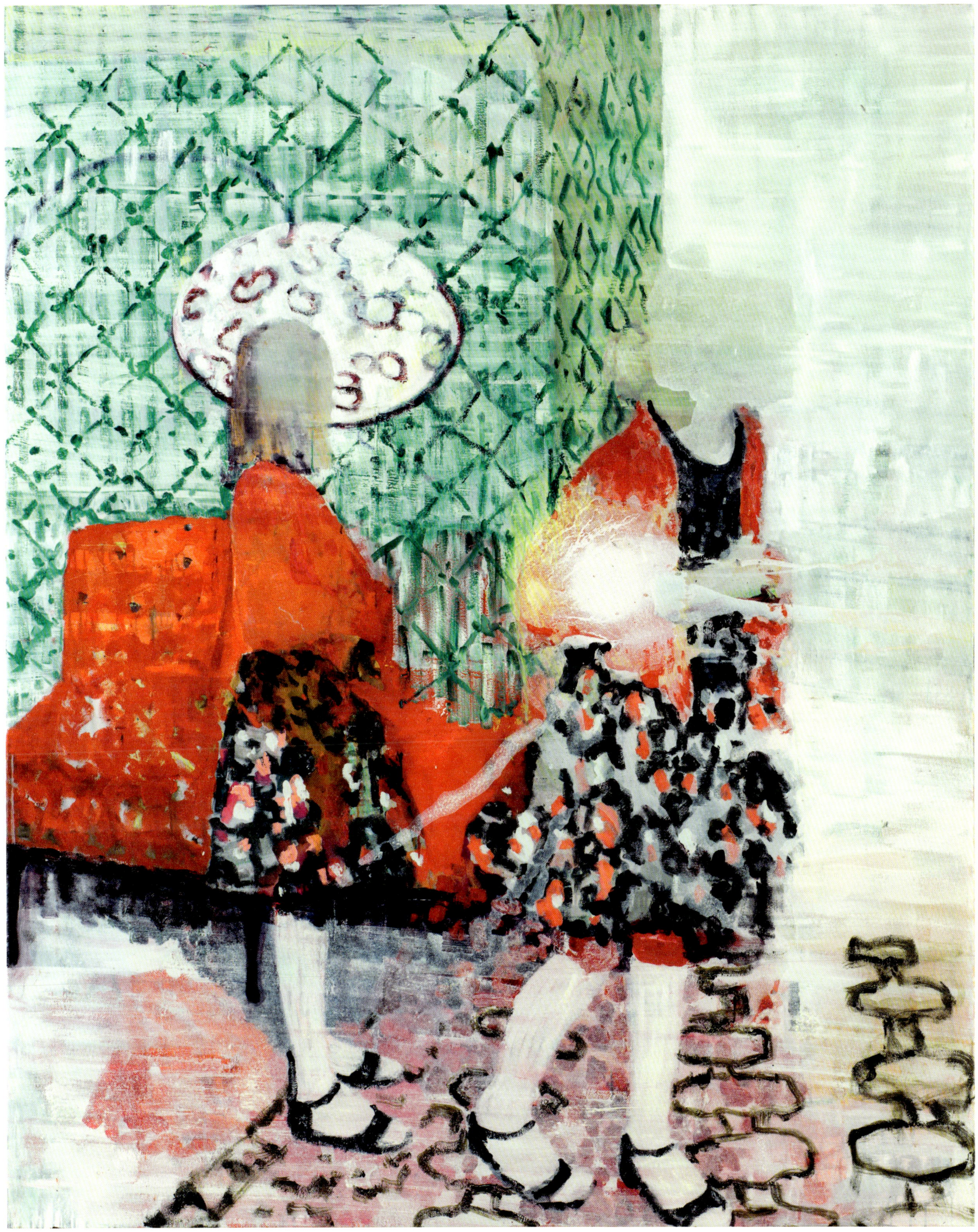

Leap Minute 2015 210×170 cm

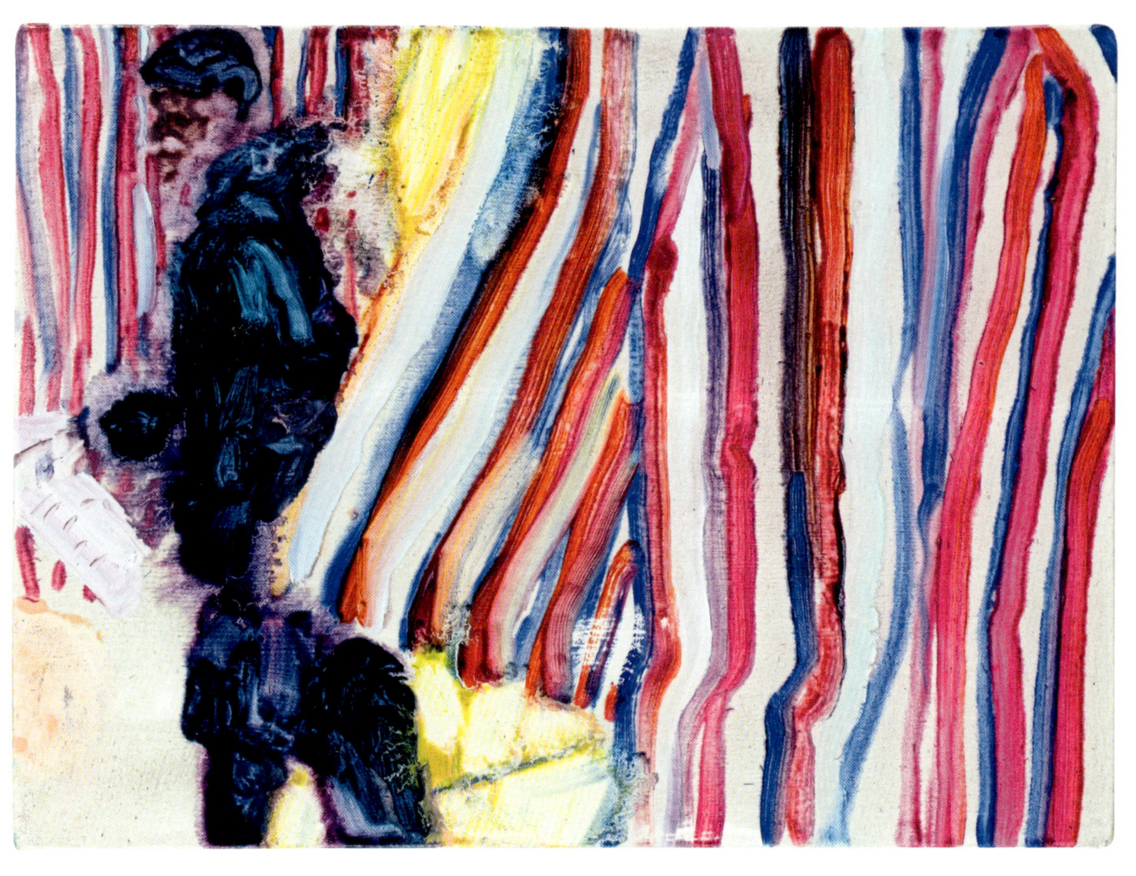

Here and there 12   2016   21.5 × 29.7 cm

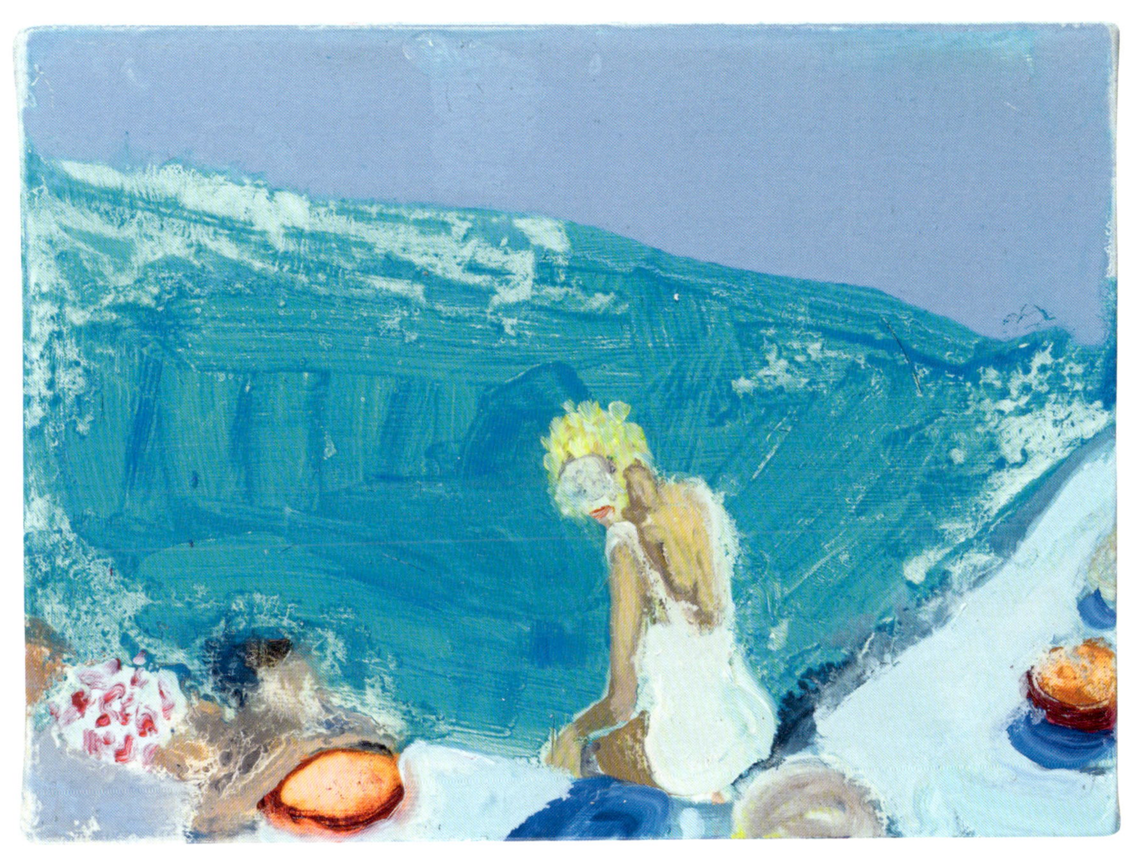

Here and there 16   2016   21.5 × 29.7 cm

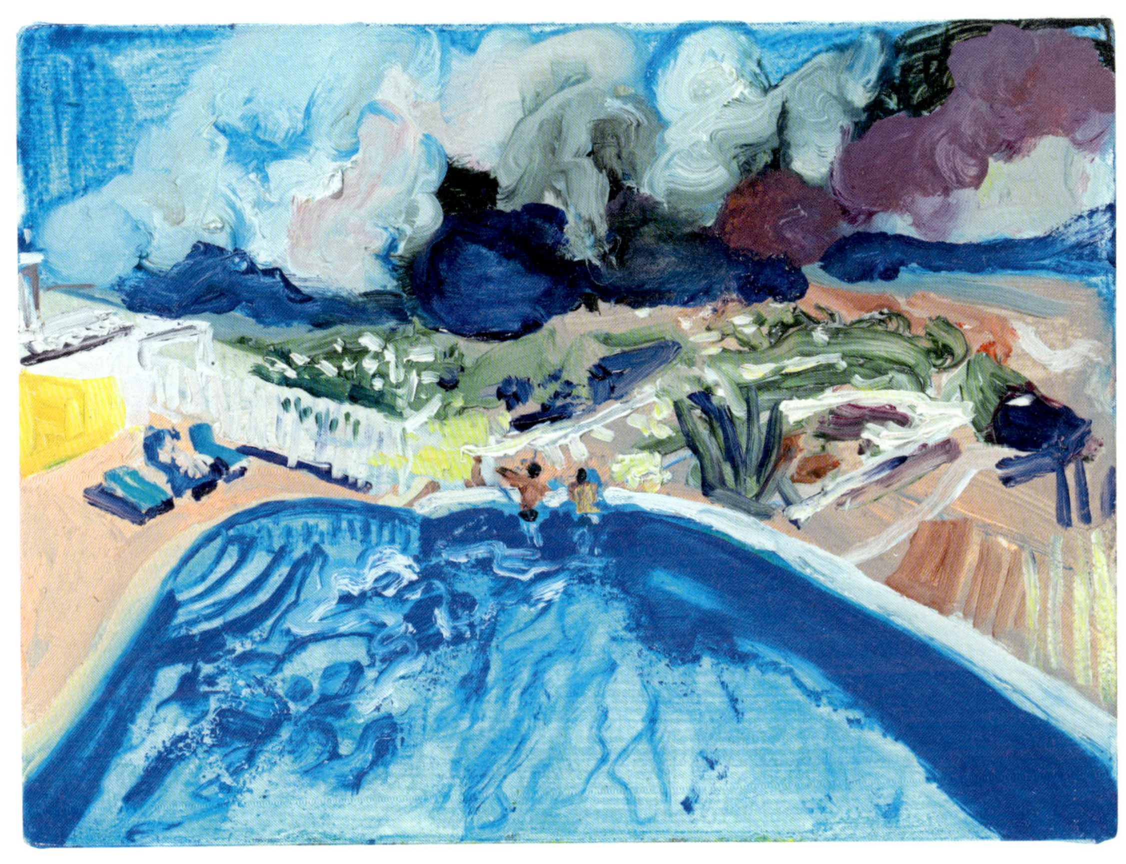

Here and there 5

2016   21.5 × 29.7 cm

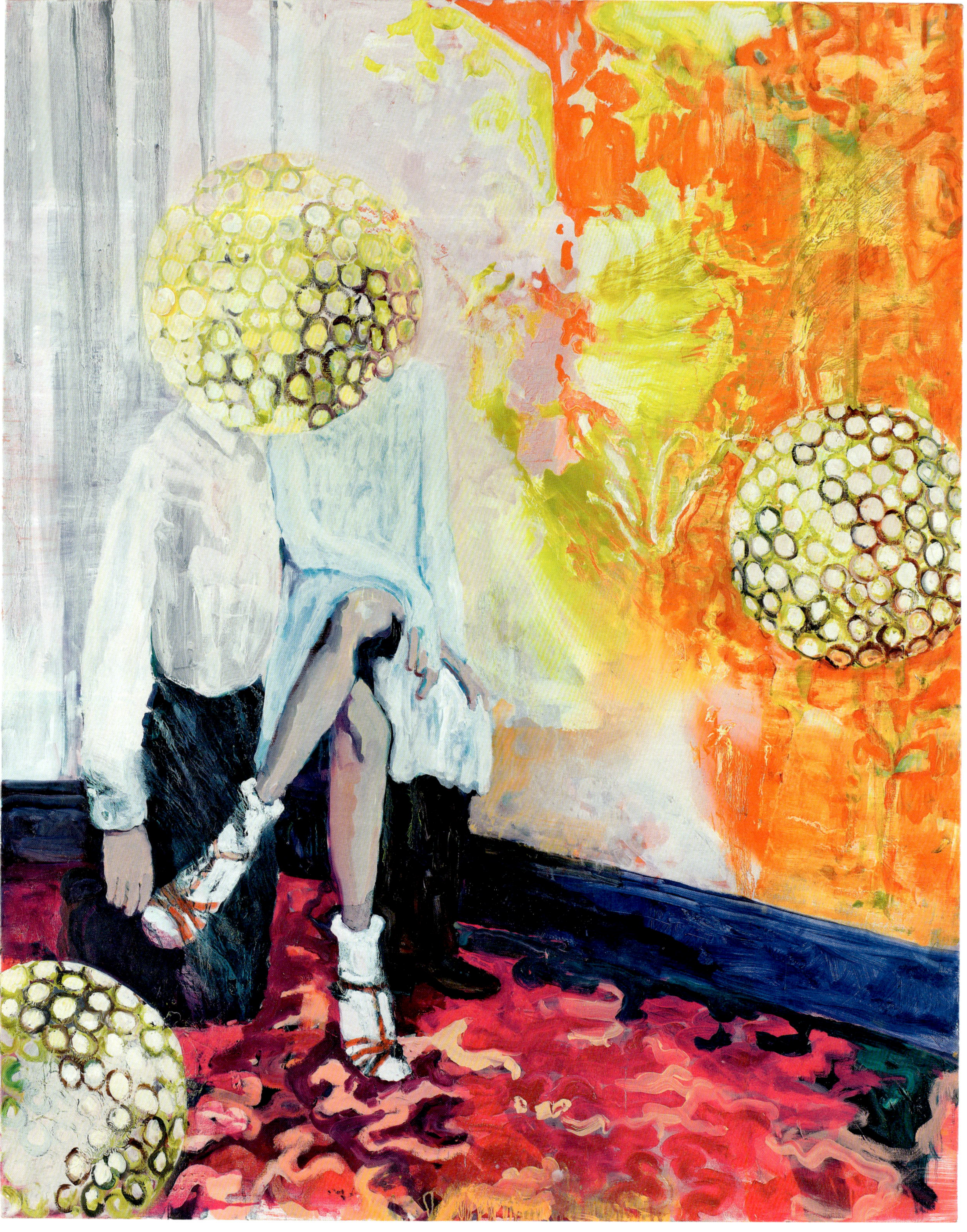

Three Balls   2017   210 × 170 cm

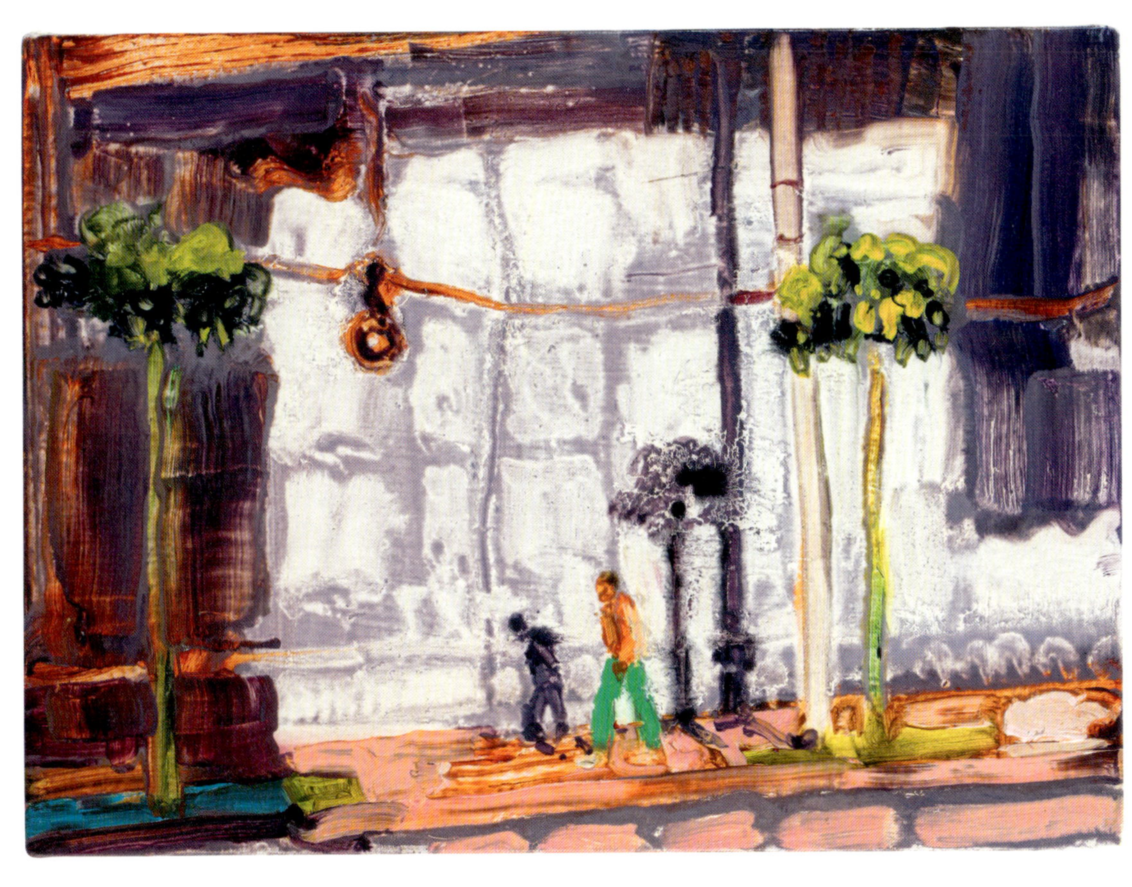

Here and there 6   2016   21.5 × 29.7 cm

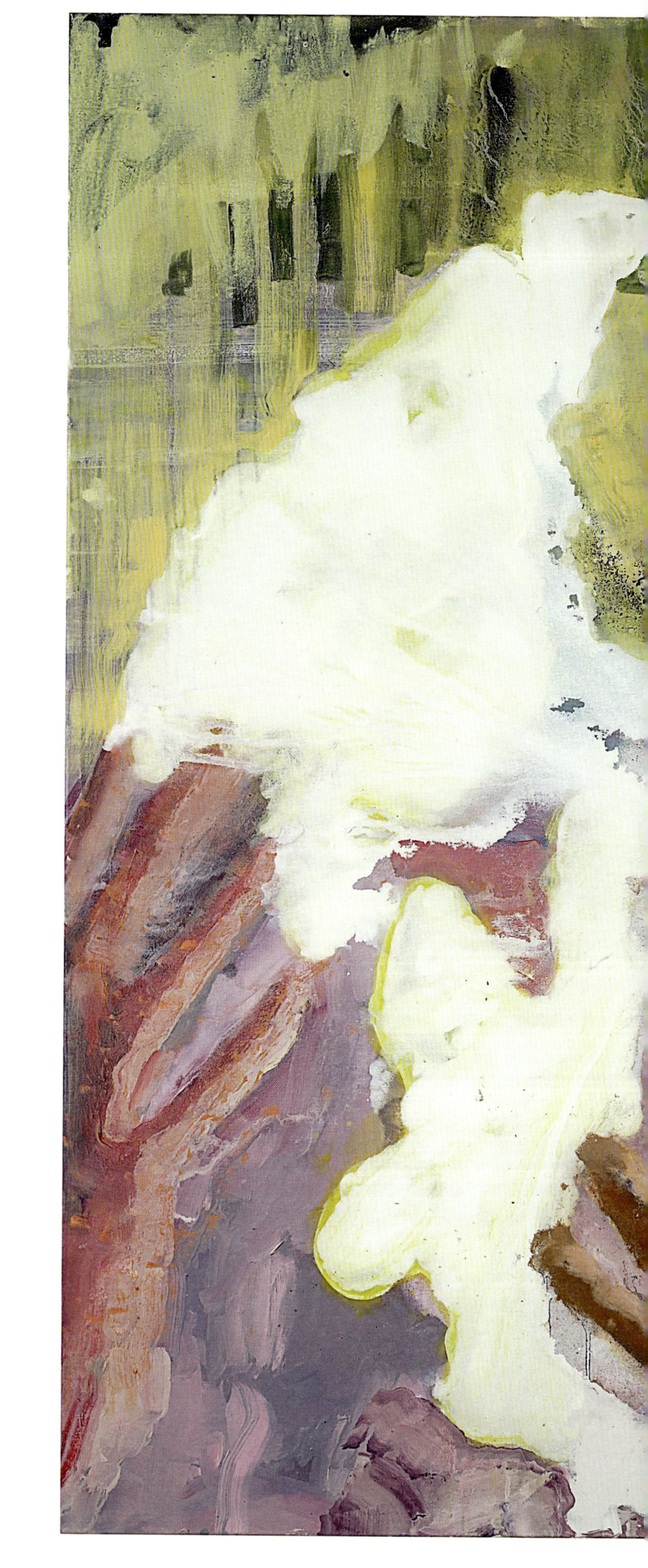

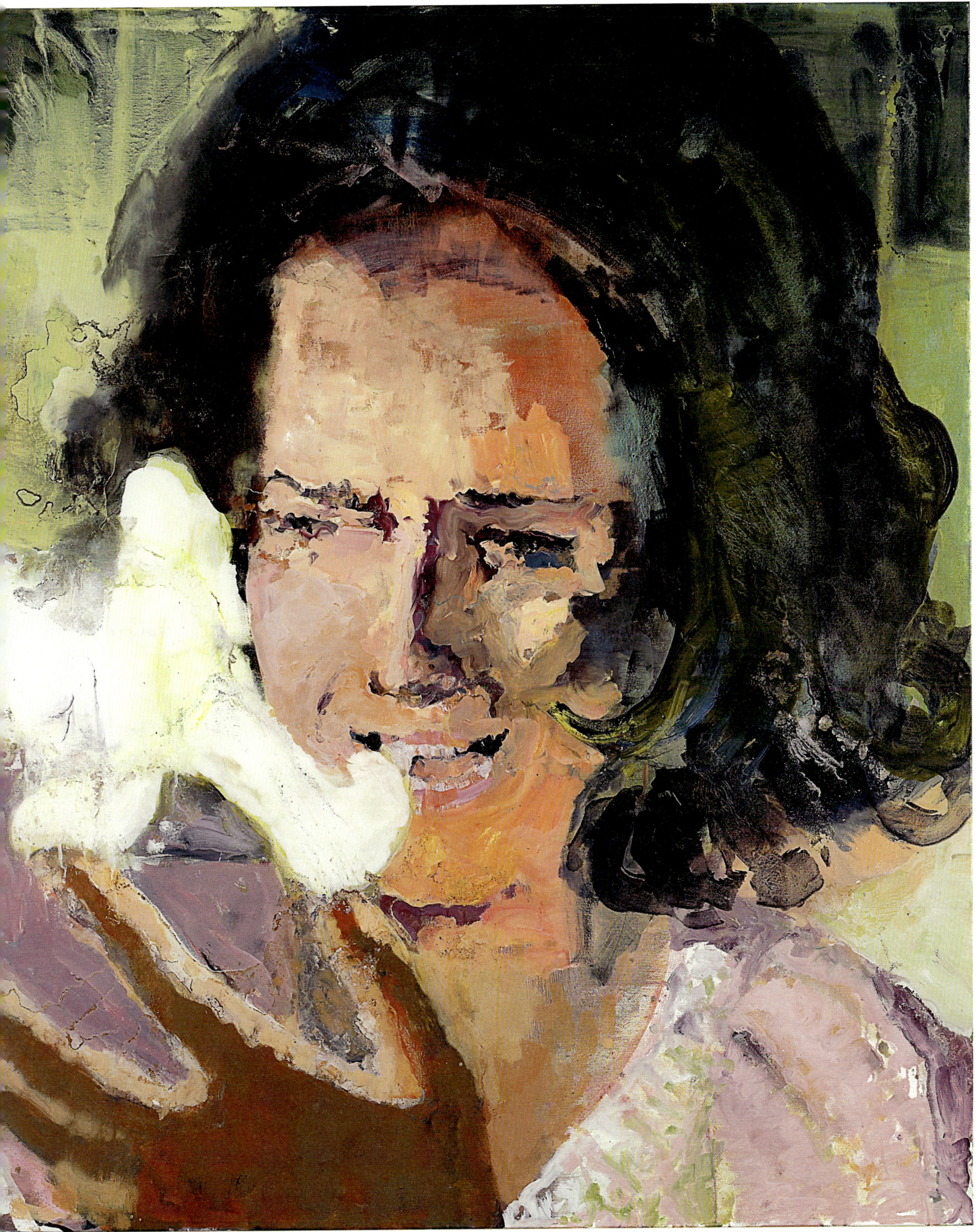

Fire at Will   2012   170 × 210 cm

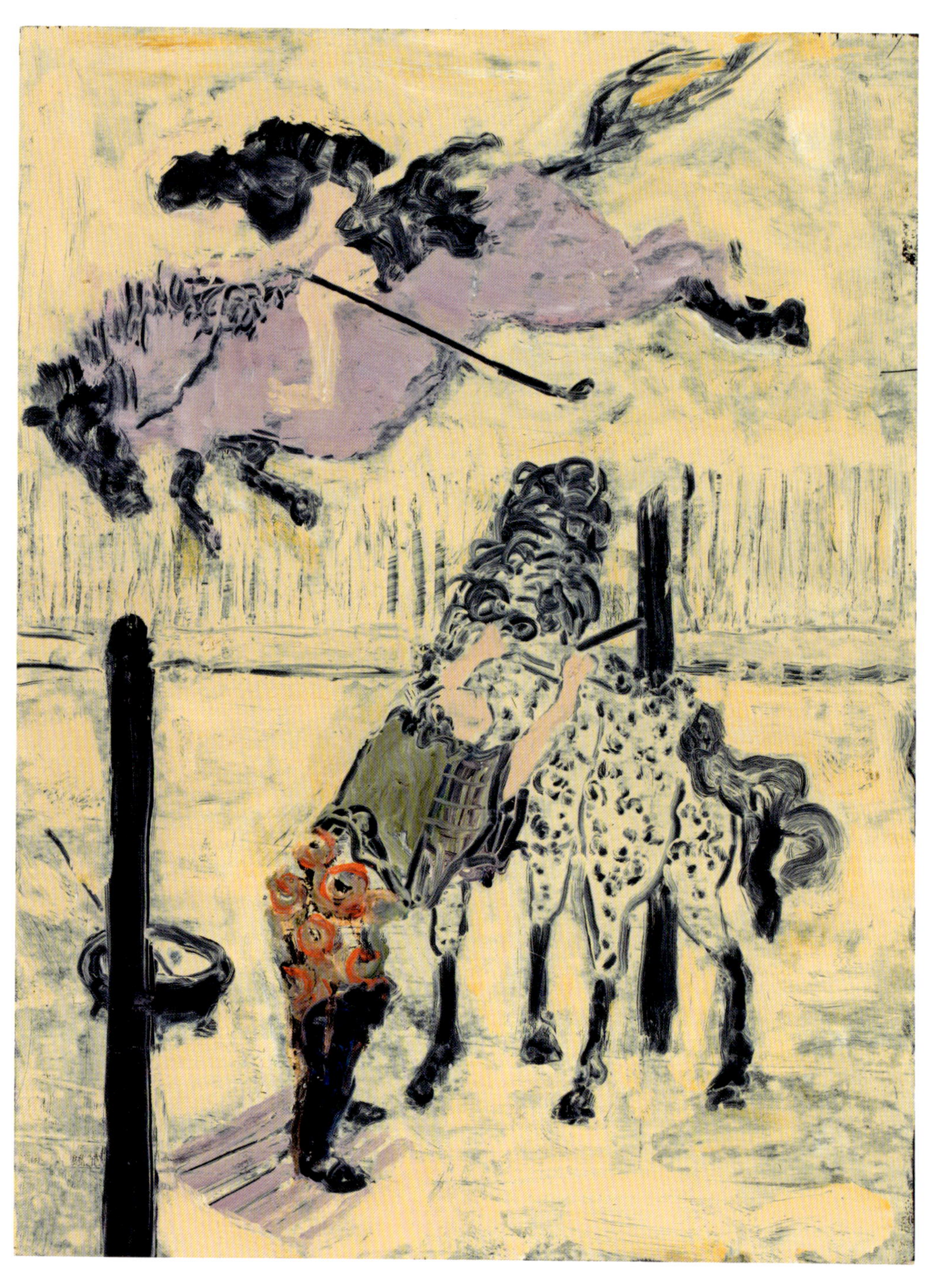

Breeding Lilac

2015   40×30 cm

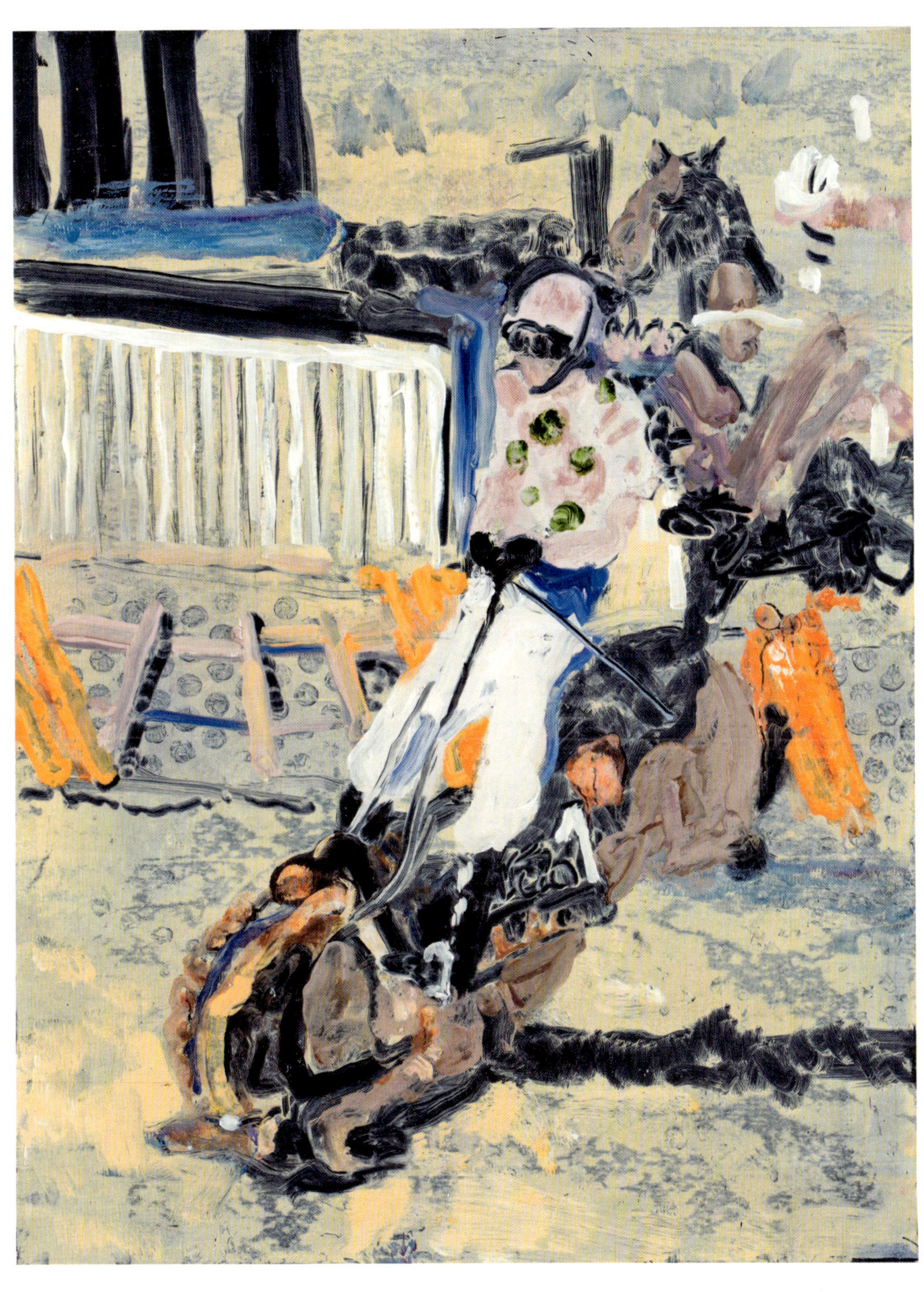

Steeple Chase

2015   40 cm × 30 cm

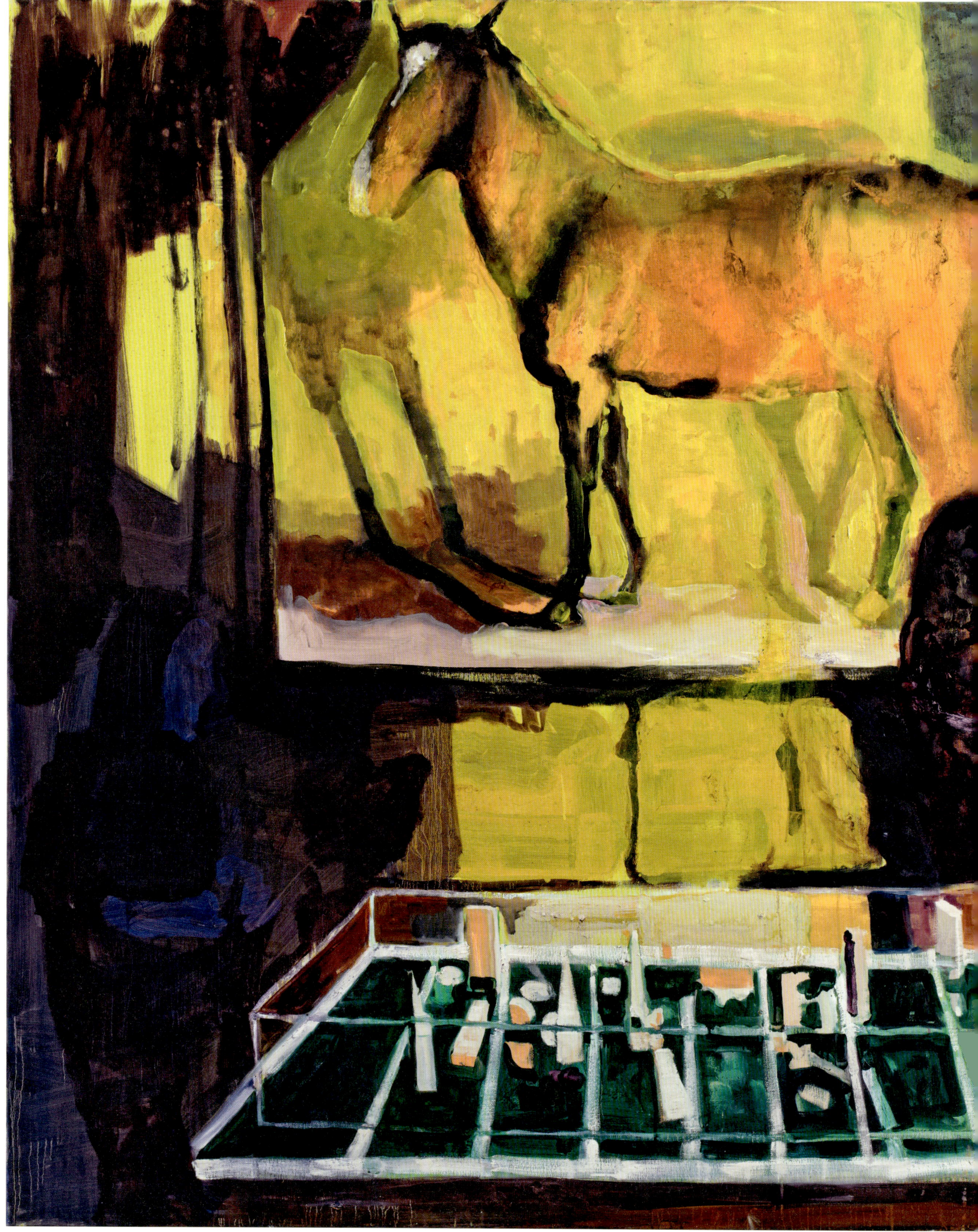

Kingdom   2016   170 × 210 cm

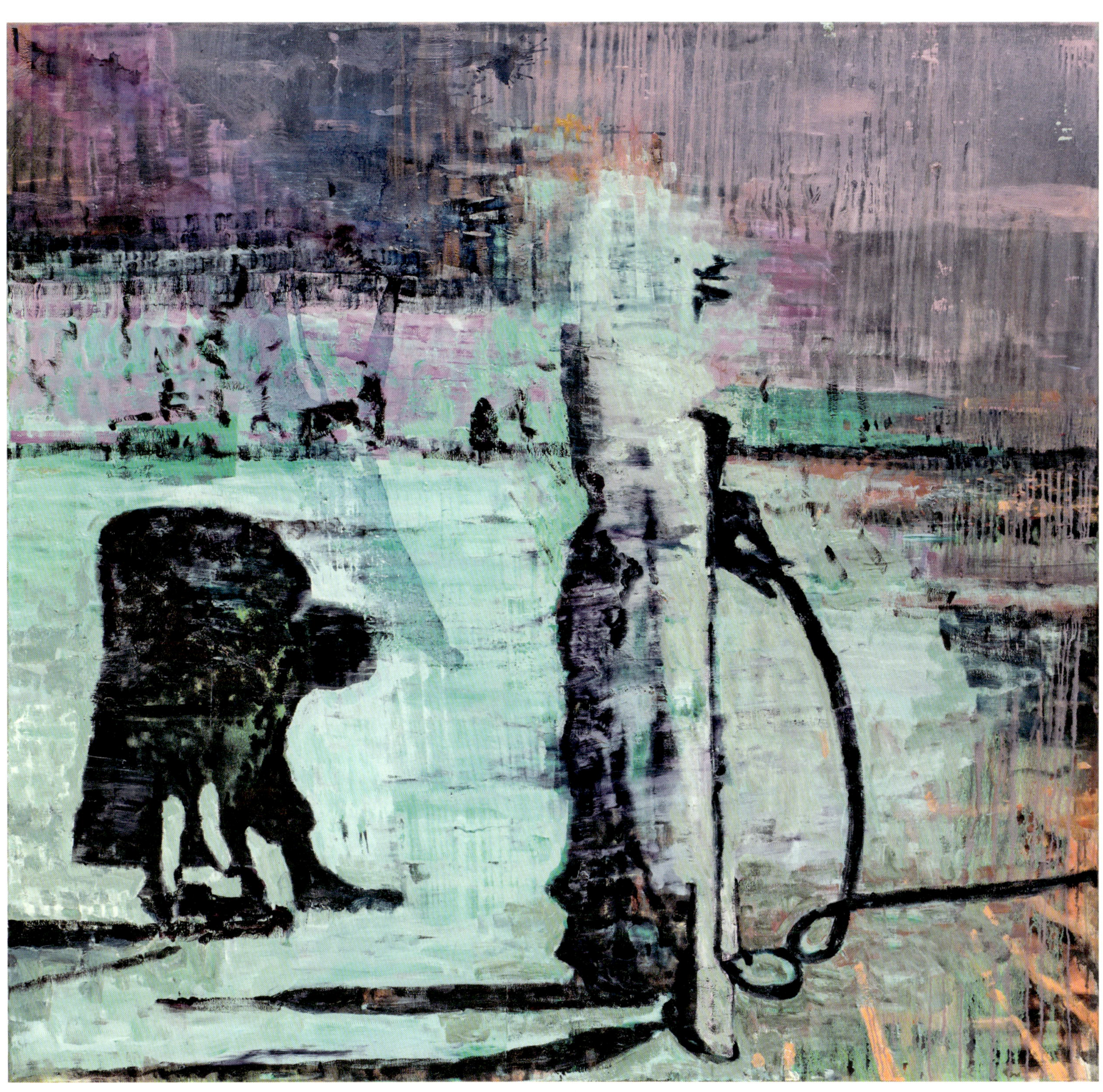

Prospectors   2015   170 cm × 180 cm

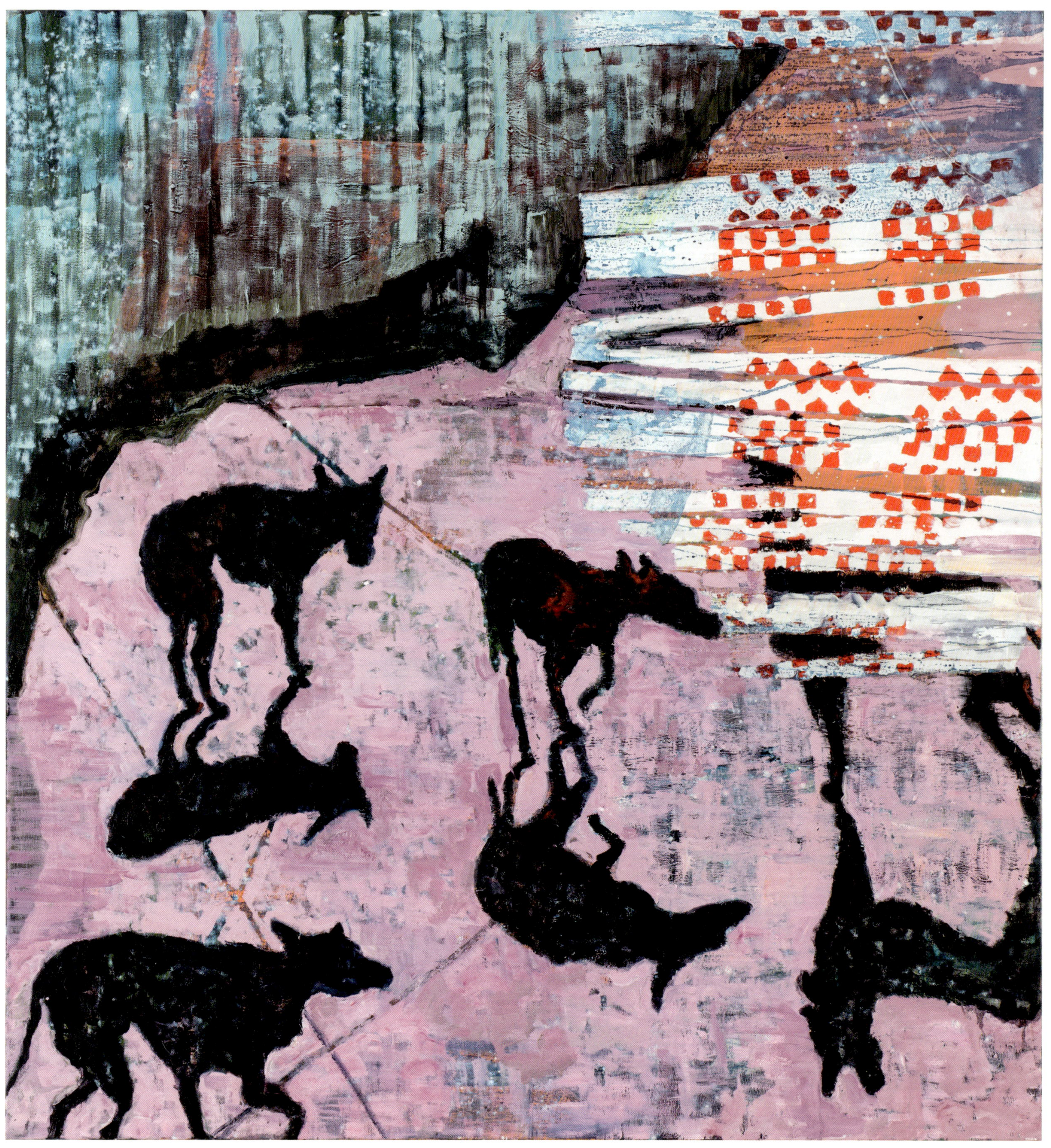

Rope Walk   2015   180 × 170 cm

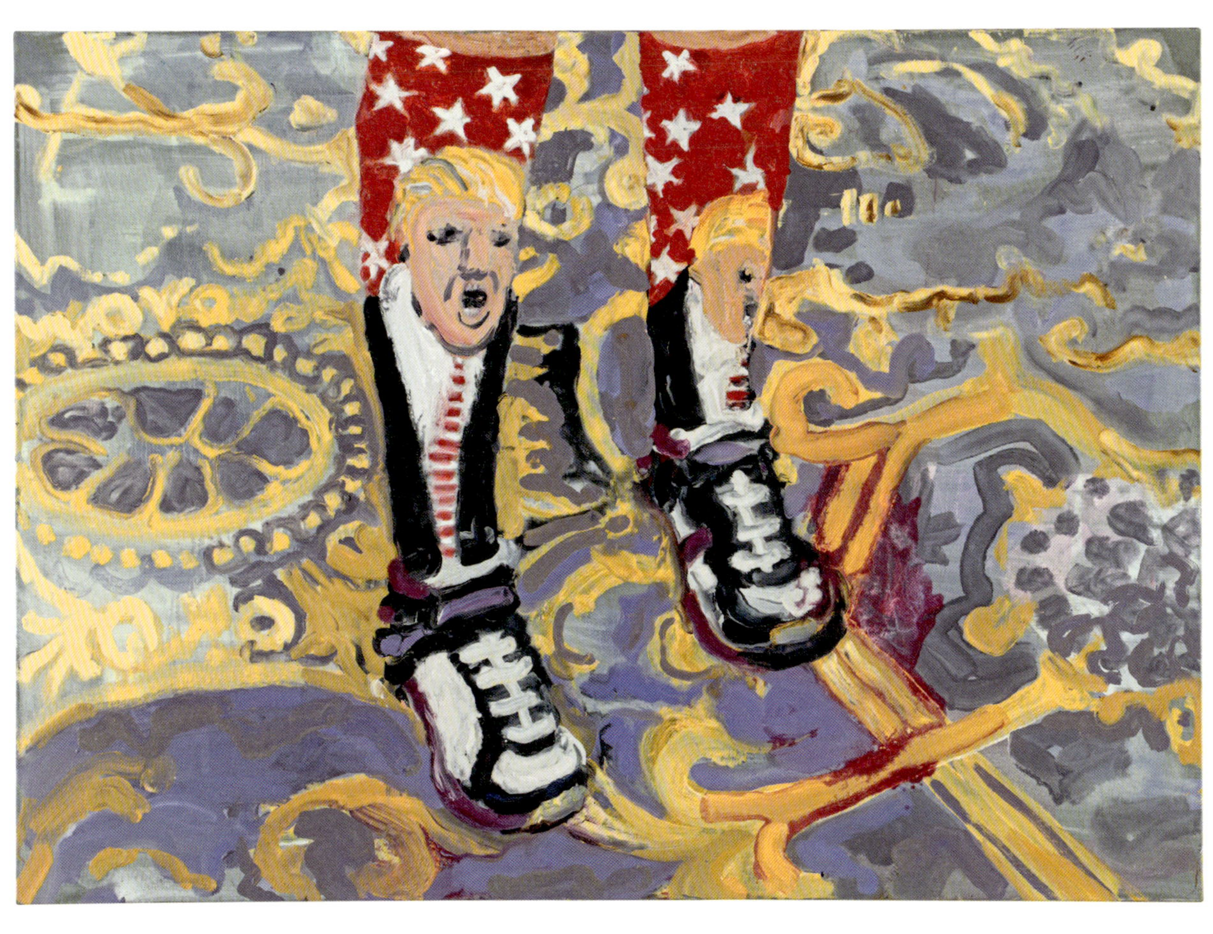

Alternative Fact   2017   100 × 120 cm

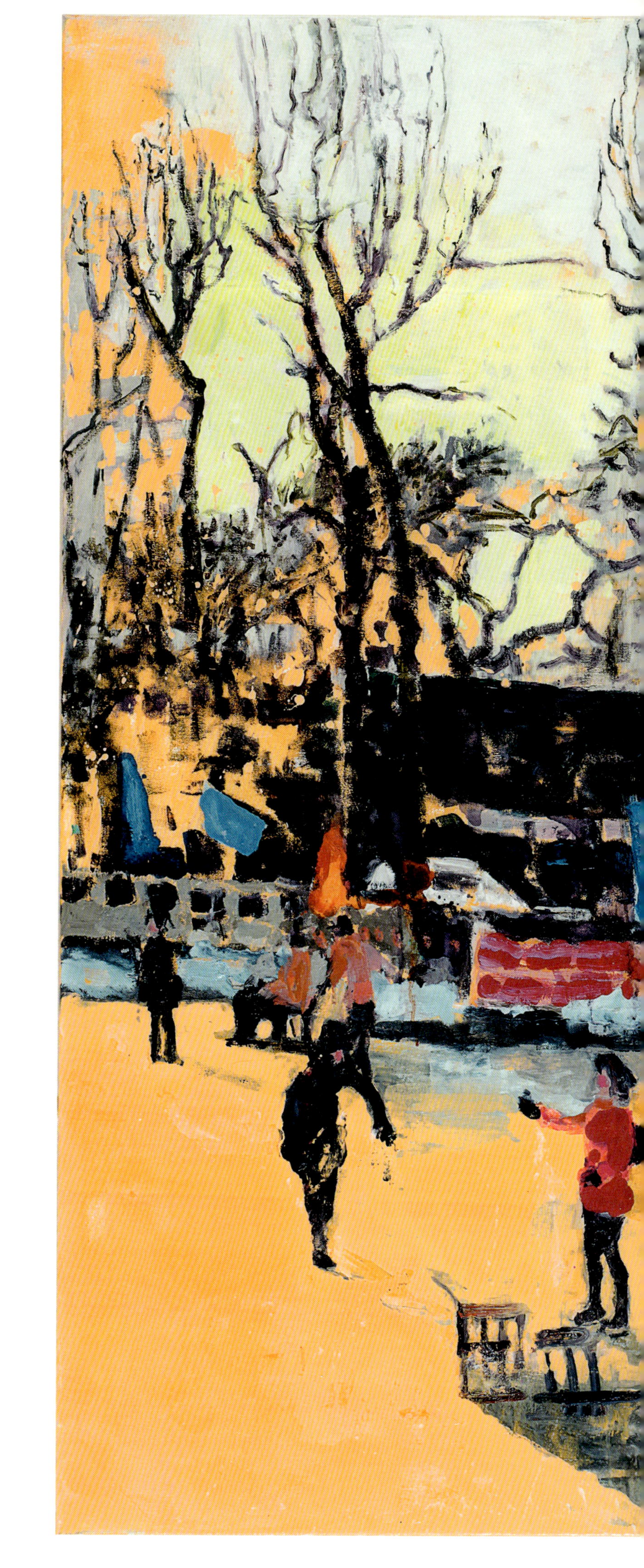

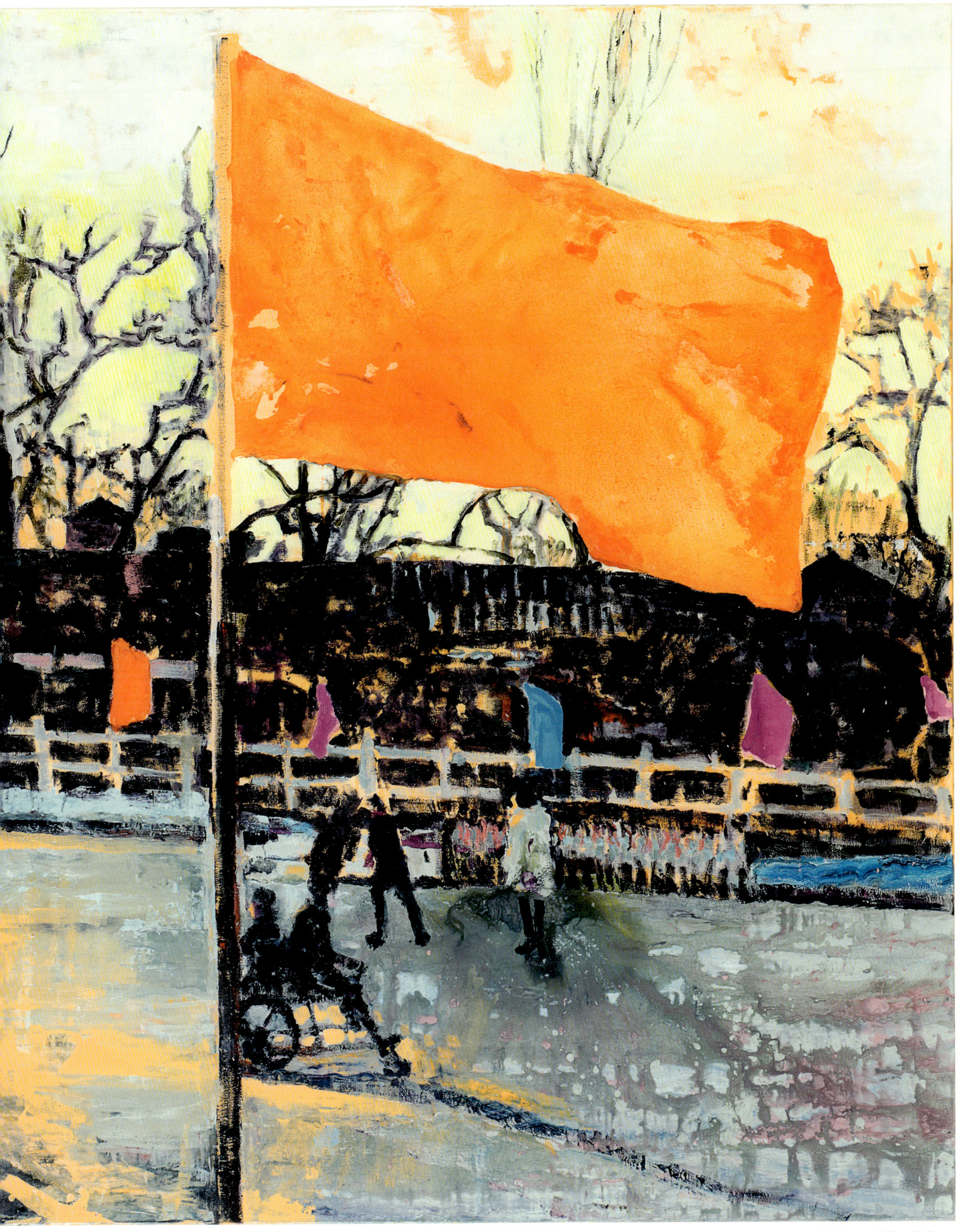

End of a Short Day   2015   170 × 210 cm

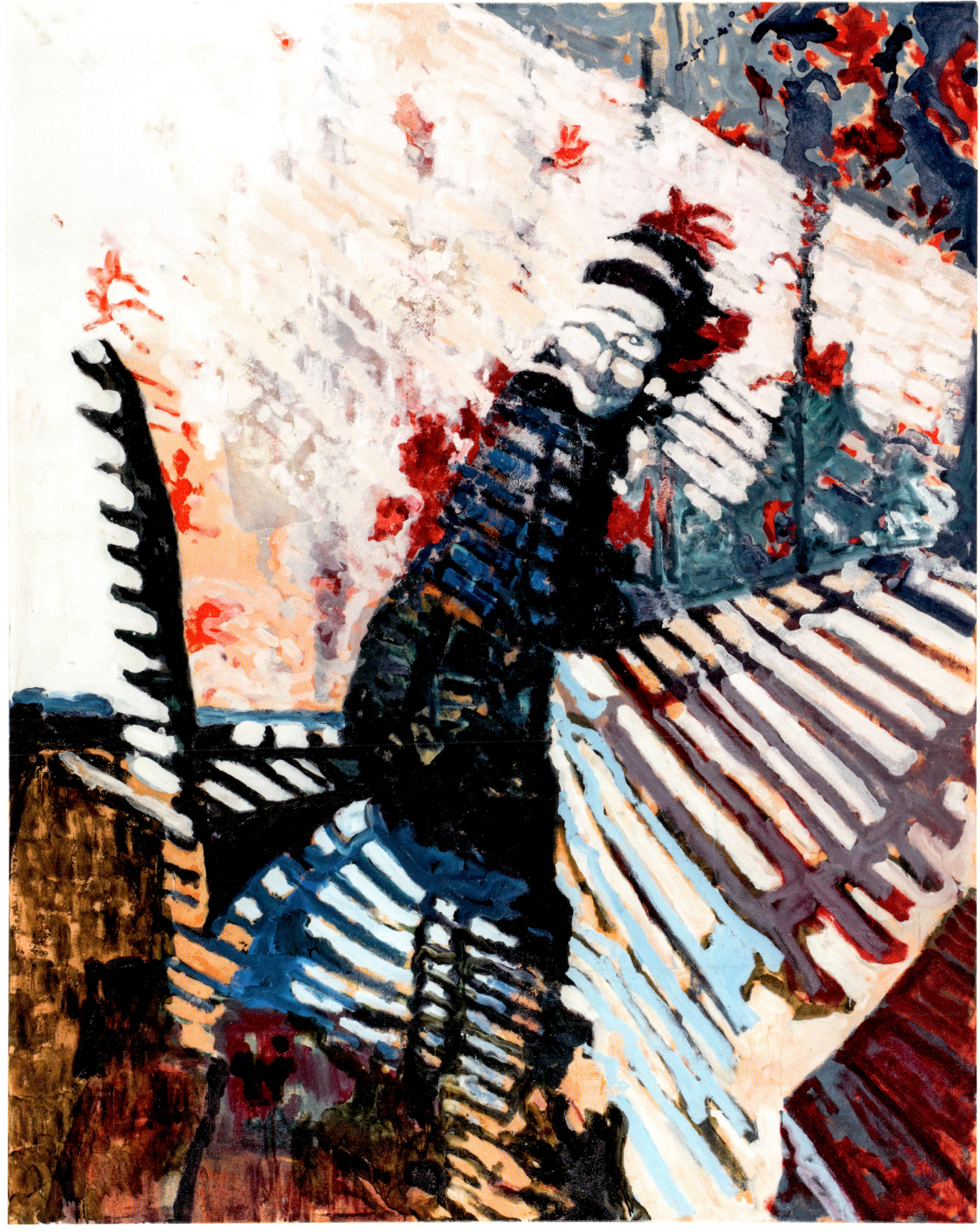

 The Elder Flower 2015 210 × 170 cm

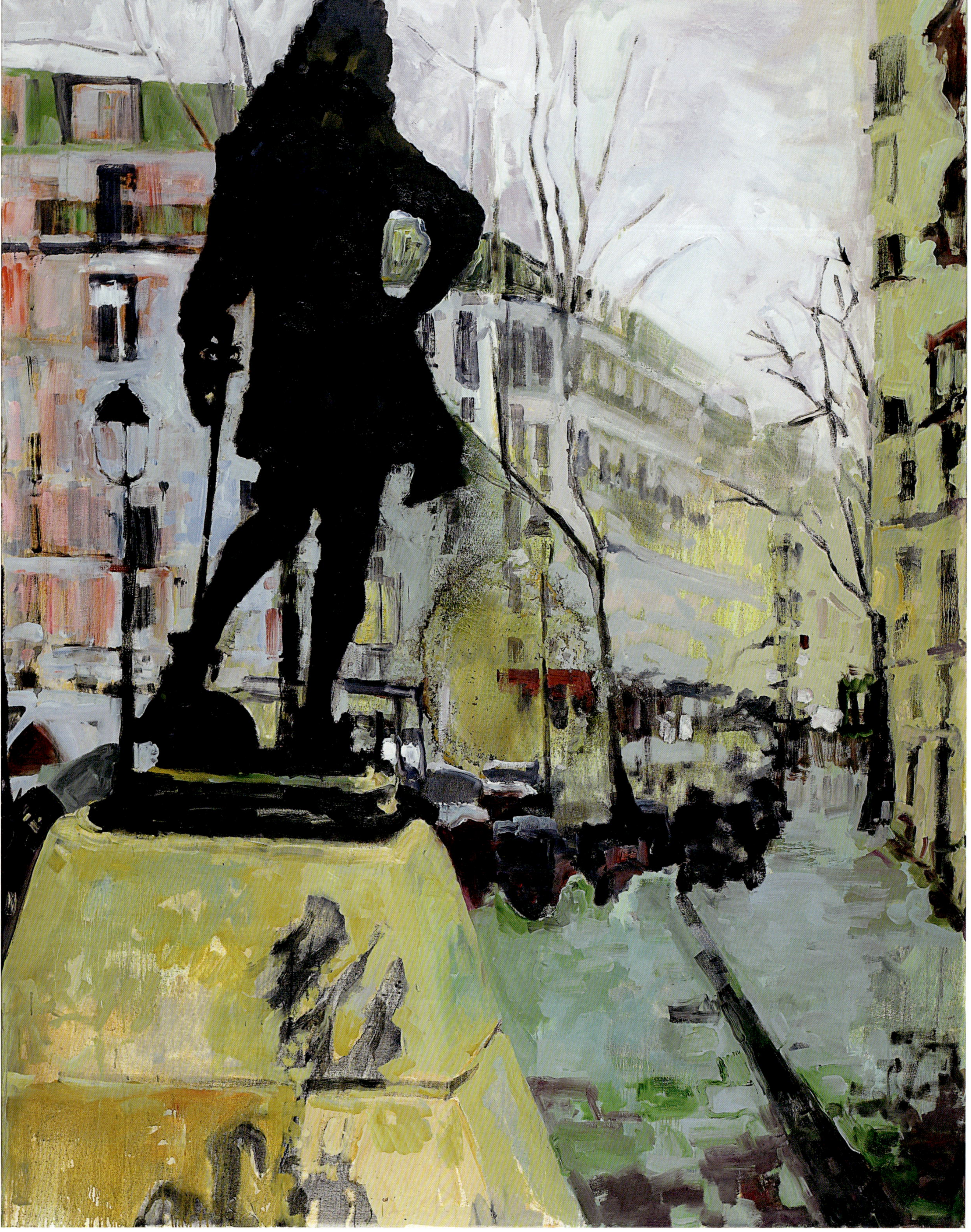

Mr Wolf   2012   210 × 170 cm

Rachel Lumsden
Return of the Huntress

[Deutsch]

Verlag für moderne Kunst

Diese Publikation und die begleitende Ausstellung bringen Rachel Lumsdens neueste Malerei mit Arbeiten der letzten Jahre zusammen. Sie bieten einen Blick auf ein Werk, das sich durch intensive Zeitgenossenschaft, Vielfalt der Bildsprache und Unkonventionalität auszeichnet.

Lumsden ist bildhungrig, mehr noch: Sie scheint sich geradezu aus der heutigen Bilderflut ernähren zu können. Alles ist ihr Recht: Zeitungsfotos, Kunstgeschichte, Traumbilder, Schaltdiagramme, Werbematerial ... Unersättlich und neugierig zugleich vertilgt sie ungeheure Mengen an Bildmaterial, das sie sich aus allen physischen Ecken und digitalen Enden zusammensucht, um damit ihr eigenes bildgebendes Verfahren zu füttern.

Dass es dabei nicht bei Sampling oder Collage bleibt, sondern am Ende Bildwelten entstehen, die sich sowohl unerwartet als auch mit grösster Selbstverständlichkeit präsentieren, ist das eigentlich Bedeutende dieses visuellen Fusionsprozesses. Es ist Lumsdens Umgang mit Farbe als Material, der das Nahtlose und Ausgewuchtete ihrer Malerei ermöglicht. In ihren Händen hat sich Farbe nicht unterzuordnen, sondern besitzt Eigenrecht und Integrität und kann so in ihrer ureigenen Natur als Substanz wirken.

Das und Lumsdens Einsicht, dass jedes Bild nur seinen eigenen Regeln gehorcht, führt zu der erstaunlichen Vielfalt ihrer Bildsprache. Stil als Visitenkarte interessiert sie nicht, sie sucht das „malerische Risiko" dort, wo sich Inhalt und Farbe abseits der Piste in die Quere kommen und vielleicht eine visuelle Lawine auslösen. Aber auch das so ins malerisch Unbekannte Losgetretene ist nicht Selbstzweck, sondern der Versuch, näher an das geheimnisvolle Leben der Bilder zu kommen, an ihren eigentlichen Puls, den Lumsden in ihrer Malerei immer wieder zu berühren vermag, ohne ihn erklären zu wollen.

Die Welt neu zeigen zu können, ist das eigentliche, sich Jahrhundert um Jahrhundert erneuernde Wunder der Malerei. Sowohl in dieser grossen Tradition als auch mitten in seiner Zeit stehend kommt uns Lumsdens Werk als eine Wirklichkeit entgegen, die zu erkunden und auszuloten der Zweck dieser Publikation und der Ausstellung ist.

Diese Einzelausstellung zeigt Rachel Lumsdens Arbeit der letzten zehn Jahre und ist die bisher umfassendste Präsentation ihrer Gemälde. Sie ist das Ergebnis einer fruchtbaren Zusammenarbeit zwischen drei Einrichtungen: der Fondation Fernet-Branca in Saint-Louis, Frankreich, dem Kunsthaus Pasquart in Biel, Schweiz, und dem Kunst(Zeug)Haus in Rapperswil-Jona, Schweiz. Wir danken Rachel Lumsden für ihr grosszügiges Engagement, das diese Ausstellung und die Publikation ermöglichte. Ebenso danken wir Bernard Jordan und den Förderinstitutionen – Kulturförderung Kanton St. Gallen, Lotteriefonds Kanton Thurgau, RHW Stiftung, Stadt St. Gallen Fachstelle Kultur, Stanley Thomas Johnson Stiftung und Pro Helvetia , Schweizer Kulturstiftung –, die uns ihre kostbare Unterstützung zuteilwerden liessen. Unser Dank geht auch an Charlotte Mullins und André Rogger für ihre scharfsinnigen Texte sowie an Thomas Bizzarri und Alain Rodriguez für die innovative und elegante Gestaltung dieser Publikation.

Pierre-Jean Sugier
Fondation Fernet-Branca

Felicity Lunn
Kunsthaus Pasquart

Peter Stohler
Kunst(Zeug)Haus Rapperswil-Jona

Anfang des 20. Jahrhunderts hielt der holländische Schriftsteller und Psychiater Frederik van Eeden schriftlich Hunderte seiner Klarträume fest. In seinem anschliessenden Roman *The Bride of Dreams* (1913) schrieb er: „Der, der träumt, ist wacher als der, der schläft" und daraus folgernd: „Der Schlüssel zum Geheimnis unseres Lebens findet sich in unseren Träumen."[1] Rachel Lumsdens Bilder scheinen unmittelbar dieser Wirkmächtigkeit der Träume und ihren nicht zu fassenden Versprechen zu entspringen. Die geisterhaften Figuren, das vielfältige Farbspektrum, die unbändigen Muster und klaustrophobischen Interieurs ihrer Bilder hinterlassen einen ähnlich intensiven Eindruck wie unvergessene Träume und eröffnen ein gefühlsgeladenes Beziehungsgeflecht, dessen Bedeutung uns in seiner Gesamtheit jedoch immer wieder auf beunruhigende Weise entgleitet. Jedes dieser Bilder nimmt das Blickfeld des Betrachters, der Betrachterin völlig ein, überwältigt die Sinne und führt uns an Orte, die einer ganz eigenen inneren Logik gehorchen. Es sind Orte, die seltsam glaubwürdig erscheinen, obwohl sie nicht selten fantastische Elemente enthalten.

Haruki Murakami – ein Schriftsteller, den Lumsden sehr schätzt und dessen Romanen eine ähnliche halluzinogene Intensität zu eigen ist – hat die emotionale Kraft von Träumen in seiner Kurzgeschichte *Schlaf* auf den Punkt gebracht. Der Erzähler beschreibt einen „dunklen, widerlichen Traum" und fährt fort: „Ich kann mich nicht an seinen Inhalt erinnern, aber ich weiss noch genau, wie er sich angefühlt hat: unheilvoll und schreckenerregend".[2] Lumsdens Bilder präsentieren sich auf ähnliche Weise, nicht als eindeutige Narrative, sondern als Bewusstseinszustände und affektive Erfahrungen.

Lumsden ist vor fünfzehn Jahren von England in die Schweiz gezogen. Gelegentlich taucht ein Motiv ihrer Schweizer Umgebung auf – wie die Schneepfähle in *Rope Walk* (2015, S. 46) beispielsweise –, doch sind es vorwiegend ihre inneren Landschaften, die sie abbildet. In ihre Arbeiten fliessen Kindheitserfahrungen, Märchen, Träume, Bilder und Fotos ein, wenn sie ihre Erinnerungen auf der Leinwand zusammenführt und verschmelzen lässt. In ihren jüngst entstandenen Bildern tritt ihr grosses malerisches Wissen, sowohl im Hinblick auf Kunstgeschichte als auch Gegenwartskunst, deutlich zutage. In *Return of the Huntress* (2016, S. 28) ist der Nachhall des Gemäldes *Jäger im Schnee* (1565) von Pieter Bruegel dem Älteren mehr als augenscheinlich, aber der Jäger (Künstler) ist nun eine Frau und alleine auf der Jagd. Sie entfernt sich von den Betrachtenden in Richtung eines verschneiten Abhangs in schwindelerregender Höhe, der den Blick auf eine moderne Stadtlandschaft unter einem viridiangrünen und magentafarbenen Himmel freigibt. Zwischen den Ästen der kahlen Bäume sickert Farbe hindurch, sie hält das Bild auf der Leinwand fest und lässt den Blick unwillkürlich zwischen der Jägerin auf ihrem Weg den Abhang hinunter und dem Verlauf der polarlichternen Farbe auf der Bildfläche hin- und herschweifen.

Angesichts der wiederholten Verwendung von Spiegel- und Rahmenmotiven in einigen erst kürzlich entstandenen Interieurs wie z. B. *Antechamber* (2015, S. 13), *Here we go Again* (2014, S. 89) und *Red Room* (2016, S. 91) stellt sich die Frage, wo eigentlich das Bilderlebnis beginnt bzw. aufhört. In *Here we go Again* dominiert ein vergoldeter Spiegel die Bildfläche, der

die Zierfiguren auf dem Kaminsims verdoppelt und den Kopf einer Frau, ein Rebhuhn auf einer Sitzstange sowie einen bewegten blauen Schatten zeigt, der dem häuslichen Umfeld entfliehen zu wollen scheint. Die Vieldeutigkeit von Édouard Manets *Bar in den Folies-Bergère* (1882) trifft hier auf das überladene Interieur von Walter Sickerts *The Mantelpiece* (ca. 1906/07), während die keramische Nachbildung eines Hundes, Porzellanfiguren von Boxern und die Figur eines Stormtroopers aus Star Wars als Erinnerungsstücke Lumsdens innerhalb des Rahmens eng beieinanderstehen.

In *Red Room* reflektiert ein ähnlicher Spiegel einen Raum, den wir selbst nicht sehen können. Der Papagei hat sich in eine Krähe mit gebogenem Schnabel verwandelt, ihr unheilvoller Schatten mahnt die Betrachtenden, dass nicht alles so ist, wie es scheint. Vielleicht verweist die heraufbeschworene Krähe auf Platons Höhlengleichnis; welche Abgründe lauern wohl im häuslichen Umfeld? Der feuerrote und kohlschwarze Raum scheint mit Möglichkeiten geradezu aufgeladen zu sein, mit einem latenten Wandel, so als könnte er jeden Moment in Flammen aufgehen oder sich auflösen, wenn der Traum endet.

Im Mittelpunkt von Lumsdens Werk steht die Figur, sei es als amorphe Form wie in *Sailing to Byzantium* (2016, S. 73) oder deutlicher umrissen wie in *Lightning Rod (Mr and Mrs Andrews)* (2016, S. 80) (In *Red Room* ist die Figur abwesend, aber ein leerer Stuhl suggeriert die Möglichkeit ihrer Anwesenheit). Sie wird niemals unmittelbar als Porträt dargestellt, sondern steht immer im Dienst des Bildes, manchmal ist sie auf eine angedeutete Form beschränkt, ein anderes Mal wird sie durch eine markante Gestaltung der

Oberfläche verdeckt (wie in *Lightning Rod*), um die Kohärenz zwischen dem dreidimensionalen Objekt und dem zweidimensionalen Gemälde sicherzustellen. Denn, auch wenn auf den grossformatigen Arbeiten von Lumsden bestimmte Subjekte – wie Figuren, Innenräume oder Stadtsilhouetten – erkennbar sind, wird doch immer der Eindruck vermittelt, dass die Farbe auf der Oberfläche die Oberhand behält.

Häufig verwendet Lumsden ungewöhnliche Motive wie beispielsweise den Doppelgänger in *Leap Minute* (2015, S. 31), die Figuren mit den Schutzbrillen in *Crow Tribe* (2016, S. 101) oder den anthropomorphen Bären in *Highway Gamblers* (2008, Abb. H, S. 128). Die Assoziation zum Unheimlichen, wie Freud es genannt hat, drängt sich geradezu auf, es bleibt aber immer die Farbe, die diese Deutung verschlüsselt. Lumsden sagt dazu: „Du begibst dich auf ein Abenteuer, wenn du malst. Auf der einen Seite möchte man bestimmte Bereiche offenlassen, die Sache nicht überziehen, aber wenn man das Subjekt kennt, fragt man sich natürlich, was sich noch dahinter verbirgt."[3] In *Leap Minute* übermalte Lumsden schliesslich die Gesichter der Mädchen und opferte ihre Identität für eine verstörende Bildwirkung. Ihre Köpfe scheinen vom Körper losgelöst und verdreht, die Tapete hinter ihnen tritt mit ihrem Muster in den Vordergrund und zieht sich bis über das Sofa. Lumsden möchte die Möglichkeit der Mehrdeutigkeit offenhalten, einen Raum, den die Betrachtenden mit ihren eigenen Ansichten füllen können. Sie vermeidet die Klarheit und gesteht der Farbe ihren eigenen Willen zu. Dabei vertraut sie den Entscheidungen, die sich während des Arbeitens ergeben und weniger einem vorab gefassten strikten Plan.

Diesen Ansatz treibt sie in ihren jüngeren Bildern auf die Spitze, vor allem bei den Interieurs, die in einem Wirrwarr aus abstrakten Zeichen auseinanderzutreiben scheinen. *The Elder Flower* (2015, S. 51) zeigt eine Frau, die im Begriff ist, sich von einem Stuhl zu erheben. Ihr Gesicht wird von lamellenartig einfallendem Sonnenlicht erhellt. Diese Form der klaren Lesbarkeit ist jedoch nur angesichts einer Reproduktion der Arbeit möglich. Steht man vor dem Original des Gemäldes, scheint sich die Oberfläche fast vollständig aufzulösen, das Sonnenlicht überstrahlt alles mit seiner weissen Fluoreszenz, die hellblauen, kobalt- und auberginefarbenen Schatten überziehen die Oberfläche des Bildes mit einem Muster, das an Eisenbahnschwellen erinnert – und das Gesicht, wenn man es überhaupt so bezeichnen möchte, besteht aus weissen und braungrauen Stellen über einem lasierten blauen Grund.

Ein einzelnes weisses Oval hält die Gesichtszüge zusammen, sodass wir ein Auge, Augenbrauen, ein Kinn erahnen können. Diese symbiotische Beziehung zwischen Oberfläche und Subjekt bezeichnet Lumsden als das „Spalten des Atoms", der Farbe wird sozusagen eine Nebenbeschäftigung als Subjekt zugewiesen, während das Subjekt selbst in Schleifen und Windungen, Mustern aus Farbe und Form explodiert.[4] Wenn beide möglich werden und zeitgleich präsent sind, erfüllt dies die Arbeit mit einer knisternden Energie.

Die Farbe ist es, die Lumsden vorantreibt, sei es das limonadenorange Leuchten von *End of a Short Day* (2015, S. 49) oder das markante Nordlicht von *Return of the Huntress*. In *Think Tank* (2015, S. 21) ist sie spärlich und spröde, in *Leap Minute* kritzelig und nervös und in *Red Room* glühend und gespenstisch. Die von ihrer Hand geführte Farbe bleibt dem Betrachter, der Betrachterin in der Kehle stecken, eine Unzahl von Farben durchdringt unseren Verstand und zielt unmittelbar ins Herz. Diese Bilder lassen sich nicht mit Abstand oder als Reproduktion betrachten, sie müssen vielmehr körperlich erlebt, gespürt und geträumt werden.

Endnoten

1   Frederik van Eeden, *The Bride of Dreams*, 1913, Auszug in: Anna Faherty (Hg.), *States of Mind: Experiences at the Edge of Consciousness*, Austellungskatalog, Wellcome Collection, London 2016, S. 112–114.
2   Haruki Murakami, „Sleep" (dt. Schlaf), in: *The Elephant Vanishes*, Vintage, London 1994, S. 105–106.
3   Aus einem Gespräch der Künstlerin mit der Autorin, 29. November 2016.
4   Ebd.

Es ist Winter, später Nachmittag, der Himmel grauviolett und smaragdgrün, das Licht gedämpft. Die Jägerin kehrt über eine Kuppe zurück zur Stadt mit ihren Bürogebäuden, Fabriken und Parkplatzdächern. Ein Hund trottet neben ihr her. Es ist sehr still.

Wir befinden uns ein Stück hinter der Jägerin, beinahe am Rande der Leinwand, wo schwarze, von schmutzigweissen Pinselstrichen unterbrochene Streifen unter dem Bann der Jägerin wie Bäume erscheinen.

Wir sind uns bewusst, wie *Return of the Huntress* (2016, S. 28), ein neues Gemälde von Rachel Lumsden, konstruiert ist, nehmen die Materialität der Farbe wahr, das dick aufgetragene Impasto über wässrig verlaufenden Nuancen, spüren das offenkundige Vergnügen daran, wie Farbe auf der Bildfläche hin- und hergeschoben und manipuliert werden kann, um Textur und Tiefe, ja auch Berührung und Klang entstehen zu lassen.

… und doch sind wir auch die Jägerin selbst, sie zieht mit uns, wir ziehen mit ihr.

All diese Qualitäten waren Rachel Lumsdens Arbeiten auch schon vor fünfzehn Jahren zu eigen. Diese Publikation und die begleitende Ausstellung machen hingegen deutlich, wie sehr sich ihre Bilder in dieser Zeit hinsichtlich Thematik und ihres Umgangs mit Farbe auch verändert haben.

Als Lumsden 2002 von London nach St. Gallen zog, war es gerade vier Jahre her, als sie ihren Master in Malerei an den Royal Academy Schools absolviert hatte. Das Vermächtnis von Francis Bacon, Lucian Freud, Frank Auerbach und anderen Malern der Londoner Schule sowie der Einfluss von Künstlern wie Peter Doig, Elizabeth Peyton oder Dexter Dalwood in den letzten Jahren haben der figurativen Malerei in Grossbritannien

eine ungebrochene Aufmerksamkeit beschert. Es ist daher kein Zufall, dass Lumsdens Herangehensweise an die Malerei viel mit ihren Vorgängern gemeinsam hat – und dass sich ihr Stil in der Schweizer Kunstszene auf augenfällige Weise abhebt.

Ihre auffallend grossformatigen Gemälde sind meistens mindestens so gross wie Lumsden selbst und erlauben ihr, eine körperliche Beziehung zu ihren Werken herzustellen, etwas, das sich auch auf den späteren Betrachter überträgt. Eindrücklich vermitteln die Bilder den Prozess ihrer Entstehung und lassen auf eine Künstlerin schliessen, die ein enormes Gespür für die Eigenschaften und Möglichkeiten ihres Materials besitzt. Lumsdens Arbeiten können nicht als narrativ bezeichnet werden, weil sie zu offen und für eine eindeutige Lesart zu mehrdeutig bleiben; es lässt sich zumindest sagen, dass es sich um atmosphärisch aufgeladene Welten handelt. Ihre Themen verbinden unbeachtete Paraphernalien des Alltäglichen mit fantastischen Elementen, autobiografische Fragmente mit dem kollektiven Unbewussten. Diese stimmen oft mit dem Zeitgeist in der Malerei, aber auch mit aktuellen sozialen und politischen Aspekten überein. Dennoch bleiben sie auf eine bemerkenswerte Weise eigensinnig und autonom. Lumsden erschafft Bilder, die eine geheimnisvolle Energie abstrahlen und zwischen Materialoberfläche und Bildlichkeit zu oszillieren scheinen.

Werkgruppen

Bis 2010 hat Rachel Lumsden das Malen in Serien bevorzugt. Diese Vorgehensweise ermöglichte ihr die Wiederholung bestimmter Bildmotive oder

Ideen über einen Zeitraum von mehreren Monaten, um die verschiedenen Aspekte eines Themas schrittweise entfalten und darstellen zu können, zum Nutzen einer stärkeren Wirkung auf die Betrachterinnen und Betrachter. Das Ergebnis war mehr als beeindruckend: Während die serielle Herangehensweise eine Art versetzten Dialog mit dem Thema entstehen liess, entwickelten die einzelnen Arbeiten eine derartige Dichte, dass es den Anschein hatte, als wären Filmsequenzen zu einem einzigen eindringlichen Bild eingedampft worden.

Im Mittelpunkt der frühen Serien steht jeweils ein klar definiertes Objekt, das Aspekte aus Lumsdens Vergangenheit verkörpert. In *Ancestral Inheritance* (1998, Abb. A, S. 127) ist auf jedem Bild ein Möbelstück aus dem Besitz ihrer Grossmutter zu sehen. Während die überlebensgrosse Darstellung des Mobiliars an die Welt der kleiner gewordenen Alice im Wunderland denken lässt, erinnert die ebenso spannende wie unheimliche Dunkelheit unter den Möbelstücken an Roald Dahl oder Edgar Allan Poe.

Auch in der nächsten Serie *Arc Light* (2001, Abb. K, S. 129) konzentrierte sich Lumsden auf einen einzelnen Einrichtungsgegenstand, in diesem Fall ein altmodischer Lampenschirm. Der finster-brütende Hintergrund der Bilder kontrastiert die Schrulligkeit des Objekts. Es sind aber die übertrieben langen, nach unten laufenden Farbtropfen, die das Bild über die schlichte Darstellung einer Figur-Grund-Beziehung hinaustragen in die düstere Interpretation eines alltäglichen Gegenstandes. Lumsdens Interesse galt hier der Frage, wie derartig banale Objekte eine psychologische Dimension annehmen können, die der Intensität eines menschlichen Porträts entspricht. In diesem

Zusammenhang ist die Tatsache bedeutend, dass Lumsden fast nie die Gesichter ihrer Figuren im Detail zeigt – vielmehr zieht sie es vor, Charakter, Stimmung oder auch Beziehungen mittels Körperhaltungen oder Bewegungen zu vermitteln und auf die Darstellung des Gesichts zu verzichten.

Ein Aspekt von Lumsdens Arbeiten, der in *Arc Light* offensichtlich wird, ist ihr Interesse an Hell-Dunkel-Kontrasten. Während das in dieser Serie durch eine künstliche Lichtquelle evident wird, ist es in späteren Bildern oft Tageslicht, das sich im Fenster eines düsteren Interieurs zeigt, oder Sonnenlicht, das den Schattenwurf der Dinge betont oder das Drama eines stürmischen und sich verfinsternden Himmels unterstreicht. Lumsden hat in dieser Serie mehrere Elemente einer Vorgehensweise eingeführt, die sie später sowohl prüfend wiederverwendet als auch weiterentwickelt.

Mit der Serie *Homeland Security* (2003, Abb. B,C, S. 127) setzte Lumsden die Erkundung der trivialen und möglicherweise anrüchigen Seiten des häuslichen Lebens fort; dabei spielten insbesondere Kultur und Traditionen ihres Heimatlandes Grossbritannien eine Rolle. Das Motiv des „Tea Cosy", einer gehäkelten Wärmehaube für die Teekanne, stand in direktem Zusammenhang mit ihrer Ankunft in der Schweiz, die zeitgleich mit 9/11 und dem Krieg in Afghanistan geschah. Verstört von der negativen Berichterstattung über Grossbritannien in der Schweizer Presse und ihrer eigenen Entwurzelung in einem fremden Land bewusst, wählte Lumsden das „Tea Cosy" als archetypisches britisches Symbol für schlechten Geschmack, das auf der Leinwand als Gruppe oder einzeln die gesamte Bildfläche füllend an die Formen manövrierenden Panzern erinnert.

In ihrem Spiel mit der Mehrdeutigkeit ging sie einen Schritt weiter, als sie in der anschliessenden Serie *Dashboard Talisman* (2005, Abb. M, S. 129) etwas Kleinem und Unbedeutendem den Status eines monumentalen malerischen Sujets verlieh: Dass Lumsden die Plüschtiermaskottchen, die in Autos vom Rückspiegel baumeln, zum Motiv grossformatiger Gemälde erhob, lässt auf eine gewisse exzentrische Beharrlichkeit in ihr schliessen. In ihrem voyeuristischen Blick über die Motorhaube entschied sie sich für eine Perspektive, die sich sowohl mit den räumlichen Bezügen als auch mit dem Tabu des Eindringens ins Private befasste und nicht an der getreuen Abbildung der Automobilisten-Fetische interessiert war.

Lumsdens Interesse an sowohl natürlichen Formen als auch an mechanischen Konstruktionen zieht sich wie ein roter Faden durch ihre künstlerische Praxis, zum Beispiel in der kürzlich entstandenen grossformatigen Wandarbeit, die sie für das Bildungszentrum Arbon im Kanton Thurgau geschaffen hat. Ein schwarzes Raster, das Assoziation an Schaltkreise und Netzknoten weckt, überzieht ein vielfarbiges Wabenmuster, das uns schon aus der Serie *Silent Inhabitants* (2006, Abb. D,E, S.127) bekannt vorkommt: In jenen Arbeiten treffen Mikrozellen und Schaltplatinen auf Blumen, Vögel und Insekten und entwickeln neue parasitäre Lebensformen, um überlebensfähig zu bleiben. *Silent Inhabitants* führt ein charakteristisches Merkmal von Lumsdens Arbeit ein, das in späteren Bildern oft anzutreffen ist – ihre Fähigkeit, Atmosphäre zu schaffen, ohne auf Erzählerisches zurückzugreifen. Für die Arbeit *Kriechstrom* (2006) hat sie beispielsweise eine Nagelbürste über die Leinwand gezogen, um unregelmässige und filigrane Linien zu erzeugen,

die an einen elektrischen Schaltplan erinnern und dem Bild sowohl Bewegungsdrang als auch das Äquivalent weissen Rauschens verleihen.

Unbehagen bleibt auch in der Werkgruppe mit dem Titel *Bird Wars* (2007-2008, Abb. F, G, S.128) allgemeiner Tenor: Vögel und Tiere in Menschengestalt vertreten den Menschen und seine Emotionen. Trotz der konventionellen Komposition mit der Kombination aus Bäumen, Figuren und Vögeln entziehen sich diese Arbeiten einer eindeutigen Lesart. Vielmehr lösen sie disparate Rückbesinnungen aus, etwa auf unheimliche Gestalten aus Kinderbüchern, Illustrationen aus Büchern des 17. Jahrhunderts, auf die gesellschaftskritischen Satiren und Karikaturen von Hogarth und Goya, auf Computerspiele.

Der Übergriff der Vergangenheit

Lumsdens Arbeiten sind immer auch in einem kunsthistorischen Kontext zu betrachten, da sie keinerlei Bedenken bei der Aneignung bestimmter Themen oder dem Umgang mit Farbe kennt: „Ich liebe Corots atmosphärisch aufgeladene Herbstlandschaften, aber auch Malcolm Morleys Malerei, die eigentlich das Gegenteil von dem ist, was ich mache."[1] So hat sie in der kleinformatigen Arbeit *Morley's Deckchair* (2015, S. 85) ihre Wertschätzung für Morleys Darstellung von Figuren in vertrauter Umgebung demonstriert. Mit ihren Bezügen auf historische Bilderwelten – wie beispielsweise barocke Kostüme und Otto Lilienthals Hängegleiter in *Bird Wars*, oder öffentliche Denkmäler wie bei *12 O'clock High* (2012, Abb. J, S. 129) und *Mr Wolf* (2012, S. 52) – komprimiert Lumsden Vergangenheit und Gegenwart und führt historische, politische und soziale Aspekte zusammen. Die Geschichte Grossbritanniens ist ein wiederkehrender Hintergrund der Arbeiten, beispielsweise die Operationszentrale aus dem Zweiten Weltkrieg in *When Push Comes to Shove* (2012, Abb. L, p. 129), der sie beiläufig Spielsalonmotive hinzugefügt hat.

Der Übergriff der Vergangenheit auf die Gegenwart kommt vor allem in der Atmosphäre von Lumsdens Interieurs zum Ausdruck. Die antiquierten Möbel, die in vielen ihrer Interieurs auftauchen – insbesondere Beistelltischchen, Lampe und Zierfigürchen – gründen die Bilder in der Muffigkeit altmodischer Wohnzimmer, die, zumindest in Grossbritannien, immer noch in einer gewissen Gesellschaftsschicht zu finden sind. Lumsdens beständiges Interesse an diesem Sujet, das in der britischen Malerei eine grosse Tradition hat, wurde vielleicht auch durch den Umstand verstärkt, dass sie schon lange ausserhalb des Landes lebt: „Einer der stärksten und nachhaltigsten Einflüsse auf meine Arbeit sind die Gemälde von Walter Sickert aus dem späten 19. Jahrhundert. Seine etwas düsteren bürgerlichen Wohnräume, aber auch seine Bilder der schmutzigeren Seiten Londons fliessen in meine Interieurs ein."[2] Die Darstellung eines Raumes kann sehr expressiv sein, wenn Objekte wie Lampen und Möbel als Stellvertreter der Figur zum Einsatz kommen und die Vieldeutigkeit des Raumes die Atmosphäre auflädt. In *Here we go Again* (2014, S. 89) ist es zum Beispiel nicht auf den ersten Blick ersichtlich, dass man einen Kaminsims und dessen Spiegelbild sieht. Die Interieurs zeigen sich in Nahsicht, bieten so einen fragmentierten Blick auf die Dinge an und nehmen zugleich den Betrachter in ihre Introspektion auf. Den unbehaglichen Eindruck, die Dinge seien nicht unbedingt das, was man zu sehen glaubt, erzeugt Lumsden in vielen ihrer Arbeiten immer wieder durch Hinzufügen von Türen, hinter denen eine andere Welt lauern könnte. Auch verwendet sie Fenster als Mittel der dramatischen Inszenierung, um ein Bild im Bild zu schaffen.

In die Farbe schlüpfen

Die doppeldeutige Lesart erstreckt sich auch auf den Herstellungsprozess der Bilder. Lumsdens Umgang mit Farbe – sowohl was die farbliche Gestaltung als auch das Material an sich betrifft – ist radikal. Farbe ist zugleich grell und schmutzig, satt und diskordant. Die Melancholie, die dem Bürgerlichen innewohnt, offenbart sich im Schmutz und der Giftigkeit verstaubter Interieurs in der Serie *Ancestral Inheritance* und weitet sich zur klaustrophobischen Atmosphäre jüngerer Arbeiten wie *Leap Minute* (2015, S. 31). Bis zu Bildern wie *End of a Short Day* (2015, S. 49) mit seinen leuchtend orangen Farbflächen hat Lumsden einer einzelnen Farbe nur selten eine solch umfassende Entfaltung zugestanden. Das geschah eher in Form öliger Auskargungen, die viel mehr reine Malerei als Darstellung sind, oder mit Terpentinlachen, die auf der Bildfläche wie tiefe Löcher wirken. Schwarz kommt eine bemerkenswert grosse Bedeutung zu: Es schimmert durch die Schichten anderer Farben oder verschmutzt diese direkt; auch haften schwarze Partikel an Objekten oder schweben in der Atmosphäre. Die Präsenz des Schwarz wird zudem als Kontrast zum Licht spürbar, das Lumsdens Arbeiten erhellt und scheinbar von innen ausleuchtet.

Bei naher Betrachtung scheinen sich aber auch die von grellem Sonnenlicht erzeugten schwarzen Schatten aufzulösen, die Farbe verrät hier wenig über das Abgebildete, das sich erst wieder aus der Ferne zu erkennen gibt. Die Formen zeigen sich an Stellen, an denen die Farbe verrinnt, besonders diffus. Der Inhalt der Arbeit wird im Zusammenwirken von Farbe und ihrer Materialität verkapselt, wobei letztere häufig eine eigenständige Ebene der Abstraktion besetzt. Durch Verwendung von Ölfarbe, die sie wiederholt mit Pinseln und anderen Werkzeugen bearbeitet, erzeugt Lumsden für grössere Bereiche einen weichen, gestischen Pinselduktus, der mit der dynamischen Pinselführung an anderen Stellen kontrastiert. Es ist von Bedeutung, dass Lumsden kaum mit mittleren Formaten arbeitet, vielmehr malt sie regelmässig kleine Bilder auf Resopal-Platten, Papier oder Leinwand. Diese können sowohl als Arbeitsskizzen für grössere Gemälde dienen, als auch als eigenständige Werke gelten.

Obwohl Lumsdens Arbeiten deutlich figurativ sind, bleibt die Rolle der menschlichen Figur mehrdeutig, nicht zuletzt, weil die Künstlerin nur selten Gesichter darstellt und somit Erzählerisches oder Psychologie vermeidet. Ihre Figuren entspringen dem trockenen Humor, der für Lumsdens Arbeiten charakteristisch ist und der die düstere Atmosphäre und beklemmende Thematik aufhellt – oder manchmal auch eine dezidierte Ironie durchblitzen lässt wie im Falle der hybriden Kreaturen in *Bird Wars* oder der Dreiecksbeziehung von Mann, Frau und Puma in *On a Sticky Wicket* (2012, Abb. I, S. 128). Häufig übermalt Lumsden einzelne Elemente eines Bildes, um etwas Anderes zur Erzeugung von Kontrast hervorzuheben: „In der Malerei geht es für mich um diesen Akt der Zerstörung, der einer Arbeit ein zweites oder gar drittes Leben ermöglicht.

Ein Beispiel dafür ist das Bild zweier Mädchen. Ich habe ihre Gesichter übermalt, obwohl sie durchaus gelungen waren, da das Bild dadurch zu einem Porträt geworden wäre, anstatt die Bewegung zwischen verschiedenen visuellen Schichten zu sein. Ich wollte, dass sich die konkrete Welt in vieldeutigeren Formen auflöst." [3]

Lumsdens Beziehung zu ihrem Material hat sich in den letzten zwei, drei Jahren verändert: Sie wagt mehr und setzt weniger auf erprobte Strategien wie früher. Sie arbeitet mit trockenem Impasto und dünnen Schichten flüssiger Farbe, um bestimmte Bereiche farblich zurückzunehmen; mitunter giesst sie auch die Farbe auf die Bildoberfläche „bis sie richtig suppig ist und ich das Gefühl habe, in Farbe zu schwimmen".[4] Indem sie Farbe über die Oberfläche zieht oder ausgiesst – ein Vorgang, der sich nur teilweise kontrollieren lässt – erzeugt sie sowohl trockene als auch klebrige Bereiche. Durch dieses Ringen – dem Dialog mit der Materialität der Malerei – öffnet sie den Raum für Unerwartetes. Lumsden beschreibt das so: „Die Malerei ist die sexy Form der Quantenphysik, jede Spur auf der Leinwand ist nicht nur ein Farbklecks, sondern auch die Darstellung einer Form. Es ist diese inhärente Dualität, die dem Bild seine Spannung verleiht. Manchmal habe ich das Gefühl, auf einer schlammigen Baustelle zu stehen, wo ich so lange zwischen Idee und Material verhandle, bis ein verlaufener Farbfleck figurativen Gehalt annimmt, der aber formbar genug bleibt, um für sich selbst, aber auch für etwas Anderes zu stehen." [5]

Der Impuls für eine neue Arbeit wird gewöhnlich von etwas ausgelöst, das Lumsden gesehen hat. Sie arbeitet intuitiv, sieht aber Intuition als ein über viele Jahre erworbenes Wissen. Insofern nutzt sie sie als entscheidende Komponente des Balanceaktes zwischen der Herstellung einer Bildwelt und der Handhabung der Farbe. Die Unberechenbarkeit des Mediums gibt Lumsden die Freiheit, Fehler oder Unfälle geradezu herauszufordern – obgleich „mit einer gewissen Antizipation des Resultats" [6], um so eher den Prozess in den Mittelpunkt zu stellen und nicht die zuvor definierte Bildidee. „Mir geht es in meiner Arbeit immer um Materialität, das geht so weit, dass ich sogar Ideen aufgebe, damit die Farbe selbst sich entwickeln kann. Jede Leinwand gleicht einem eigenen Universum mit jeweils unterschiedlichen Regeln, auf die zu reagieren ich fähig sein muss. In mir ist die Erkenntnis gereift, dass Malerei nur auf der Leinwand stattfindet und zwar im Moment des Malens selbst. Ich kann zwar Themen recherchieren, nach inspirierenden Materialien suchen, in Photoshop mit Kompositionen experimentieren und Skizzen anfertigen, aber all das bleibt immer nur Vorbereitung für den Moment, in dem Farbe auf Leinwand trifft."[7]

Mit leichtem, tänzelndem Schritt kehrt die Jägerin zurück. Der Hund streicht um ihre Beine, schnüffelt an der Beute, die sie über der Schulter trägt.

Am Waldrand hält sie kurz inne, ihr Blick schweift über die abendliche Stadt. Es ist sehr still. Dort unten wird sie ihre Bilder ausbreiten, damit die Anderen sie sammeln, betrachten und studieren können, bis alle gesättigt ihrer Wege ziehen.

Endnoten

1 Aus einem Gespräch zwischen der Autorin und Rachel Lumsden am 15. August 2015.

2–7 Ebd.

Ein Flugzeug ist auf einer mittagshellen Landebahn geparkt, die Bemalung des Hecks zu verschwommen, um es einer Nation zuzuordnen. Vielleicht eine Szene in den Tropen, wofür neben dem in der Hitze flimmernden Flugzeugheck auch eine Palme und die Silhouette einer krausköpfigen Rückenfigur im Vordergrund sprechen. Eine Passagiertreppe ist dem Flugzeug angedockt, doch niemand scheint sie benützen zu wollen – eine seltsam still gestellte Szene, allenfalls mit leicht mulmigen Assoziationen an früher gesehene Bilder von Flugzeugentführungen. Oder eine Allee entlang der Umfassungsmauer der Verbotenen Stadt in Peking: Baumschatten – in dichtem Takt über den gekalkten Gehweg, eine ebenso weiss bemalte Sockelzone und die leuchtend chinesisch rote Mauer geworfen – ziehen den Blick in eine unbestimmte Tiefe, die man zu Fuss nicht unbedingt weiter erkunden möchte. Und wie ist das mit dieser nächtlich verlassenen Parkfläche, wo die hoch auf eine Stange gesetzte Überwachungsbeleuchtung für irreale Klarheit sorgt? Wirkt dieses gleissende Licht, von einem milchigen Hof umfangen, nun beschützend für die wenigen anwesenden Fahrzeuge, oder nicht eher selber bedrohlich?

Dies nur drei Stimmungen aus jenen skizzenhaften Arbeiten, die Rachel Lumsden „zwischendurch" malt. Mit *Here and there* (2016) übertitelt und als Serie nummeriert, sind es briefpapiergrosse, spontan gemalte Werke, die meist auf Fotografien von zuvor gesehenen Szenen im Alltag beruhen. „Here and there" (englisch für „zwischendurch, gelegentlich") nennt sie die Künstlerin, und sie dienen ihr als Freiraum zur Ideenfindung für ihre grossformatigen Gemälde, in denen sie komplex verwobene Bildwelten schafft.

Dass auf jenen grossen Leinwänden die ihren eigenen Regeln gehorchende Farbmaterie eine hohe Präsenz erlangt und damit oft das Thema selber mitbestimmt, ist für die Künstlerin integraler Teil der Bildaussage: Farbmaterie versinkt in der Leinwand, verschwimmt gegeneinander, taucht in gewandelten Konsistenzen wieder auf, überlagert sich – ein Entstehungsprozess, der das Bildthema dem Lauf des Malstoffs folgen lässt.

Da kleiner im Format und schneller gemalt, sind die „zwischendurch" entstandenen Arbeiten im Farbauftrag trockener; homogen sind die Flächen neben- oder übereinandergesetzt. Frisch und mit einer gewissen Sprödigkeit liegt das Thema vor uns, und einzig bezeugen zuweilen einige Laufspuren die vorausgegangene Malmechanik. Am stärksten ist es indes sicher die expressive und durchwegs leuchtende Farbpalette, mit welcher sich Rachel Lumsden in dieser neueren Studienreihe von ihren dunkeltoniger gemalten Grossformaten absetzt. Die dort aufgebaute „Murkiness" (Rachel Lumsden) – eine bewusste Eintrübung des Sujets und Verunklärung des Kontexts, um in dieser thematischen Offenheit die oben beschriebene Freiheit für die Malerei selbst zu erringen – ist in den unlängst entstandenen kleinen Arbeiten einem rigoroseren Licht und damit einem höheren Grad an Unmittelbarkeit gewichen. So wie sich die von der Künstlerin in den Blick genommenen Lichtquellen gewandelt haben: An die Stelle eines indirekten Scheins durch etwa einen wild gemusterten Lampenschirm in einem Londoner Interieur sind die unverblümt härteren Lichtverhältnisse im öffentlichen Aussenraum getreten.

Auf thematischer Ebene ist eine Verschiebung vom persönlich-häuslichen „Interieur" zu einem distanzierten und neutraleren „Exterieur" zu beobachten – letzteres „Exterieur" eine Gattung der Kunst, die es in einer klassischen Einteilung noch nicht gab, welche indes im Übersetzungsschwung eines Interviews mit der Künstlerin unlängst für ihr Werk lanciert wurde. Tatsächlich ist es eine sehr wichtige Eigenart der Malerei Rachel Lumsdens, dass sie zwischen zwei Kulturen, in Grossbritannien und in der Schweiz, entsteht. So hat das Interieur in der britischen Kunst eine lange Tradition, die weit ins 20. Jahrhundert hineinreicht; andererseits ist die Malerei im deutschsprachigen Raum reich an expressiven Landschaften. Die Künstlerin schöpft fruchtbar aus beiden Welten, und es liesse sich behaupten, dass sich in den intuitiv „zwischendurch" entstandenen Arbeiten zwei Haltungen am besten vereinen. Denn als so definierte „Exteriors" sind sie nicht Spiegelungen einer persönlichen Befindlichkeit der Künstlerin, wie es die Malereien in einem klassisch deutschen (oder schweizerischen) Expressionismus wären. Wie in Lumsdens grossen „Interieurs" – deren „Murkiness" die Künstlerin oft aus einer Reibung mit den frugalen Innenräumen Walter Sickerts entwickelt, einem für sie wegweisenden Maler der englischen Frühmoderne – geht es ebenso um eine malerische Analyse der inneren Beschaffenheit dieser Bildwelten selbst: Wie generieren sie sich in ihrer Materialität, was sind ihre ureigenen Teile, wie reagieren sie untereinander? Und dann: Wie kann die Farbe zu einem Äquivalent für diese interne Bildmechanik finden?

Doch wie die vorangegangenen Darstellungen der gleichsam archetypischen Londoner „Bedsits" – dichte Interieurs, wo jeder Gegenstand der sehr persönlichen Lebenswelt eines

zusammengefassten Wohn- und Schlafraums
einzuordnen ist – zeigen auch Lumsdens „Exteri-
eurs" keine von Menschen unbelasteten Aussen-
räume. Sehr wohl sind Spuren von den Bewoh-
nenden auch dieser Räume vorhanden, doch als
Personen rücken bestenfalls noch Staffagefigu-
ren ins Bewusstsein. Sie bestimmen auch nicht
den Raum als offenkundig Abwesende mit, wie
es in Lumsdens grossen „Interieurs" häufig der
Fall ist. Tatsächlich ist es diese zuweilen abrupte
Verweigerung einer Erzählung, die uns vielleicht
am meisten in den „zwischendurch" gemalten All-
tagsszenen überrascht. Denn so selbstverständ-
lich sie als scheinbar fadengerade Kompositionen ihre Themen darbieten, so eigengesetzlich
bleiben sie in deren Lesarten – das Geschenk
einer Malerei, die mit Lust aus vielen Bildquel-
len schöpft und in einer unbeschwerten Aneignung der Motive eine spezifische Schlussform
der malerischen Abstrahierung findet.

Rachel Lumsden wurde 1968 in Newcastle-upon-Tyne (GB) geboren. Sie lebt und arbeitet in St. Gallen und Arbon (CH) sowie in London.

1995–1998
The Royal Academy Schools, London, Post Graduate Studies in Painting (MA)

1987–1991
Nottingham Trent University, Bachelor of Arts (Honours) Fine Art

Förderungen und Stipendien

2016
Förderbeitrag Kanton Thurgau (CH)

2014
Werkbeitrag Kanton St. Gallen (CH)

2012
VisarteOst Artist-in-Residence, Cité Internationale des Arts, Paris (FR)

2011
Internationaler Kunstpreis, Vorarlberg (AT)

2009
Förderpreis Stadt St. Gallen (CH)

2008
Artist-in-Residence der Stadt St. Gallen, La Fabrik, Berlin (DE)

2005
Werkbeitrag Stadt St. Gallen (CH)

2001
Kunstpreis, The Pollock-Krasner Foundation, New York (USA)

1998
CrestCo Art Prize, The Bank of England (GB), David Murray Prize (GB), Landseer Prize (GB)

Einzelausstellungen

2018
Kunst(Zeug)Haus Rapperswil-Jona (CH)

2017
Fondation Fernet-Branca, Saint-Louis (FR)

Kunsthaus Centre d'art Pasquart, Biel / Bienne (CH)

2015
The Other Island, Galerie Bernard Jordan, Zürich (CH)

Straight Flush, Galerie Bleisch, Arbon (CH)

2013
Drunk in Charge of a Bicycle, Kunstraum Kreuzlingen (CH)

Six Impossible Things Before Breakfast, Kunstplattform Akku, Luzern (CH)

2012
What's the Time, Mr. Wolf?, Galerie Schönenberger (CH)

2009
Man & Beast, Kunstraum Engländerbau, Vaduz (FL)

2008
Bird Wars, Katharinen, St. Gallen (CH)

2006
Silent Inhabitants, Kunsthalle Arbon (CH) (2-person show)

Dashboard Talisman, Galerie Christian Röllin, St. Gallen (CH)

2004
Misplaced, Vertigo Gallery, London (GB) (2-person show)

2001
Arc-light, Bridlesmith Gallery, Nottingham (GB)

Arc-light, The Spitz Gallery, London (GB)

1999
Foreign Body, Rivington Gallery, London (GB)

Gruppenausstellungen

2017
London meets Altdorf, Haus für Kunst Uri (CH)

2016
Im Rausch – zwischen Höhenflug und Absturz, Kunstmuseum Thurgau (CH)

Werkschau Thurgau, Kunstraum Kreuzlingen (CH)

Ausgezeichnet!, Museum Bickel, Walenstadt (CH)

London Art Fair, Long & Ryle Gallery, London (GB)

2015
20/21 Art Fair, Long & Ryle Gallery, London (GB)

London Art Fair, Long & Ryle Gallery (GB)

Twopack, Erfrischungsraum, Luzern (CH)

Grosse Regional, Kunst(Zeug)Haus Rapperswil-Jona (CH)

2013
Werkschau Thurgau, Bleisch Galerie, Arbon (CH)

Die zweite Dekade, Kunsthalle Arbon (CH)

2012
Central Booking in Berlin, K-Salon, Berlin (DE)

La Suisse est une ville, Salles d'exposition de la Cité internationale des arts, Paris (FR)

2011
The Open West, Cheltenham (GB)

2010
Arthur#5, Kunsthalle, Toggenburg (CH)

Narrative Sequencing, CBA Gallery, New York (USA)

Let the Yangzte Flow, Hubei Institute of Fine Art, Wuhan (CN)

2009
Heimspiel, Kunstmuseum St. Gallen (CH)

12/132 Biennial, Alte Fabrik, Rapperswil-Jona (CH)

Works on Paper, Raab Gallery, Berlin (DE)

AIR 2 Artists in Residence, Substitut, Raum für Aktuelle Kunst aus der Schweiz, Berlin (DE)

2008
Memory Happens, Christies auction, Kaiser Wilhelm Memorial, Berlin (DE)

Fünf Frauen für den Kaiser, Galerie Siguaraya, Berlin (DE)

2005
Berliner Liste, Messe für aktuelle Kunst, Berlin (DE)

2003
Reduced, Century Gallery, London (GB)

2000
Paint!, Vertigo Gallery, London (GB)

Publikationen

2016
Im Rausch–zwischen Höhenflug und Absturz, Kunstmuseum Thurgau, Verlag für moderne Kunst

2013
Drunk in Charge of a Bicycle, Paintings and Everything in Between, Texts: Axel Jablonski, Robert Guy Wilson, Schwabe Verlag, Basel

2012
Eine Begegnung mit der Sammlung, VP Bank-Kunststiftung Text: Brigitte Ulmer

2011
Sammlung Credit Suisse Scheidegger & Spiess, Zürich

2010
Let the Yangzte Flow , Katalog FH Zentralschweiz, Hochschule Luzern

2008
Rachel Lumsden,

Paintings 1998–2008, Texts: Felicity Lunn, Uwe Wieczorek, Bucher Verlag (AT)

Sammlungen

Regierungsgebäude Kanton Thurgau (CH), Crédit Suisse Kunstsammlung, Zürich (CH) UBS Art Collection, Zürich (CH) VP Bank Kunstsammlung Vaduz (FL), Kanton St. Gallen Kunstsammlung, St. Gallen (CH), Stadt St. Gallen Kunstsammlung St. Gallen (CH), Privatsammlungen (GB), (CH), (FL), (USA), Asia

Dozentur

Seit 2007 Hochschule Luzern Design und Kunst / University of Lucerne for applied Arts and Sciences (CH)

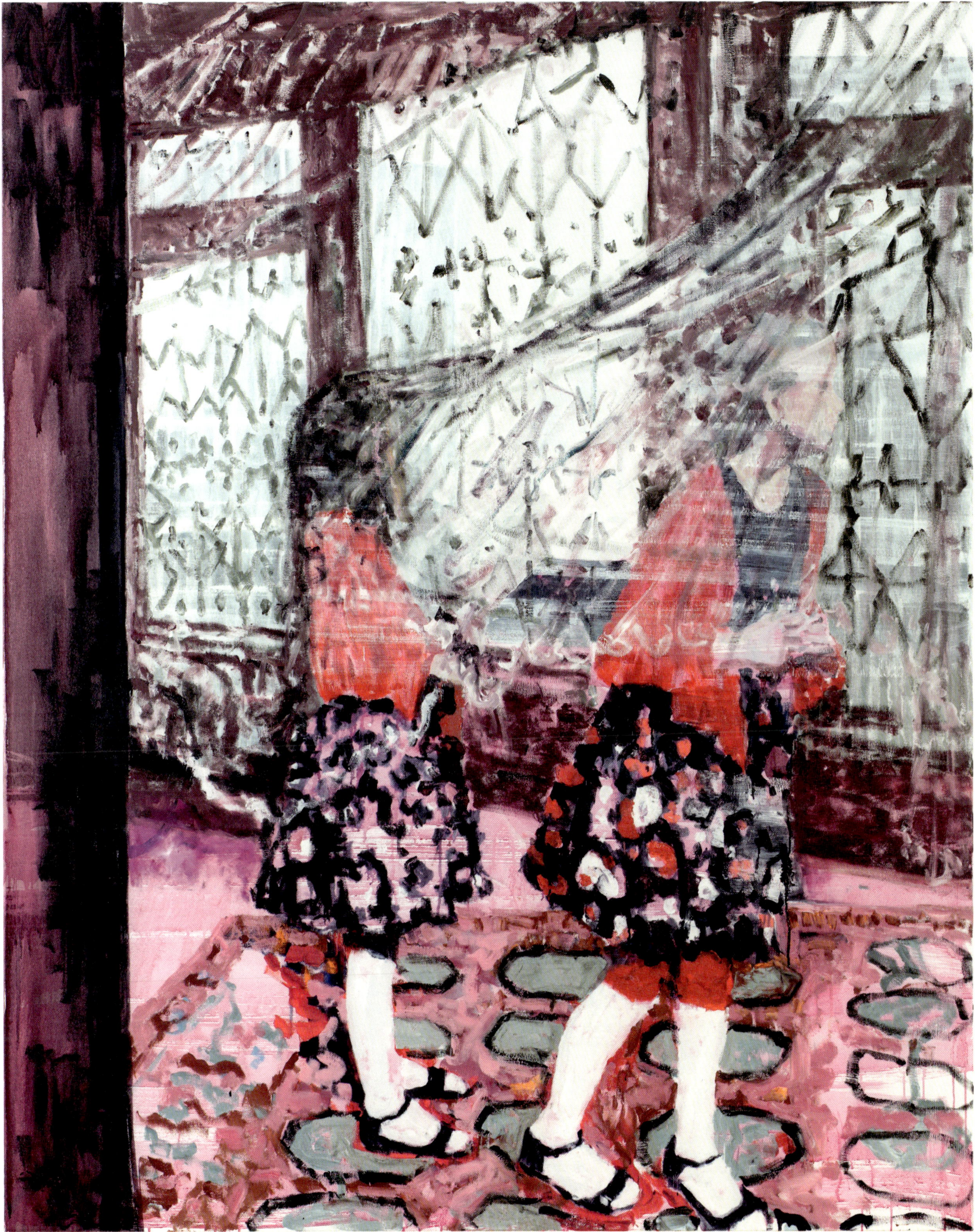

In the Fold   2015   210 cm x 170 cm

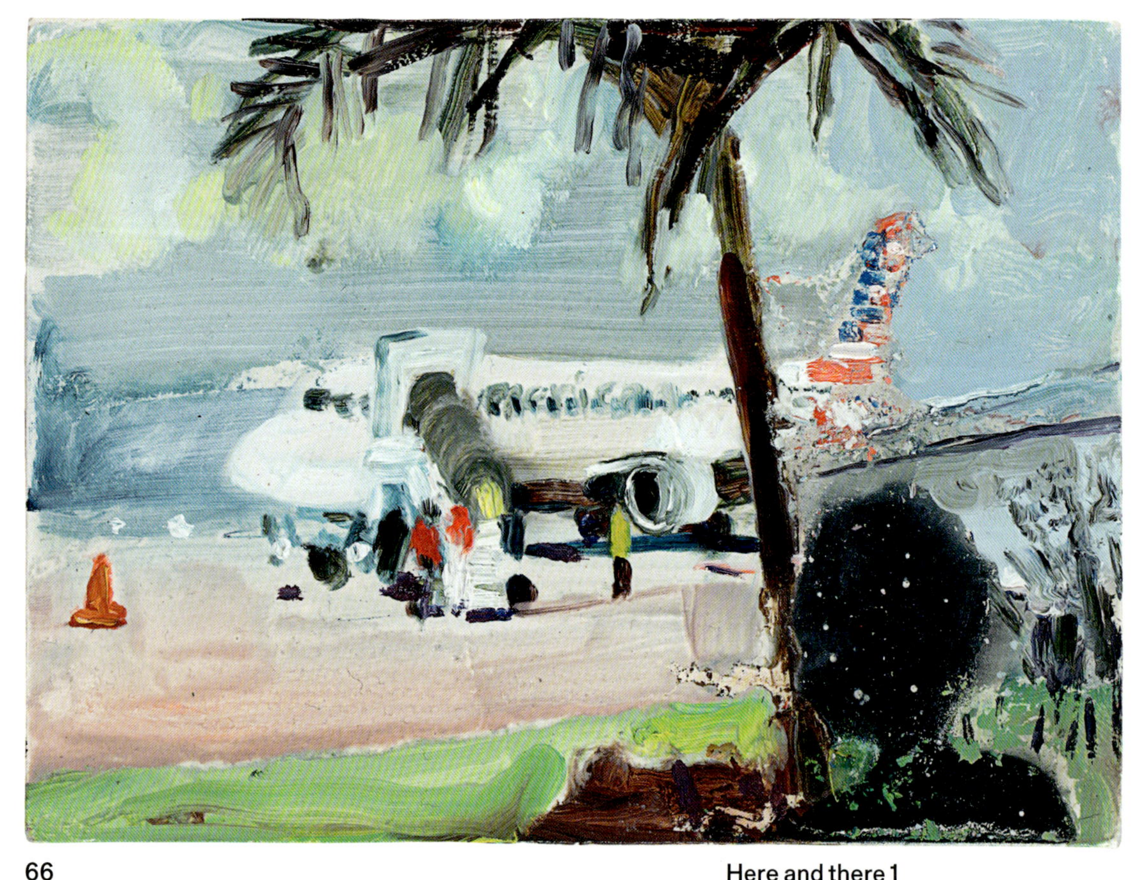

Here and there 1

2016   21.5 × 29.7 cm

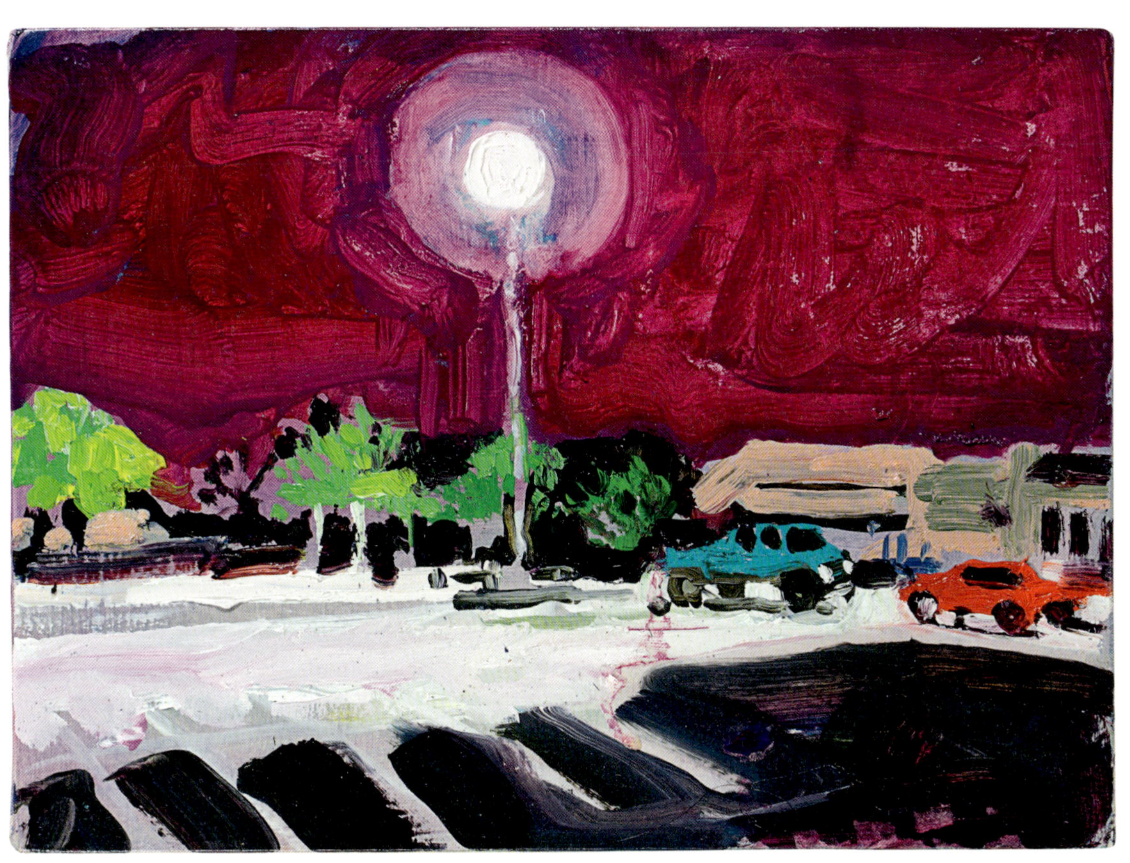

    Here and there 3   2016   21.5 × 29.7 cm

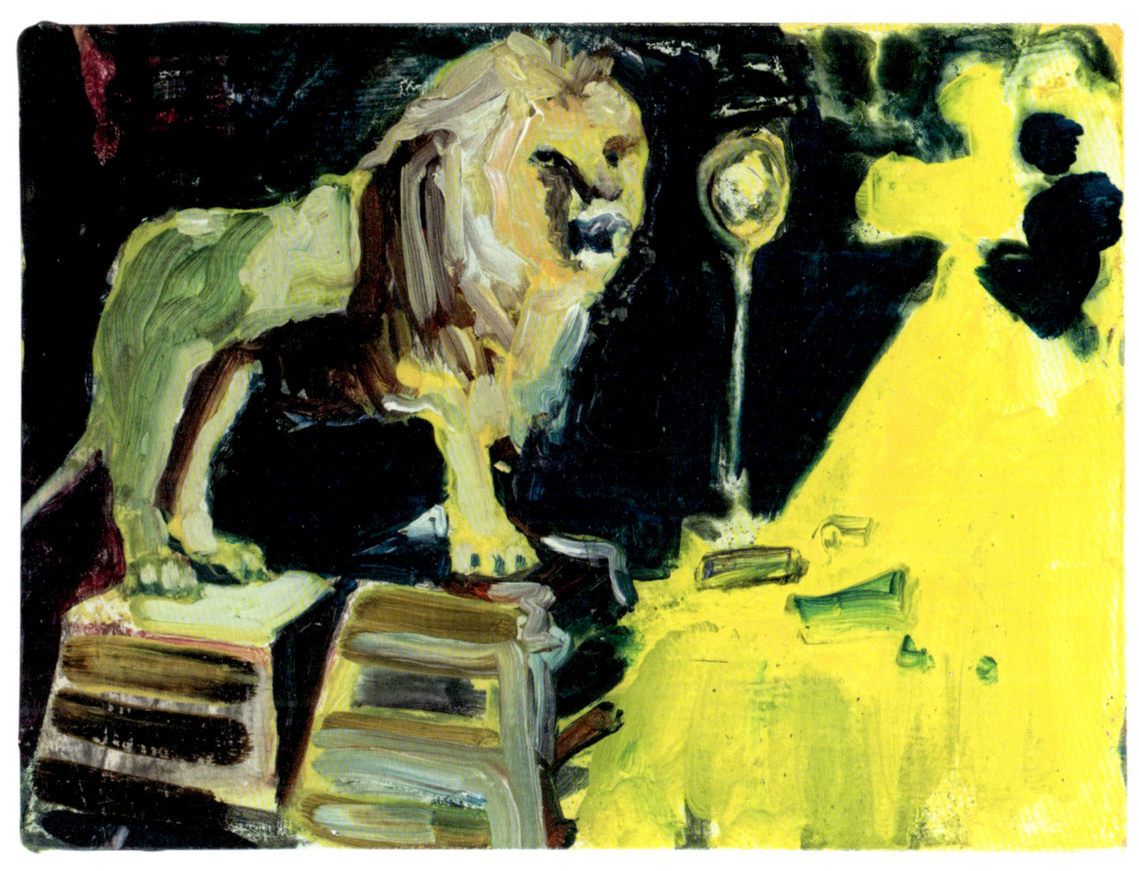

Here and there 18

2016   21.5 × 29.7 cm

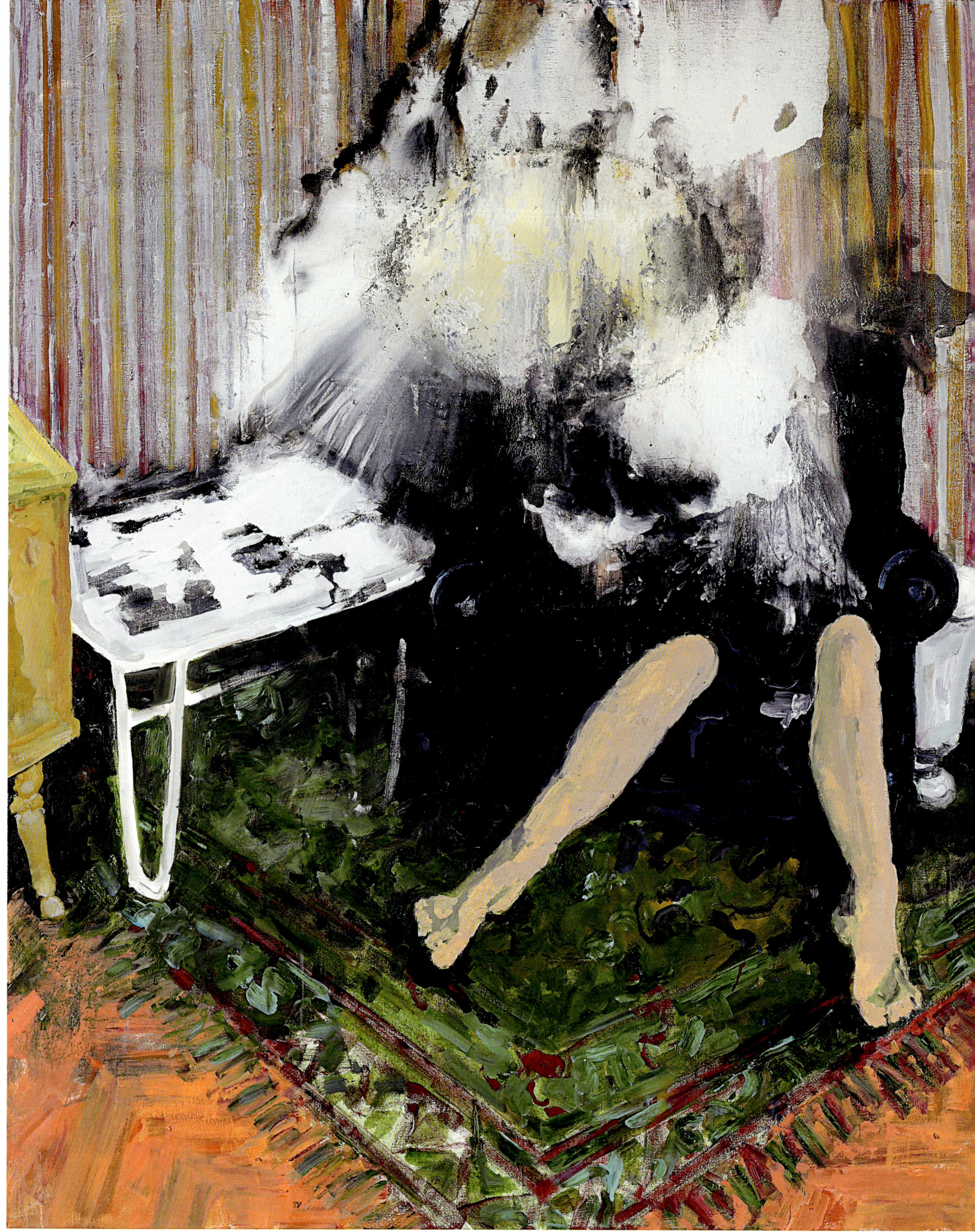

Armchair Thriller   2012   170 × 210 cm

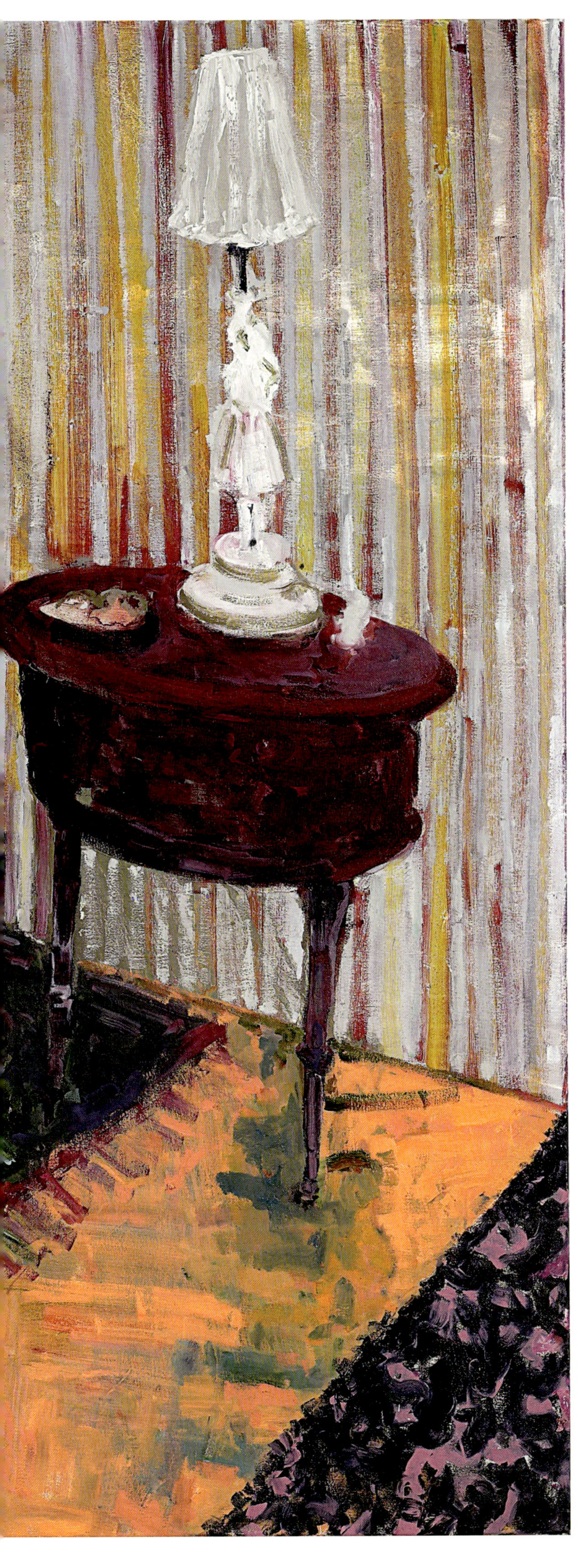

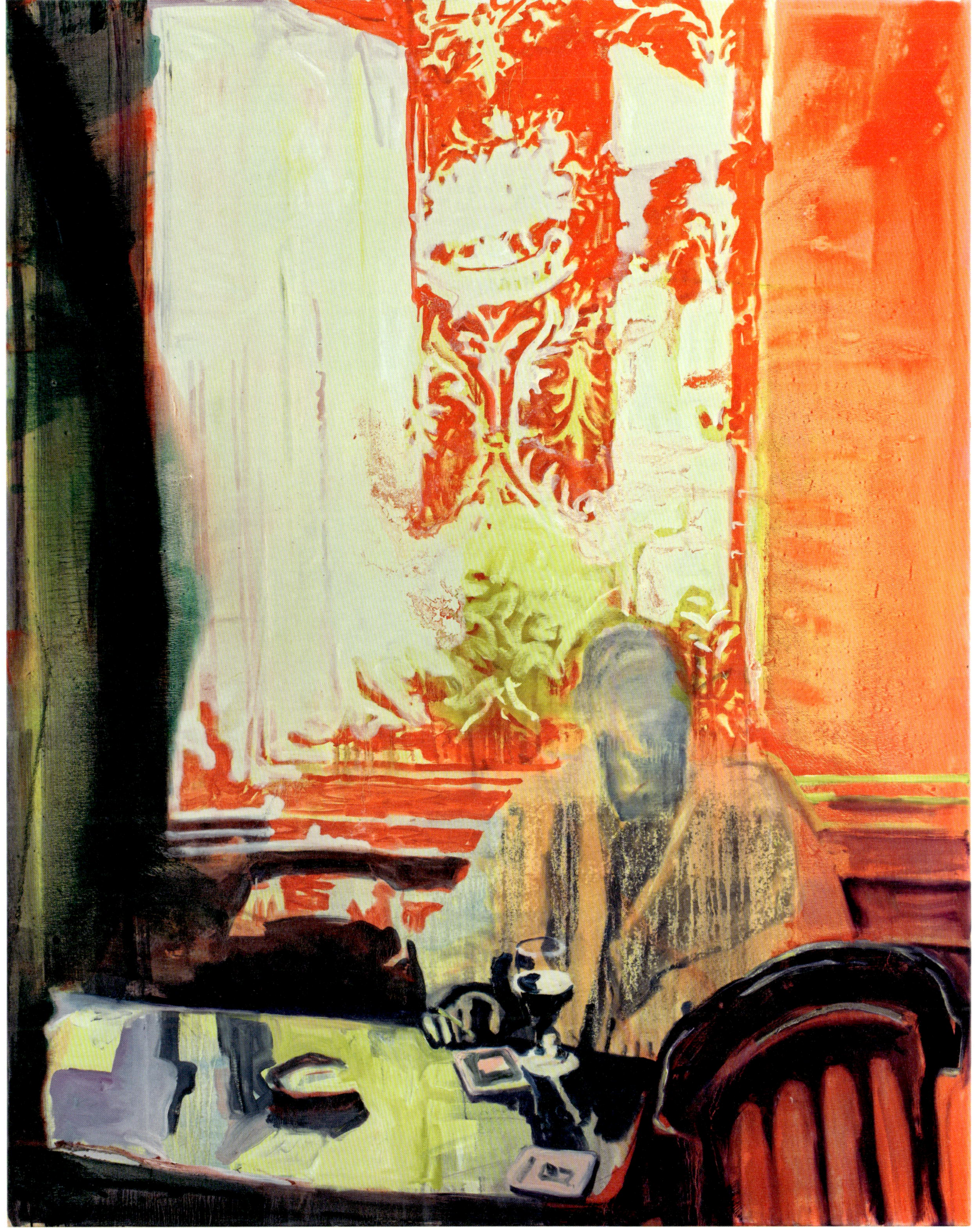

Sailing to Byzantium 2016 210 × 170 cm

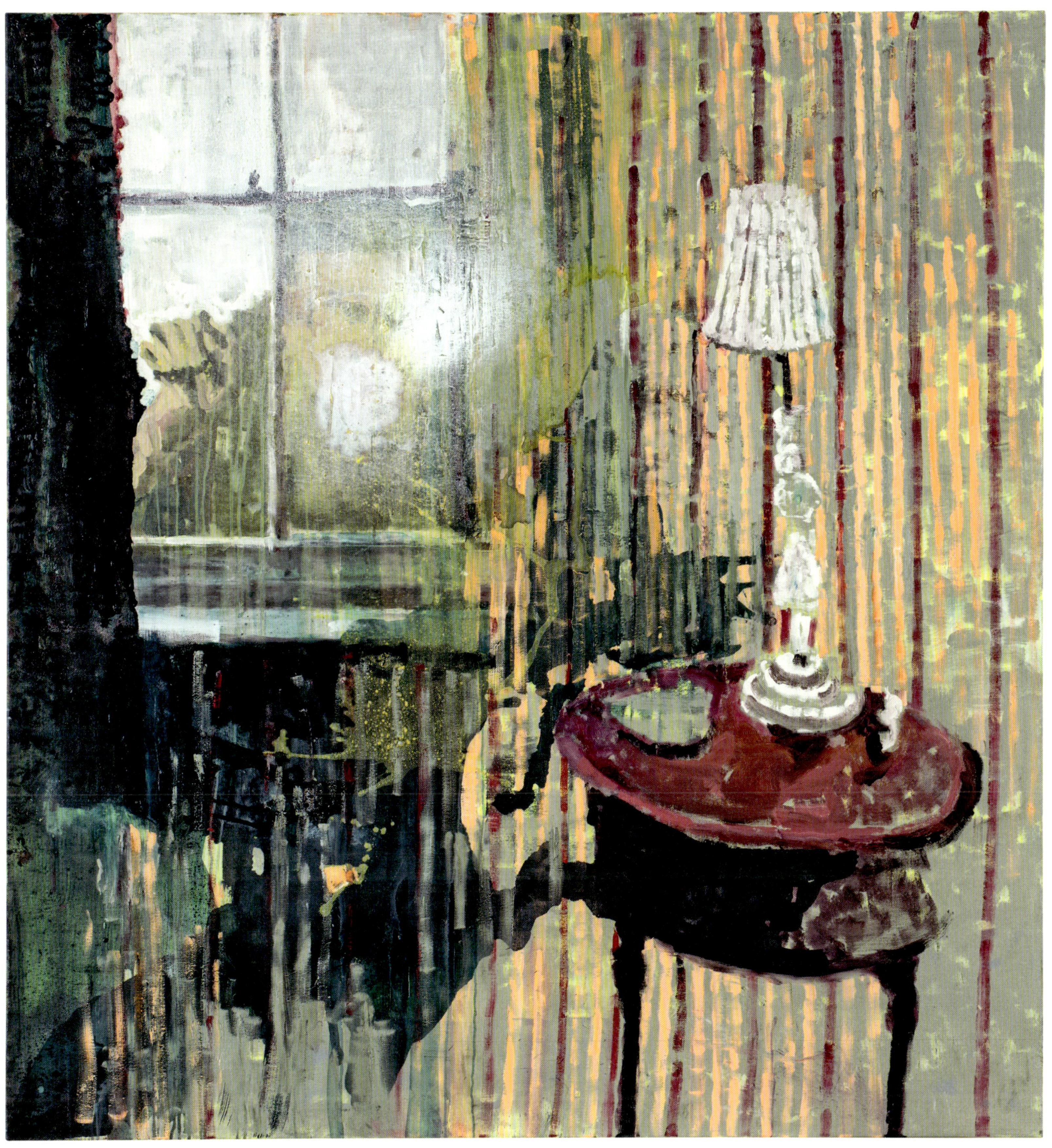

Apply Within

2015   180 × 170 cm

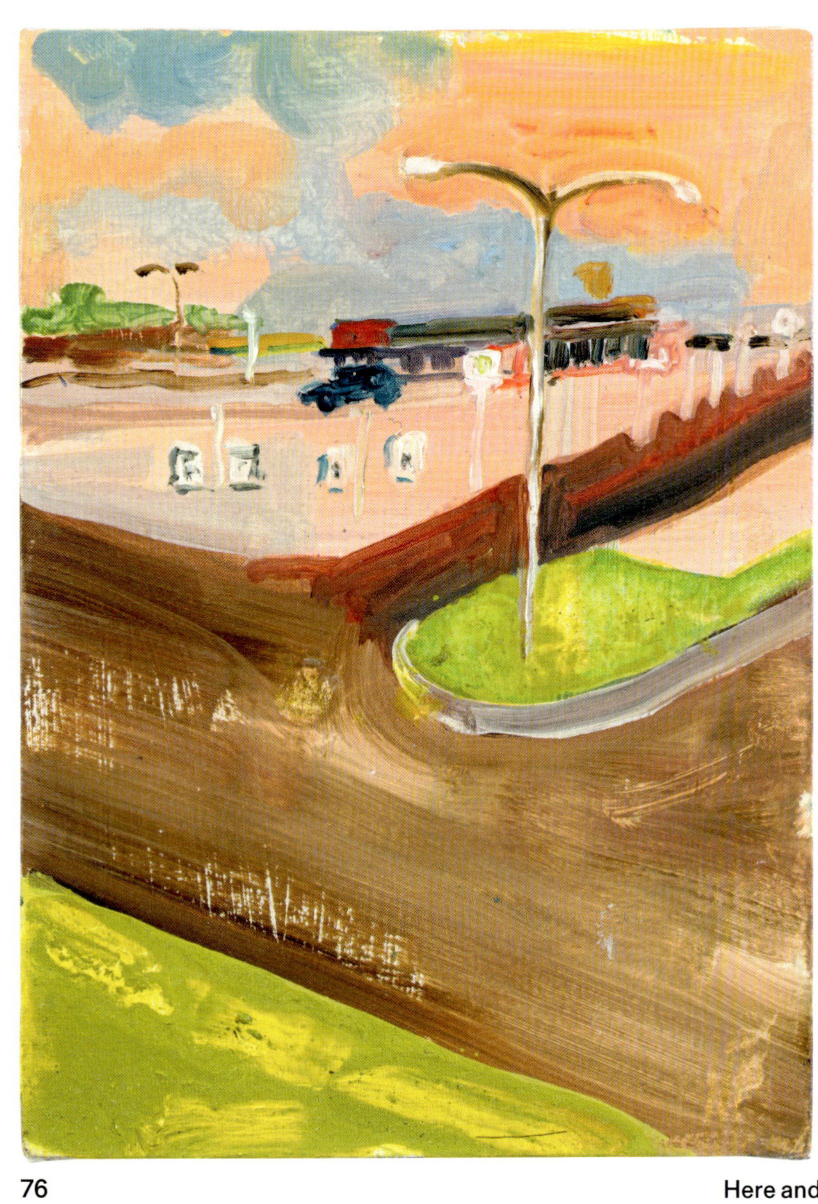

Here and there 9   2016   29.7 × 21.5 cm

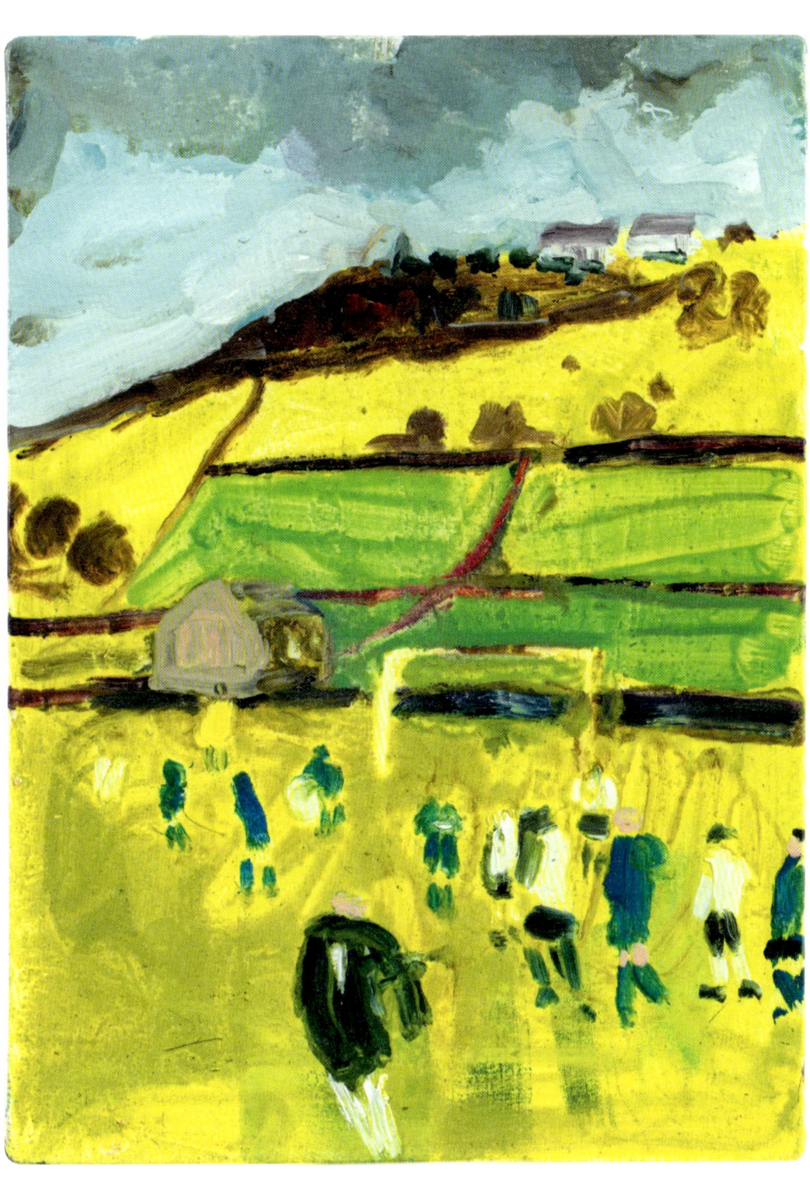

Here and there 13

2016   29.7 × 21.5 cm

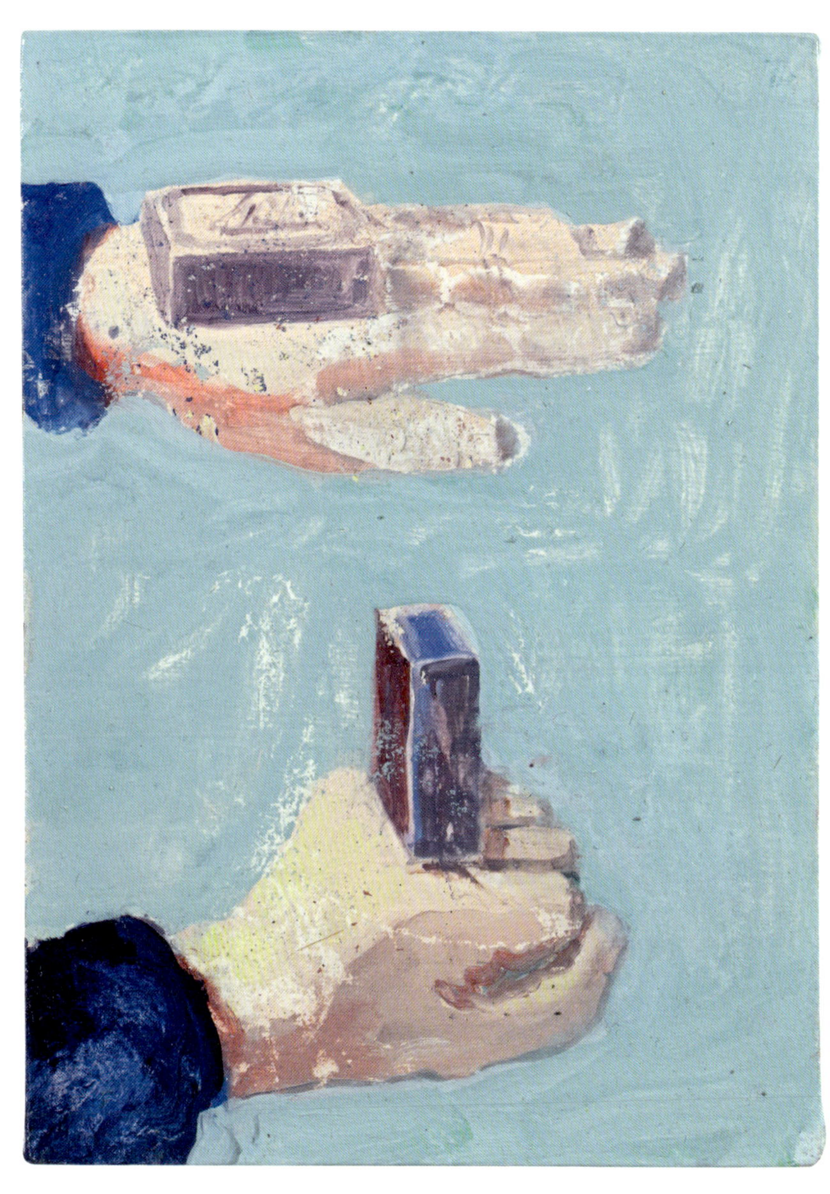

Here and there 17   2016   29.7 × 21.5 cm

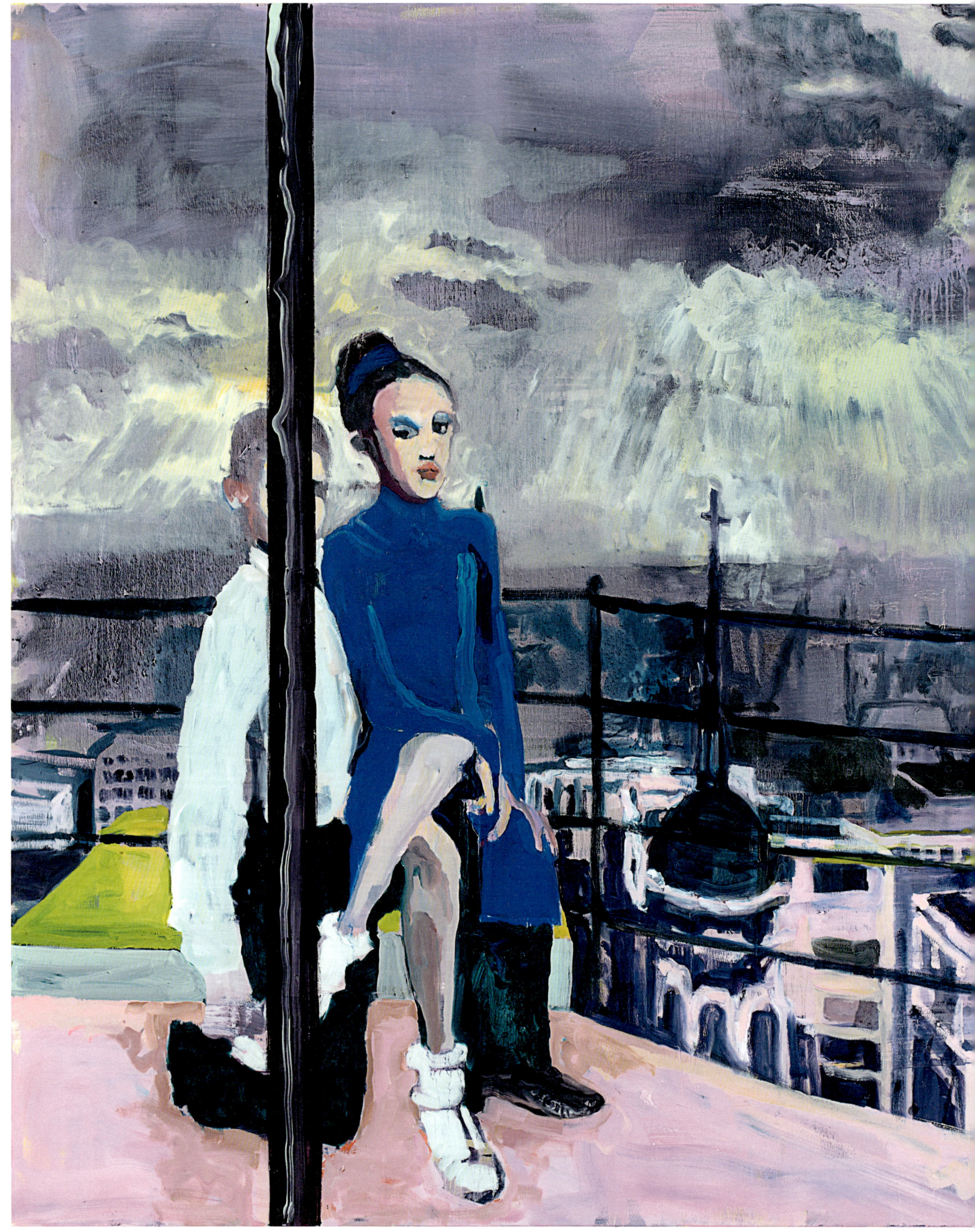

 Lightning Rod (Mr & Mrs Andrews) 2016 190 × 230 cm

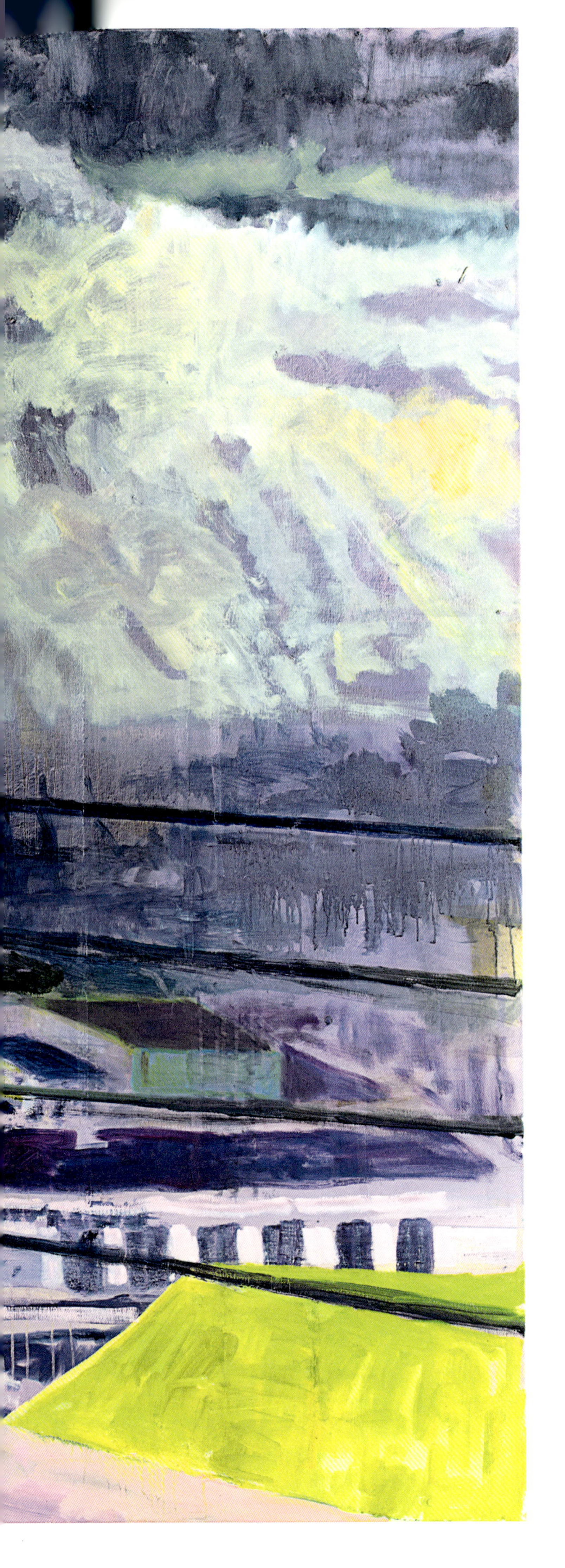

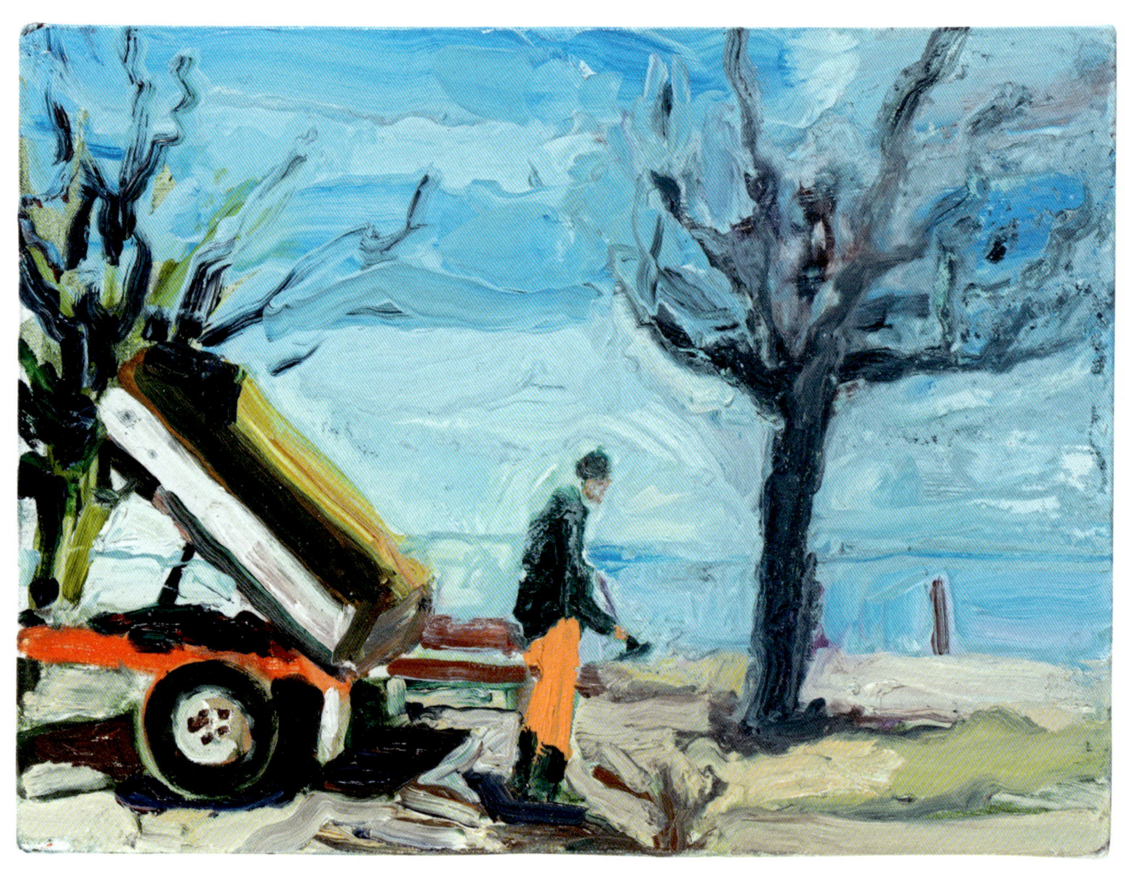

Here and there 15

2016   21.5 × 29.7 cm

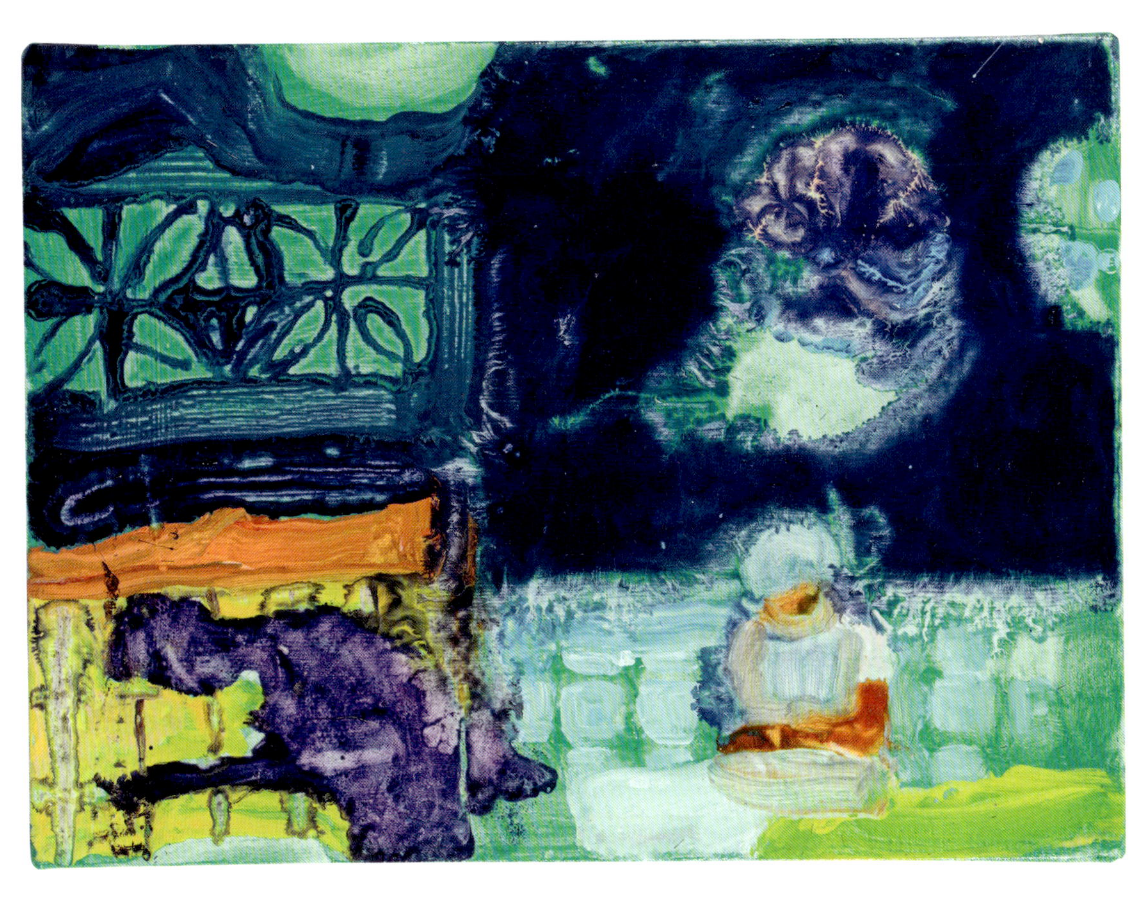

Here and there 4   2016   21.5 × 29.7 cm

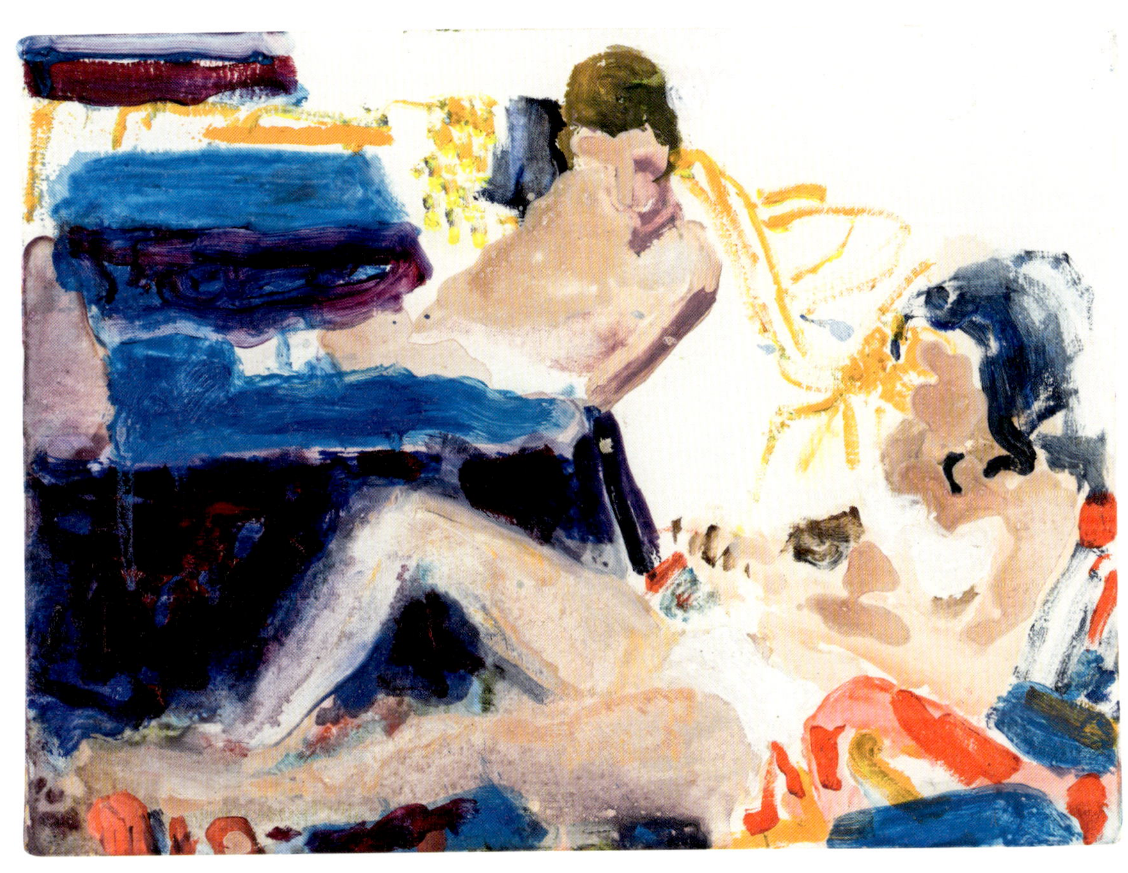

Morley's Deckchairs

2015   21 × 29 cm

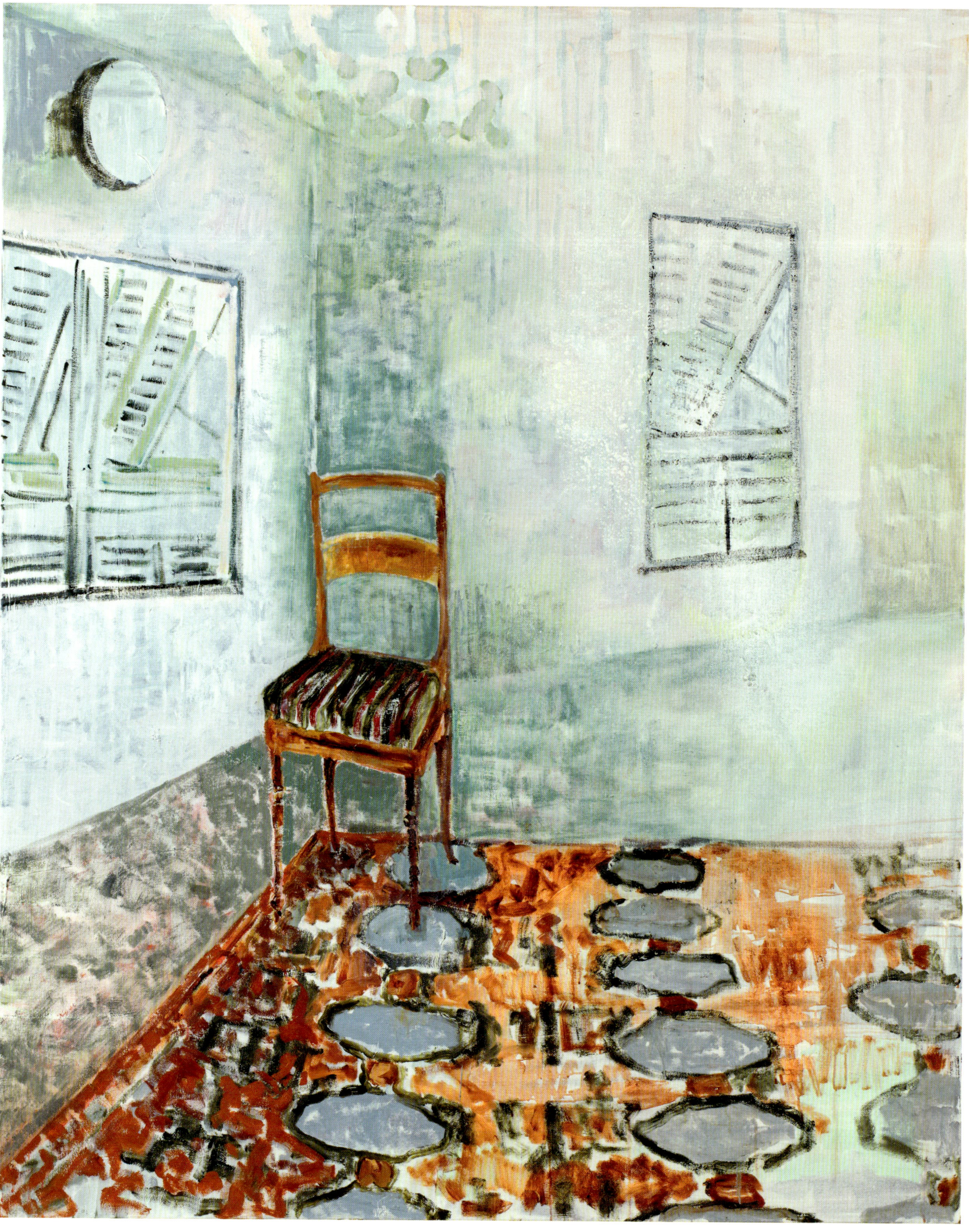

Captain Kirk

2015   210 × 170 cm

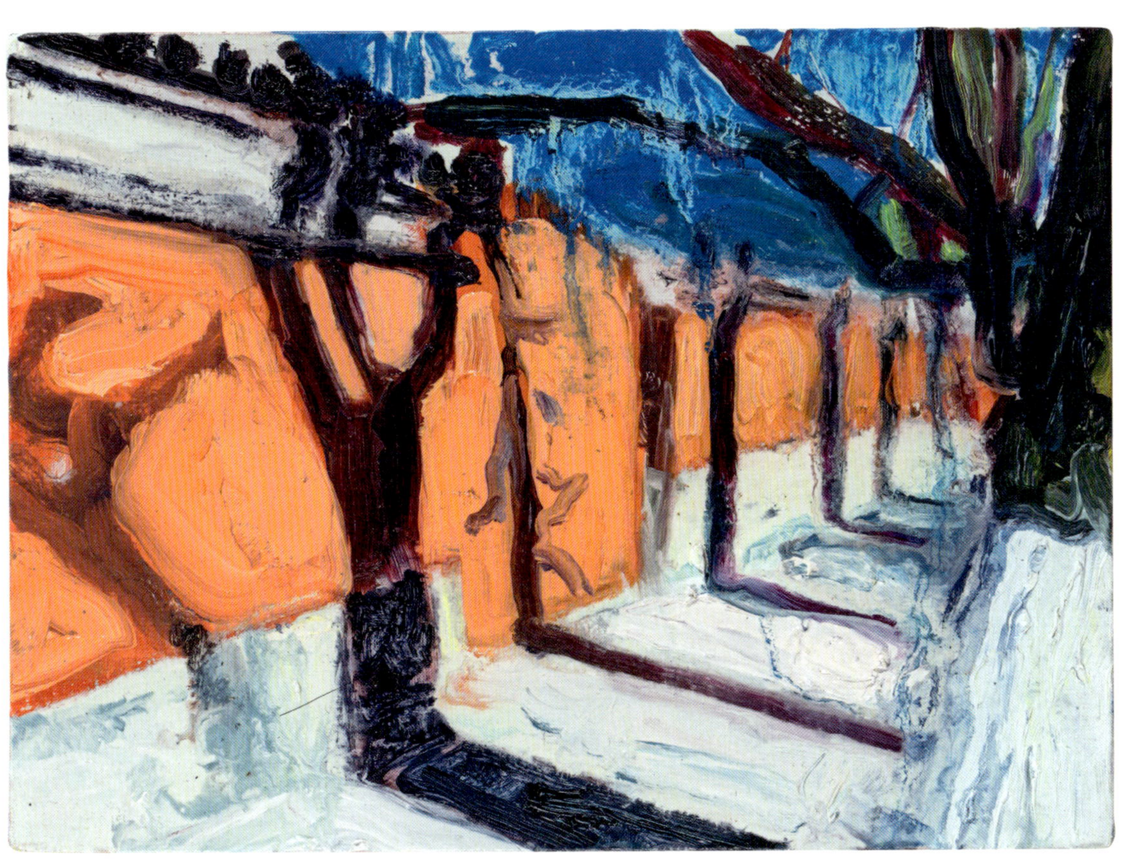

Here and there 2

2016   21.5 × 29.7 cm

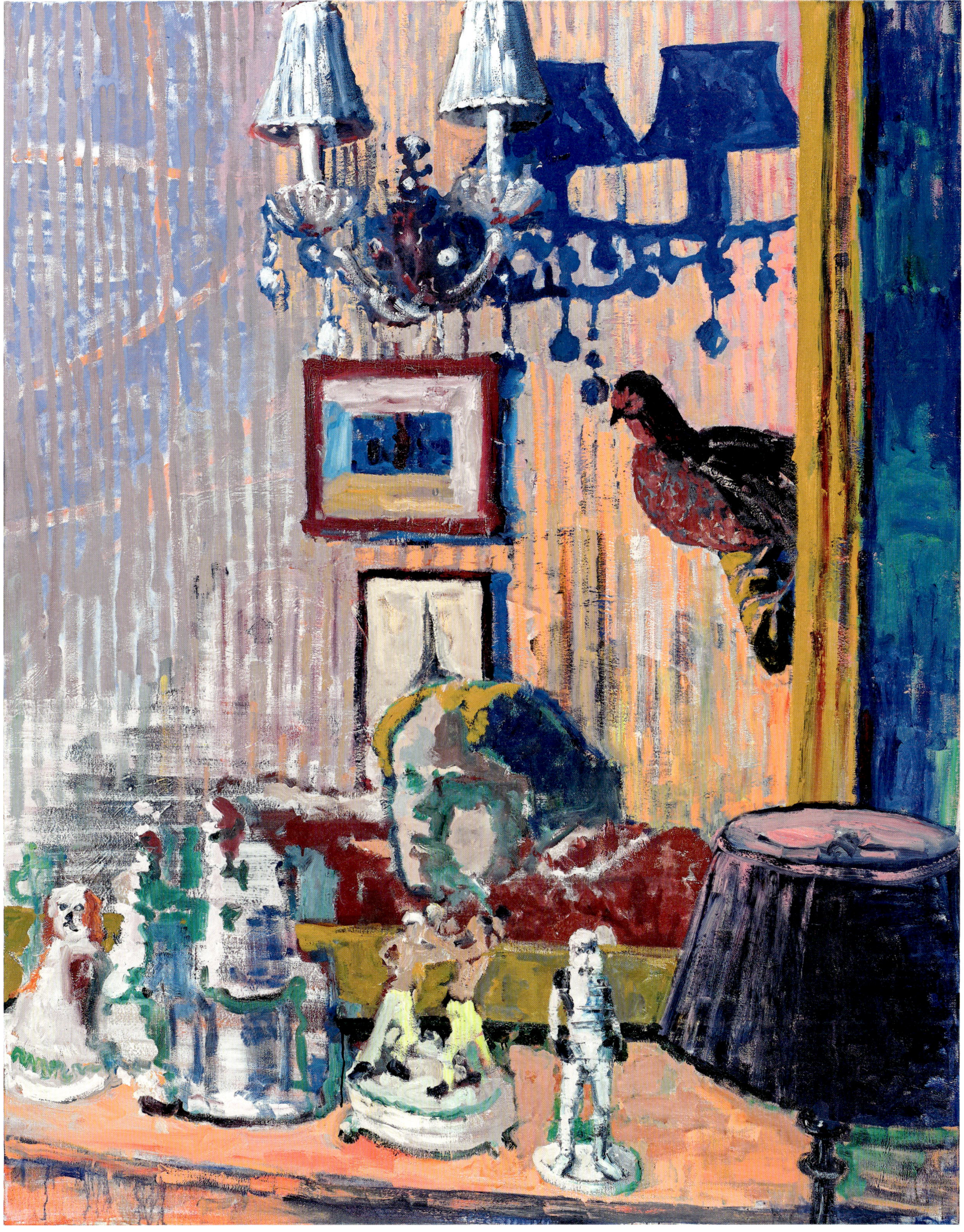

    Here we go Again   2014   210 × 170 cm

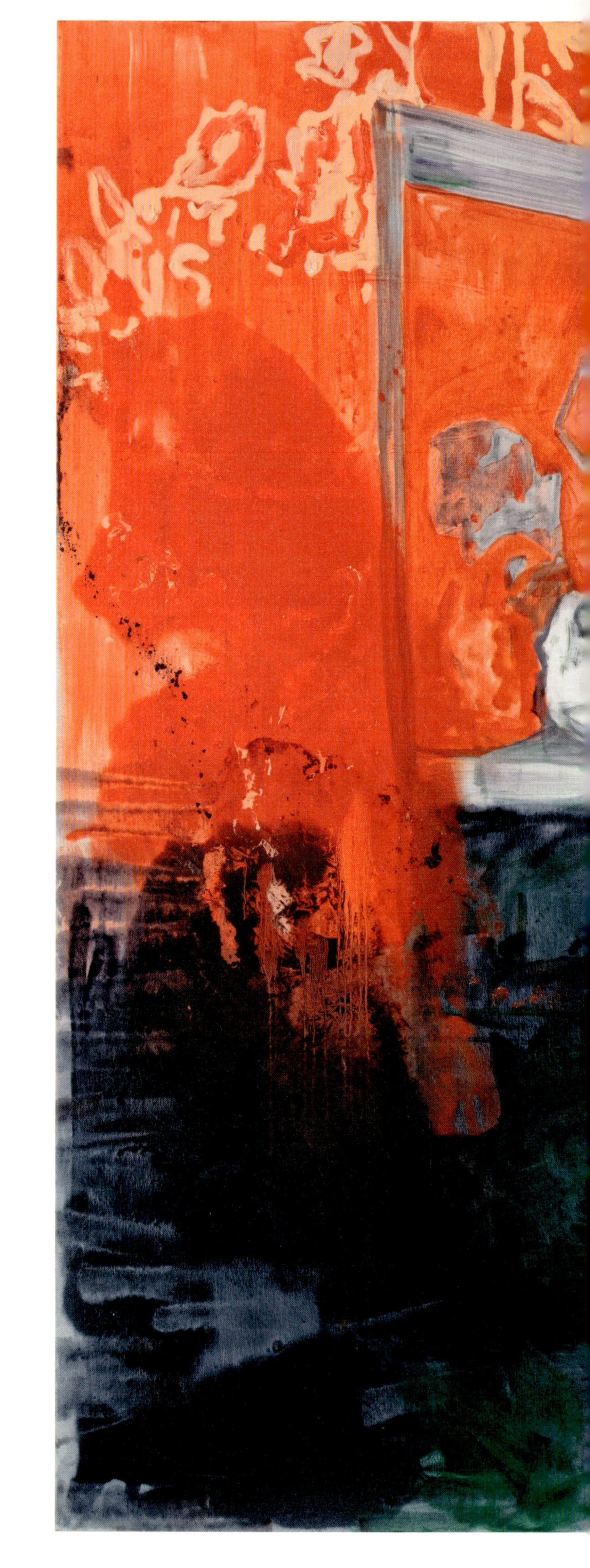

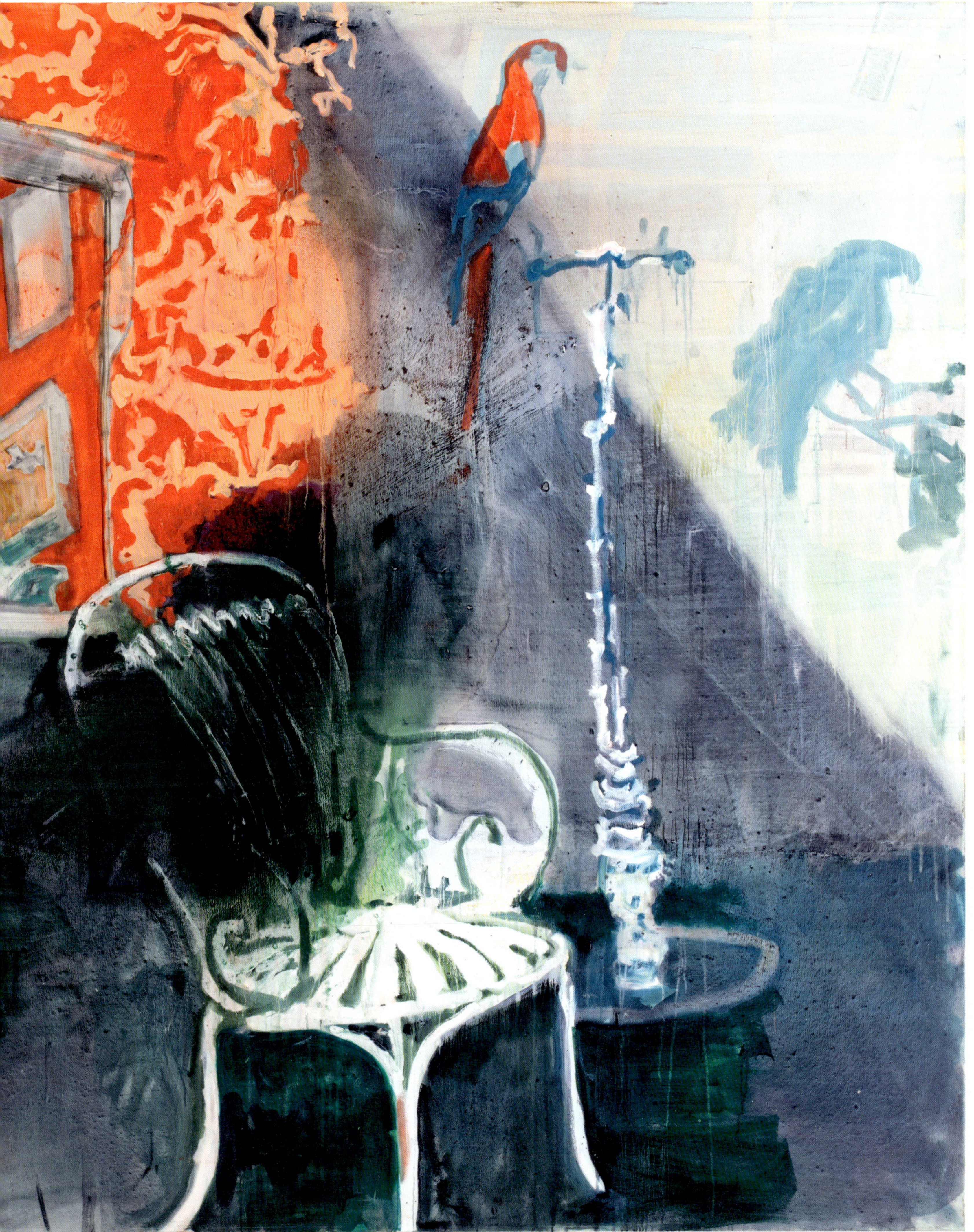

Red Room 2016 190 × 230 cm

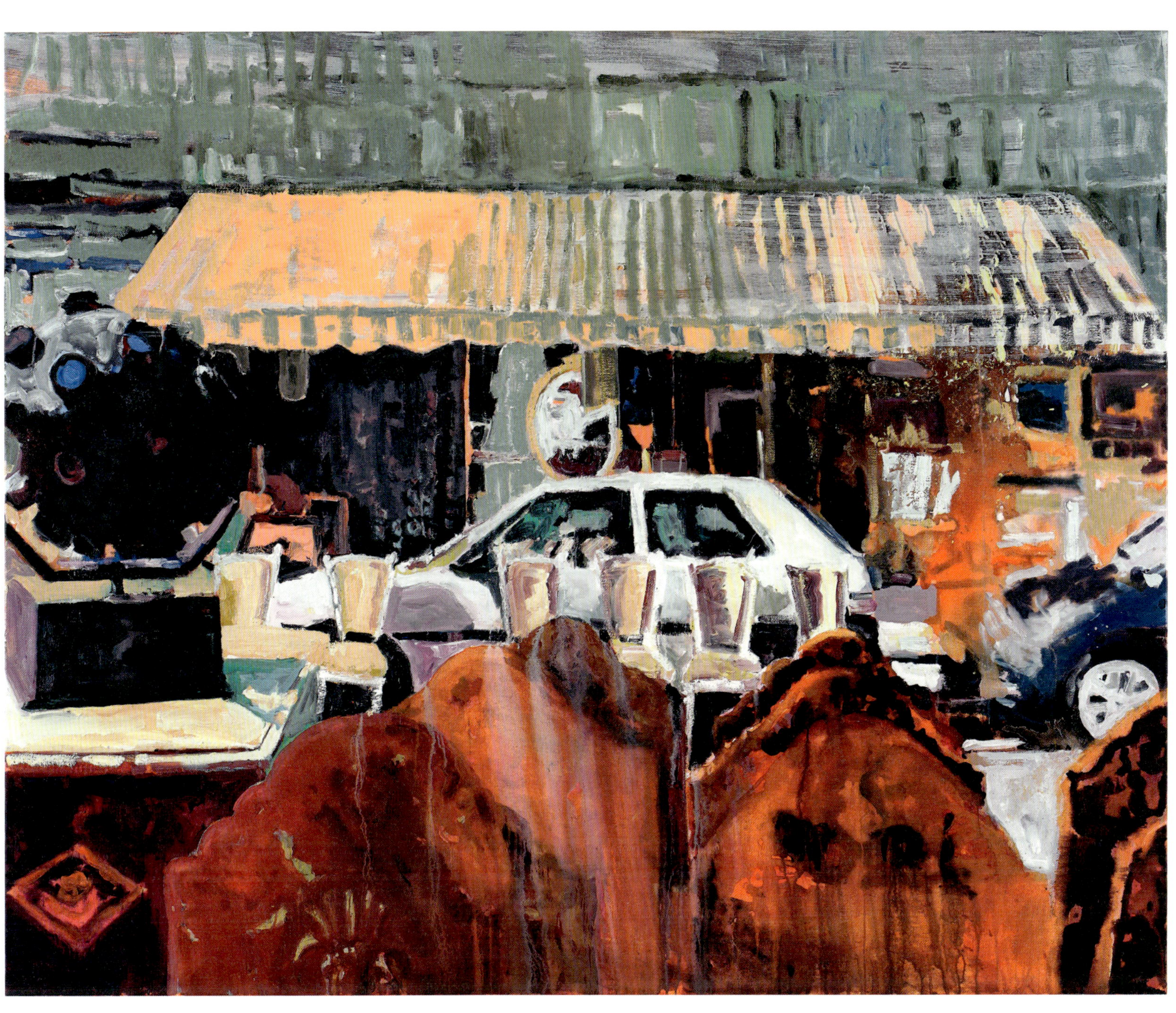

Emporium   2014   170 × 210 cm

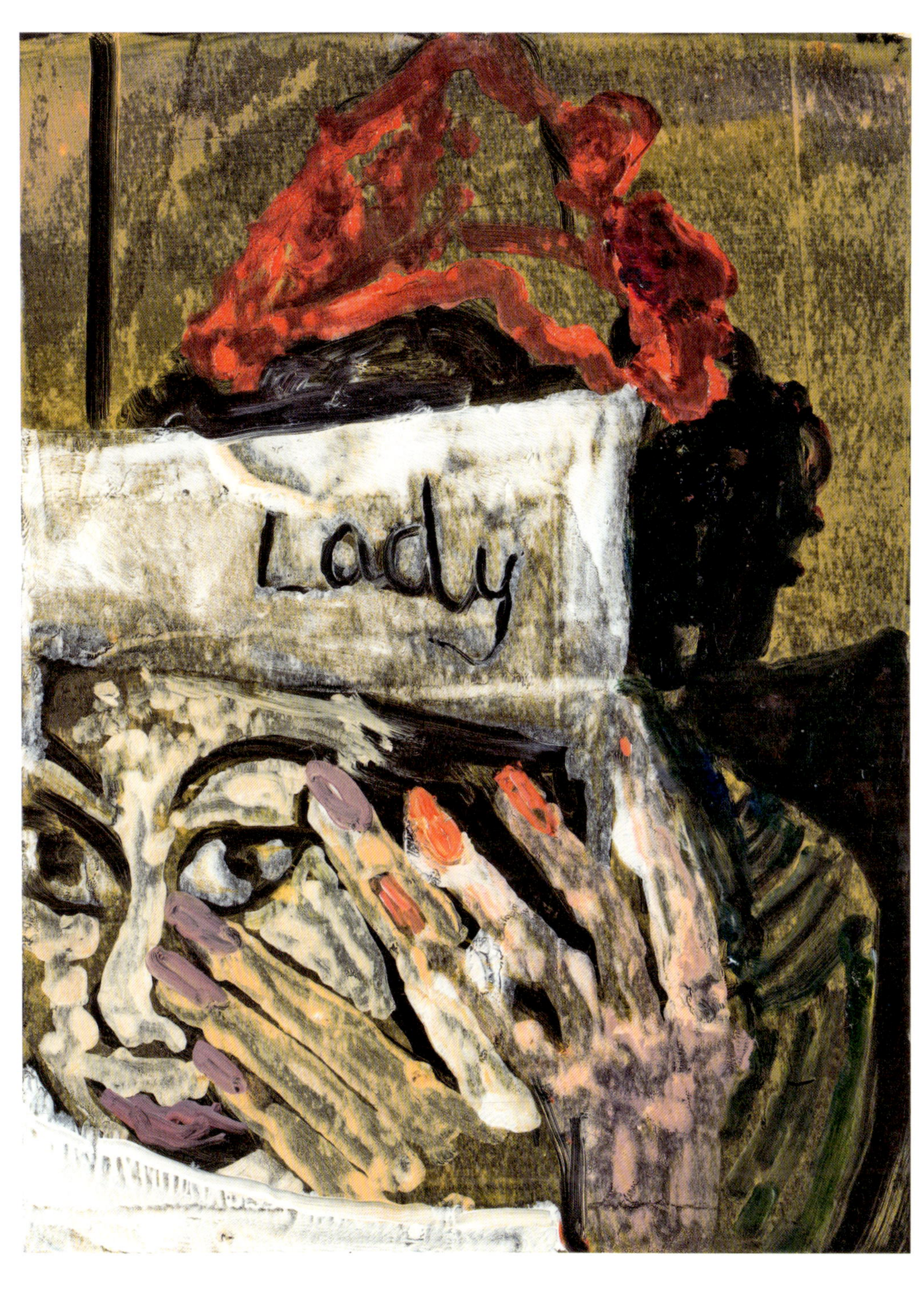

Lady   2015   40 × 30 cm

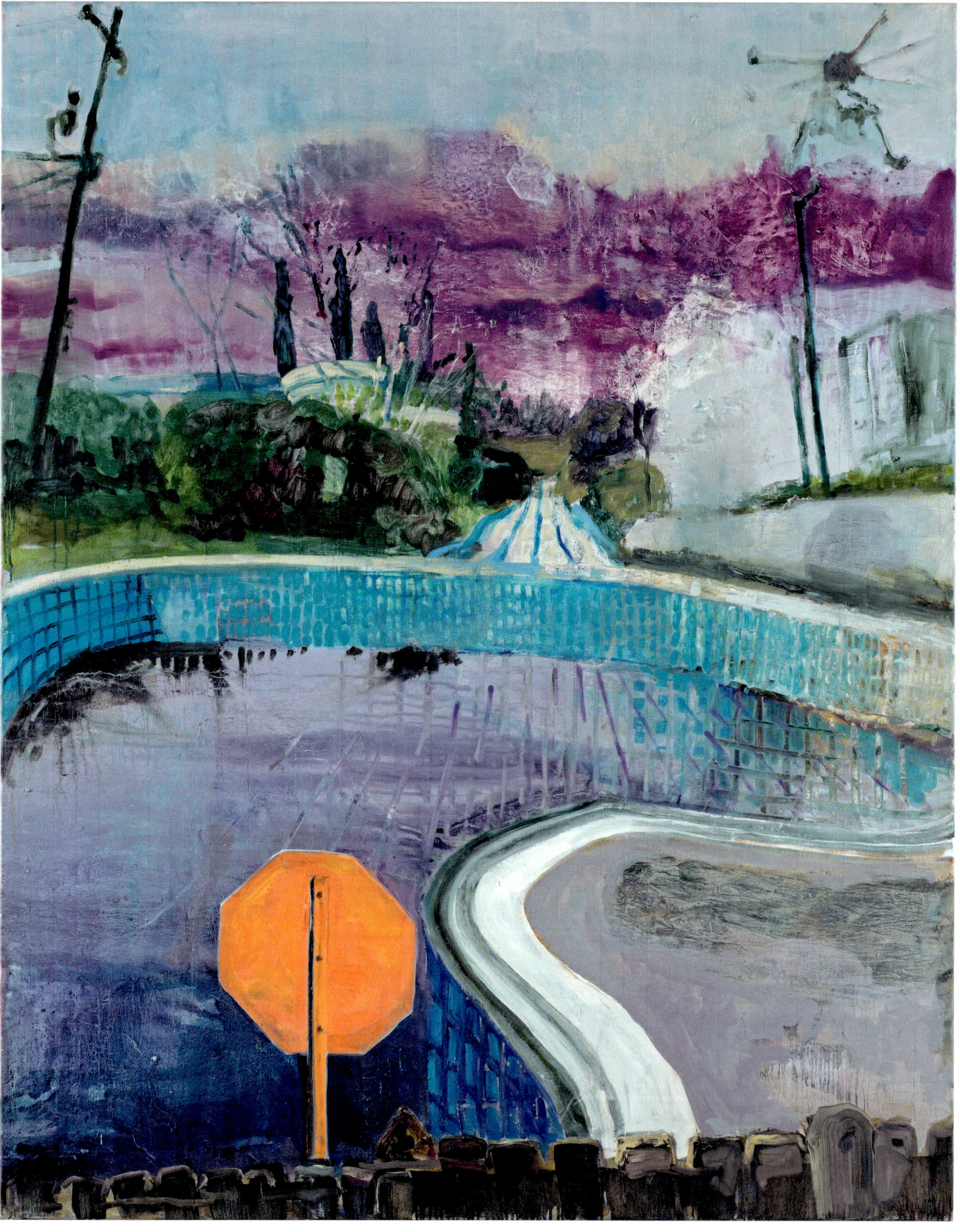

The Fence 2017 210 × 170 cm

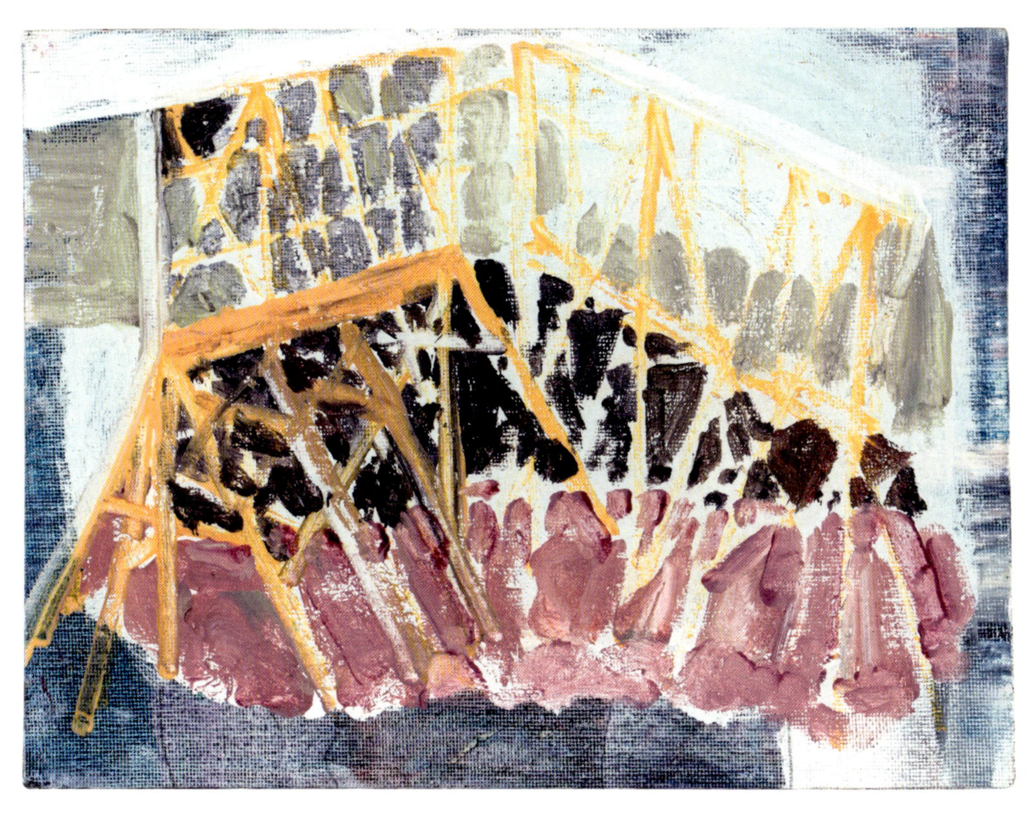

A-Frames 2015 18 × 24 cm

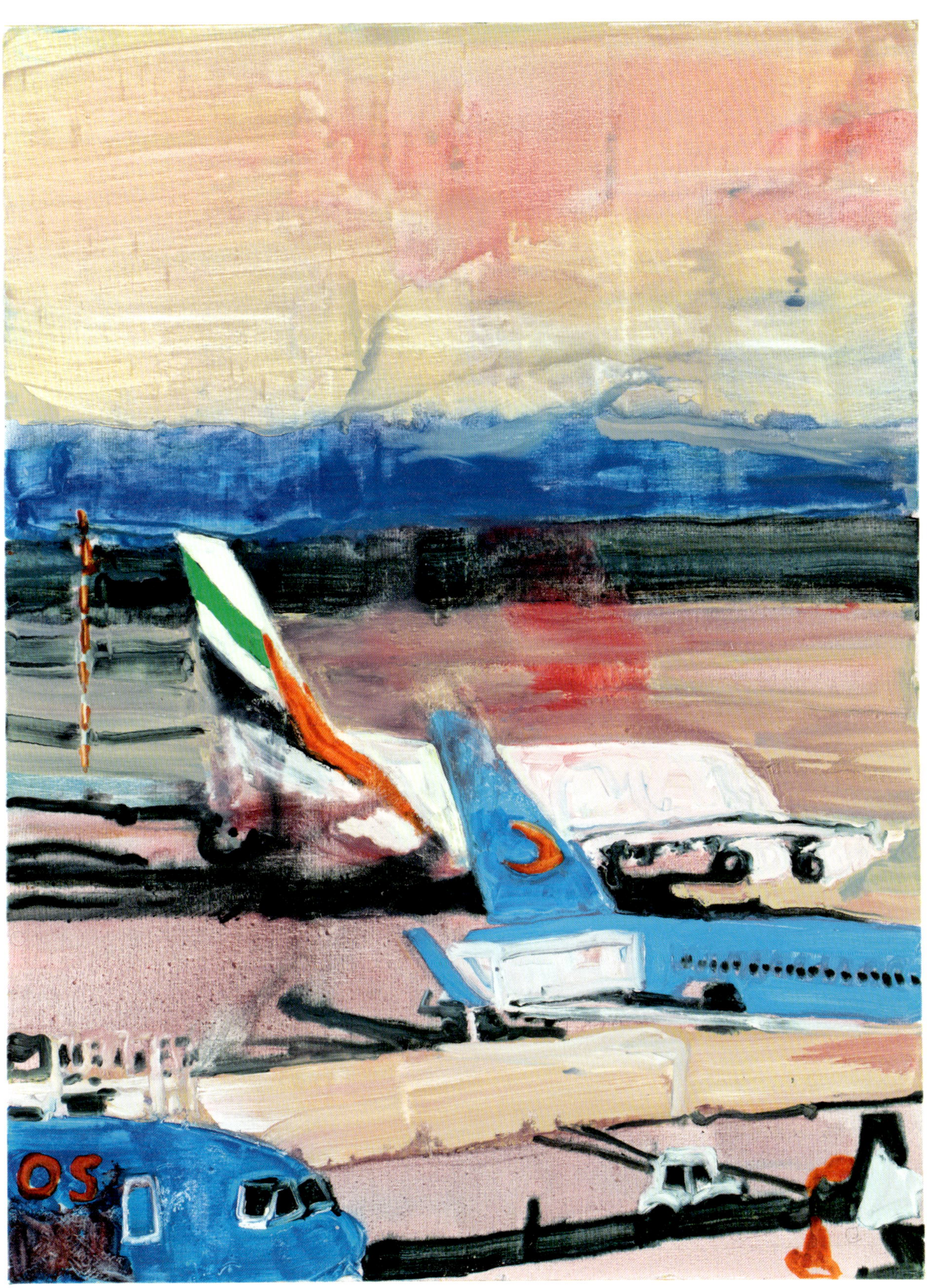

Causeway   2017   160 × 120 cm

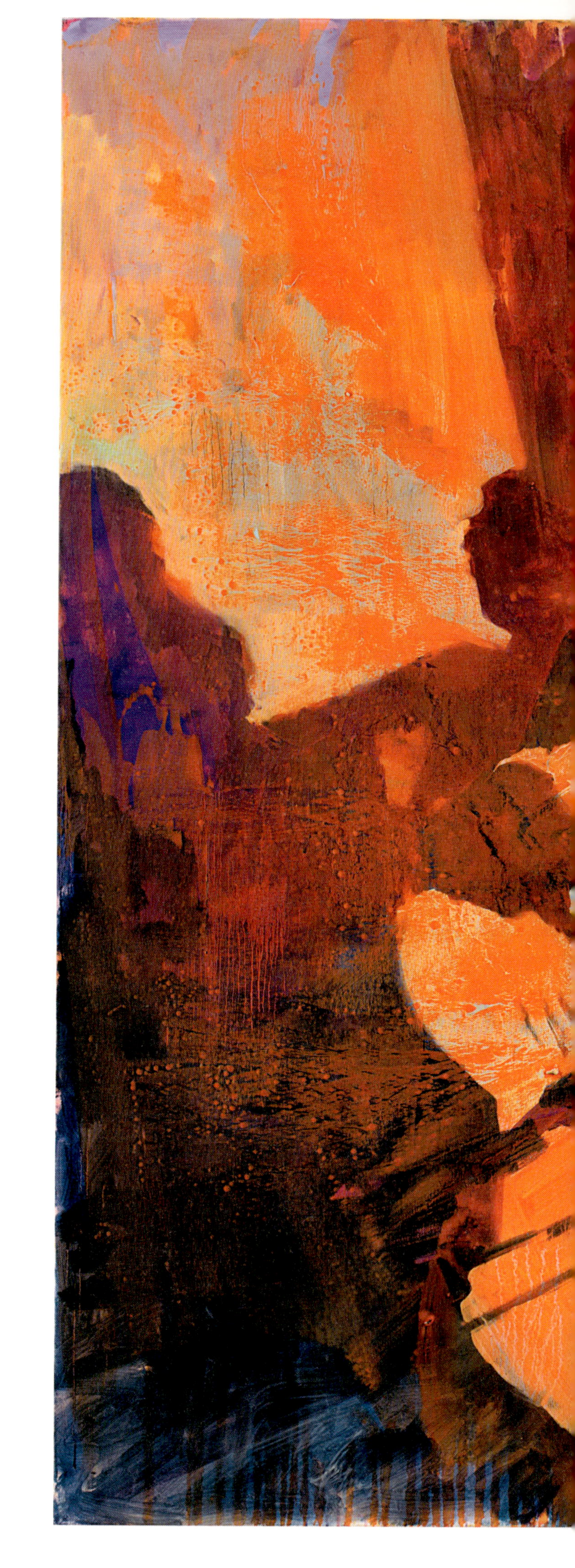

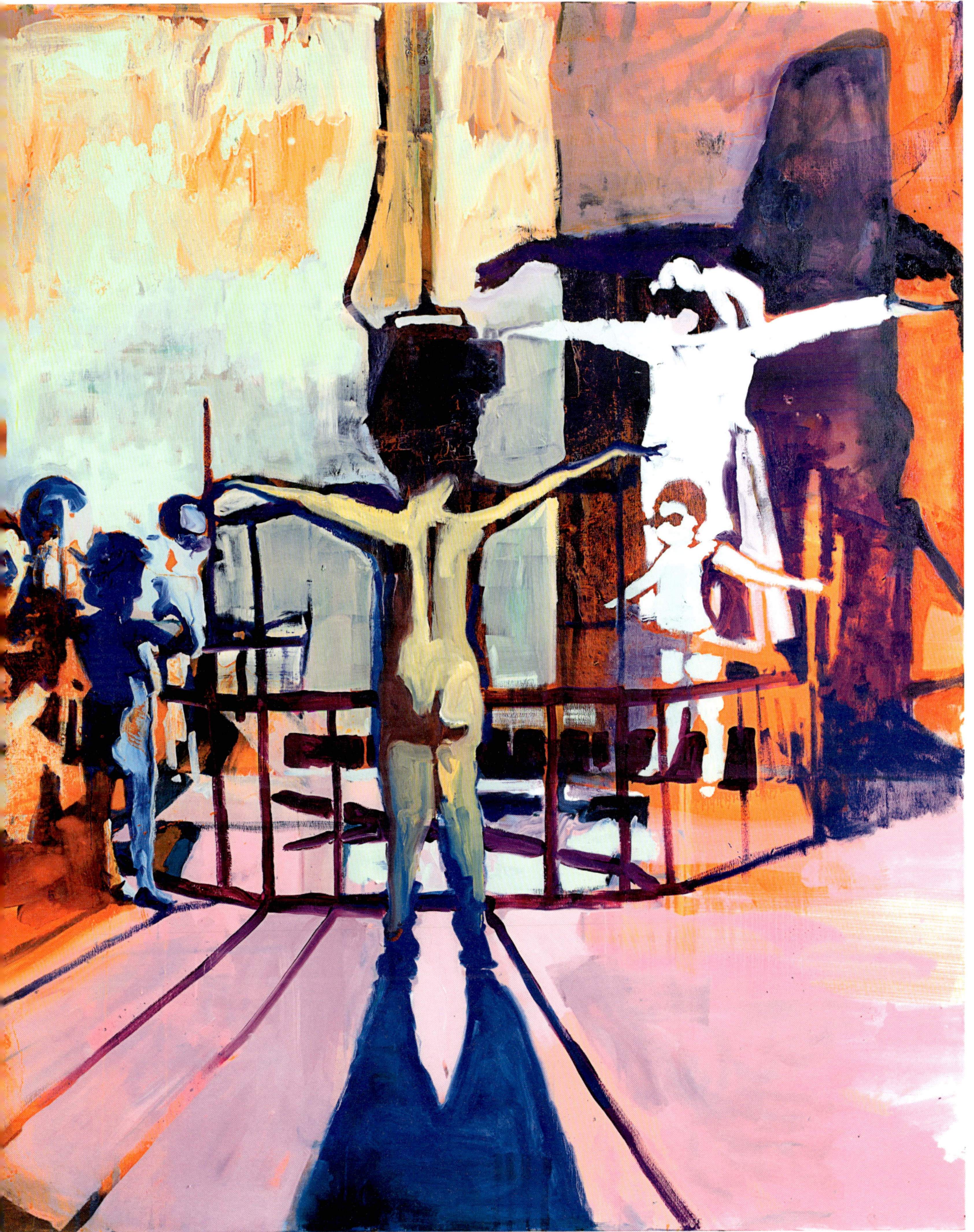

Crow Tribe

2016   200 × 240 cm

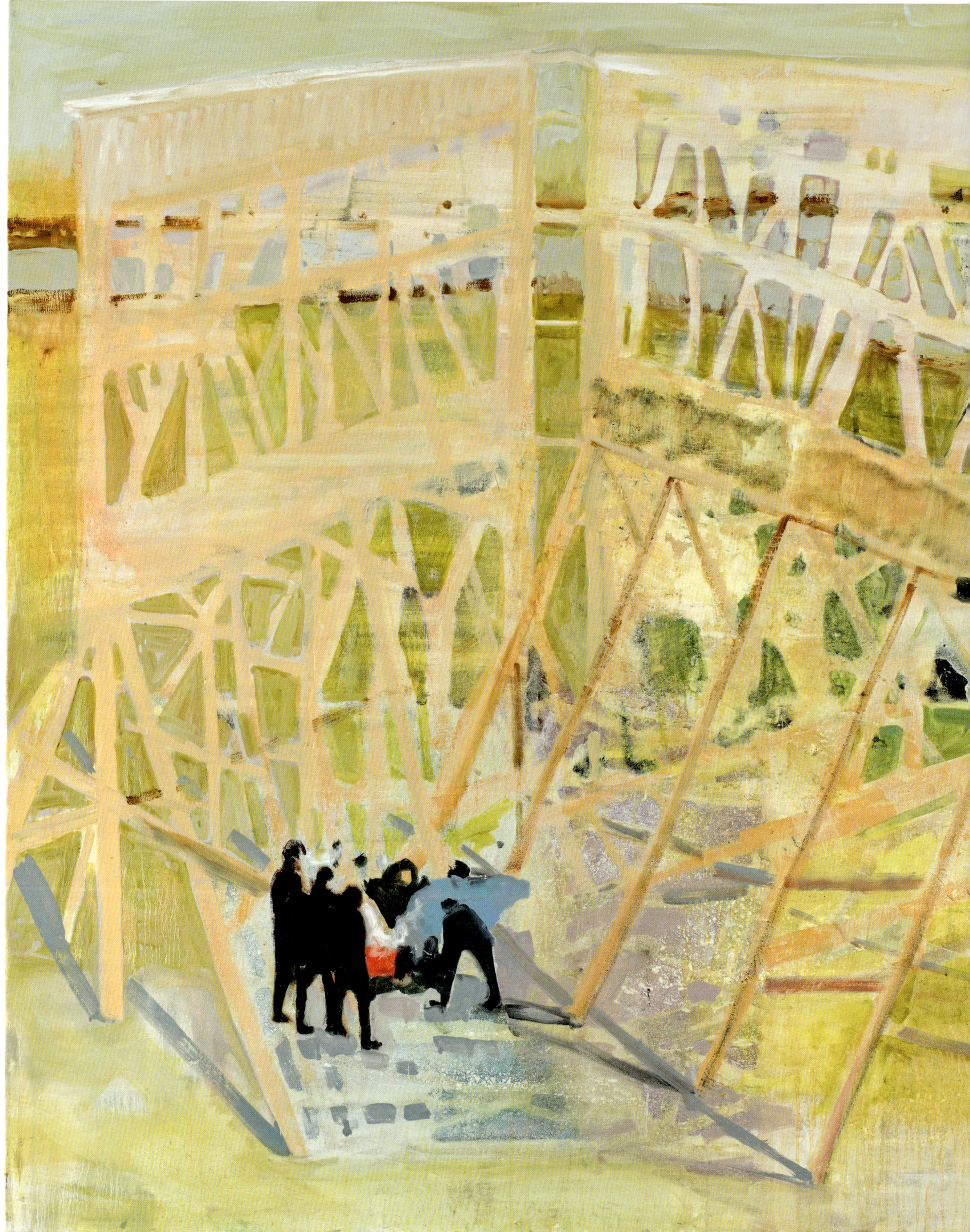

Estuary   2017   170 × 210 cm

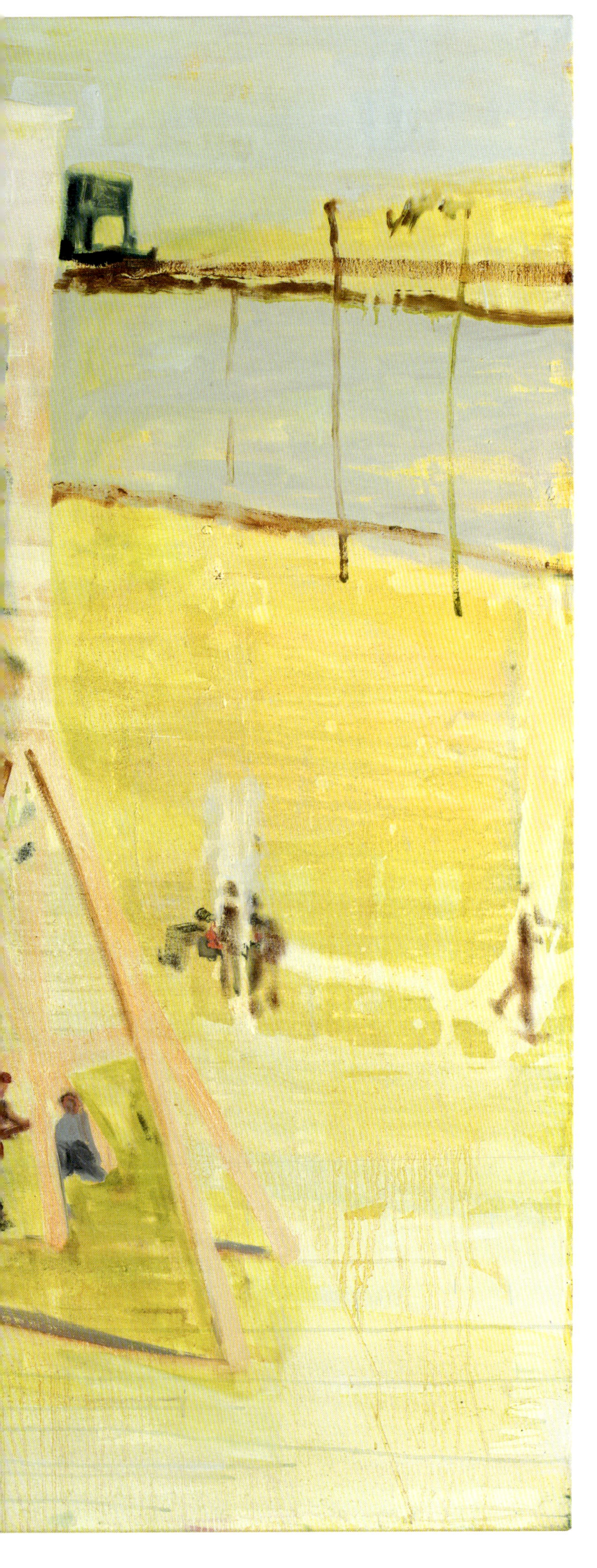

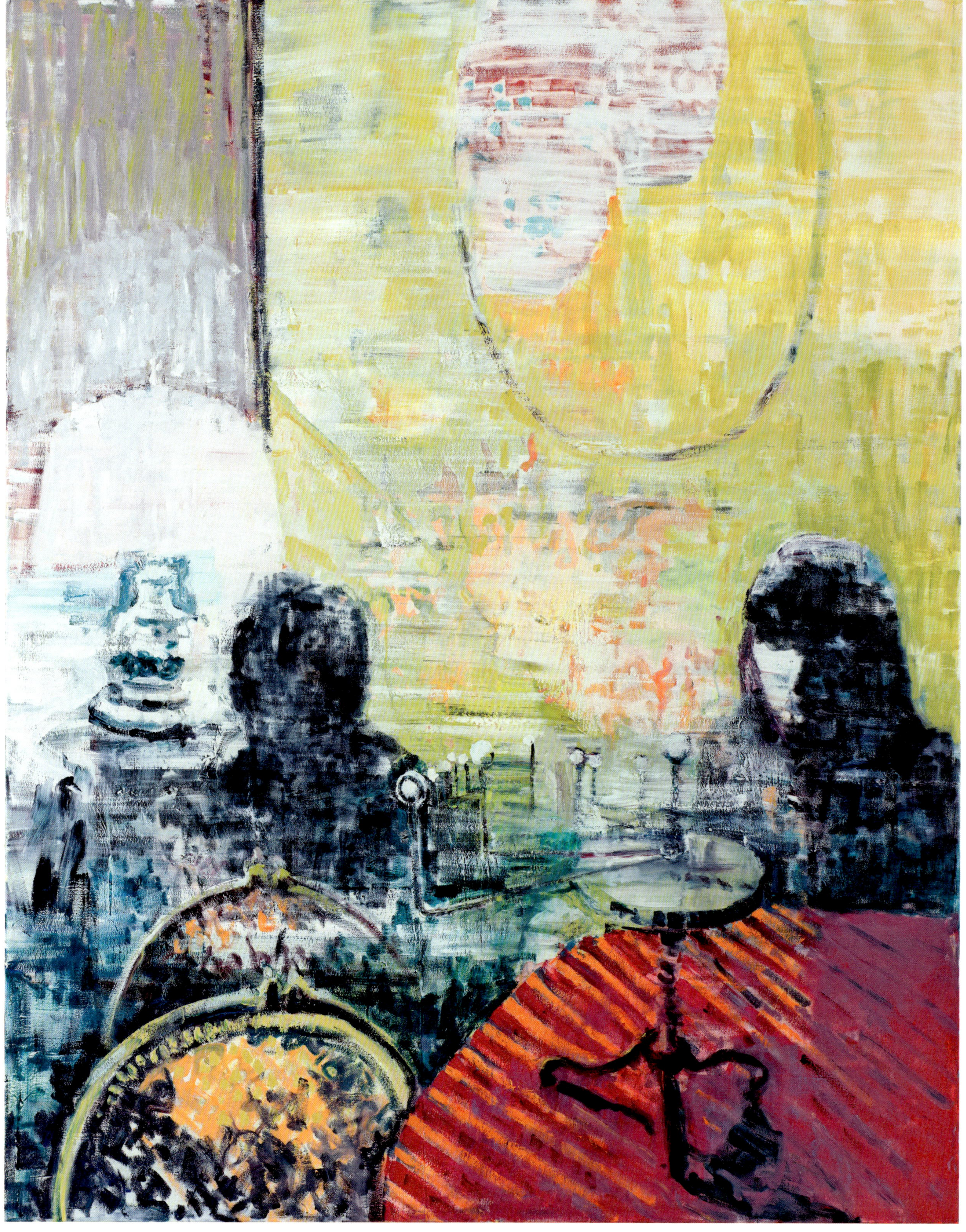

Hovercraft

2015   210 × 170 cm

Rachel Lumsden
Return of the Huntress

[Français]

Verlag für moderne Kunst

Cette publication, de même que l'exposition qui l'accompagne, présentent les tableaux les plus récents de Rachel Lumsden et ses œuvres de ces dernières années. Elles proposent un regard sur un travail qui se caractérise par son intense contemporanéité, la diversité de son langage pictural ainsi que son non-conformisme.

Rachel Lumsden est avide d'images, et plus encore : elle semble pouvoir se nourrir indéfiniment du flot de celles qui inondent notre quotidien. Tout lui est bon : photos de presse, histoire de l'art, images oniriques, schémas de circuits, matériel publicitaire… Insatiable et curieuse, elle consomme d'énormes quantités d'images, qu'elle puise dans l'univers physique et numérique pour alimenter son propre processus visuel.

Ce qui constitue la véritable signification de ce processus de fusion visuelle, est le fait qu'il ne se réduit pas à l'échantillonnage ou au collage mais qu'il en résulte au bout du compte des mondes visuels qui se révèlent à la fois de façon inattendue et avec la plus grande évidence.

Chez Rachel Lumsden, c'est l'usage de la couleur en tant que matériau, qui active de façon homogène une surface picturale en perpétuel bourgeonnement. Entre ses mains, la peinture ne saurait jouer un rôle mineur. Gardant toute son autonomie et son intégrité, elle agit telle une substance, conformément à sa propre nature.

Outre ce phénomène, l'idée chez Rachel Lumsden que chaque peinture n'obéit qu'à ses propres règles entraîne une étonnante diversité de son langage pictural. Le style en tant que marque de fabrique n'intéresse guère l'artiste ; elle recherche bien plus le « risque pictural », là où contenu et peinture s'affrontent « hors piste », et peuvent déclencher une avalanche visuelle. Or cette ouverture sur de nouvelles voies n'est pas non plus une fin en soi, mais plutôt une tentative pour se rapprocher de la mystérieuse vie des tableaux et de prendre leur pouls, de ressentir au plus près la matière de la peinture, sans chercher d'explications.

Renouveler la vision du monde, siècle après siècle, tel est le véritable miracle de la peinture. Entre cette grande tradition et au cœur de son époque, le travail de Rachel Lumsden vient à notre rencontre, telle une réalité. Une réalité que cette publication, de même que l'exposition, se propose d'explorer en profondeur.

Cette exposition personnelle, qui donne à voir le travail des dix dernières années de Rachel Lumsden, constitue la présentation la plus complète de ses peintures à ce jour. Elle résulte également d'une collaboration fructueuse entre trois institutions : la Fondation Fernet-Branca à Saint-Louis, France, le Centre d'art Pasquart à Bienne, Suisse et le Kunst(Zeug)Haus à Rapperswil-Jona, Suisse. Un grand merci à Rachel Lumsden pour son généreux engagement qui a permis la réalisation de cette exposition et de la publication. Nous remercions également Bernard Jordan, ainsi que les sponsors – Kulturförderung Kanton St. Gallen, Lotteriefonds Kanton Thurgau, RHW Stiftung, Stadt St. Gallen Fachstelle Kultur, la Fondation Stanley Thomas Johnson et Pro Helvetia, Fondation suisse pour la culture – pour leur bienveillante participation. Nos remerciements vont également à Charlotte Mullins et André Rogger pour leurs textes perspicaces, de même qu'à Thomas Bizzarri et Alain Rodriguez pour la conception innovante et élégante de cette publication.

Pierre-Jean Sugier
Fondation Fernet-Branca

Felicity Lunn
Centre d'art Pasquart

Peter Stohler
Kunst(Zeug)Haus Rapperswil-Jona

À l'aube du XXᵉ siècle, l'écrivain et psychiatre néerlandais Frederik van Eeden s'emploie à consigner des centaines de rêves lucides qui ont jalonné ses nuits. Dans le roman qui suivra, *The Bride of Dreams* (1913), il écrit : « Celui qui rêve est plus éveillé que celui qui dort ». Et de conclure : « La solution du secret de nos vies réside dans nos rêves[1]. » Les peintures de Rachel Lumsden semblent directement liées au pouvoir des rêves et à leurs promesses intangibles. Avec leurs figures fantomatiques, leurs spectres de couleurs d'une grande richesse, leurs motifs turbulents et leurs intérieurs claustrophobes, ses peintures influent sur l'esprit avec une intensité semblable aux rêves inoubliables, offrant tout un réseau de connexions émotionnelles, dont la signification générale reste néanmoins cruellement inaccessible. Chacune de ces œuvres emplit notre champ de vision et submerge nos sens en nous transportant ailleurs, en des lieux qui possèdent leur propre logique interne, des lieux qui paraissent étrangement plausibles, bien qu'ils incluent souvent des éléments fantastiques.

Haruki Murakami – un écrivain que Lumsden admire, et dont les romans témoignent tous d'une intensité hallucinogène – a condensé la puissance émotive des rêves dans une nouvelle intitulée « Sommeil ». Le narrateur évoque un « rêve sombre et glauque », qu'il explicite en ajoutant : « dont j'avais oublié le contenu précis, mais qui m'a laissé une impression sinistre[2] ». De la même manière, les peintures de Rachel Lumsden apparaissent non pas comme des narrations précises, mais comme des états d'esprit, comme des expériences troublantes.

Voilà quinze ans que Rachel Lumsden a quitté l'Angleterre pour venir s'établir en Suisse.

Il est possible de retrouver au fil de ses œuvres un motif qui reflète cet environnement helvétique – comme en témoignent notamment les piquets à neige dans *Rope Walk* (2015, p. 46) – mais le paysage de l'artiste reste essentiellement intérieur. Expériences de jeunesse, contes de fées, rêves, peintures ou photographies sont autant d'éléments qui exercent un impact sur son travail lorsqu'elle se réfère à ses souvenirs et les enjoint de fusionner sur les toiles. Sa profonde connaissance de la peinture, aussi bien historique que contemporaine, ressort nettement dans ses travaux récents. *Return of the Huntress* (2016, p. 28) fait manifestement allusion aux *Chasseurs dans la neige* (1565) de Pieter Bruegel l'Ancien, mais dans le cas présent, le nombre des chasseurs est réduit à un seul personnage, qui se trouve être une femme (l'artiste). Elle s'éloigne du spectateur pour se diriger vers un vertigineux remblai enneigé qui surplombe un paysage urbain contemporain, sous un ciel viridien et magenta. La peinture filtre entre les branches des arbres squelettiques, épinglant l'image à la superficie de la toile et forçant l'œil du spectateur à osciller entre deux pôles : suivre du regard la chasseresse descendant le remblai, ou deviner l'aurore picturale à travers la surface.

Dans plusieurs intérieurs récents de Rachel Lumsden, tels *Antechamber* (2015, p. 13), *Here we go Again* (2014, p. 89) ou *Red Room* (2016, p. 91), l'emploi répété de miroirs et de cadres pose la question de savoir où commence et s'achève l'expérience visuelle. Dans *Here we go Again*, un miroir entouré d'un cadre doré domine le plan pictural, doublant la présence des bibelots qui ornent le dessus de la cheminée, mais révélant aussi une tête de femme, une perdrix sur un perchoir, ainsi

qu'une ombre bleu vif qui menace de se libérer de son origine domestique. L'ambiguïté qui règne dans *Un bar aux Folies Bergère* (1882) d'Édouard Manet vient percuter l'intérieur encombré de *The Mantelpiece* (1906–1907 env.) de Walter Sickert, à mesure que des souvenirs de la vie de Rachel Lumsden – un chien en céramique, des pugilistes en porcelaine, la statue d'un combattant d'unité de choc – s'entassent dans le cadre. Dans *Red Room*, un miroir similaire reflète une pièce que nous ne pouvons voir par nous-mêmes. Le perroquet sur son support se mue en un corbeau à bec crochu, silhouette menaçante qui rappelle au spectateur que les choses ne sont pas toujours ce qu'elles paraissent être. Peut-être le corbeau évoqué fait-il allusion aux ombres de Platon sur le mur de la caverne ; le monde domestique n'est-il donc pas digne de confiance ? La pièce rouge feu et noir de charbon semble chargée de possibilités, de changements latents, comme si elle pouvait se consumer ou se dissoudre spontanément lorsque le rêve prend fin.

La figure humaine est à l'épicentre du travail de Rachel Lumsden, que ce soit sous une forme vague, comme dans *Sailing to Byzantium* (2016, p. 73), ou plus clairement délinéée, comme dans *Flagpole* (2016, p. 80). (Dans *Red Room*, elle est absente mais une chaise vide suggère l'éventualité d'une présence.) Si elle ne fait jamais l'objet d'un portrait, en revanche, elle est là au service de la peinture, tantôt réduite à une forme ou une apparition évocatrice, tantôt oblitérée par un geste superficiel hardi (comme dans *Flagpole*) pour maintenir la tension entre le sujet tridimensionnel et la peinture bidimensionnelle. Car même si bon nombre de grands formats de Rachel Lumsden comportent des sujets reconnaissables

– personnages, intérieurs, profils urbains –, on a toujours l'impression que c'est la surface picturale qui prime.

Souvent, Rachel Lumsden est attirée par des motifs inhabituels, tels les sosies dans *Leap Minute* (2015, p. 31), les personnages à lunettes dans *Crow Tribe* (2016, p. 101) ou l'ours anthropomorphe dans *Highway Gamblers* (2008, Fig. H, p. 128). Il y a là plus qu'une simple allusion à ce que Sigmund Freud a qualifié d'*unheimlich* (inquiétant), mais en fin de compte, c'est la peinture qui codifie cette lecture. Selon les termes mêmes de l'artiste, « on part à l'aventure lorsqu'on peint. En un sens, on se dit 'n'en fais pas trop, laisse quelques zones libres', mais ensuite, on a l'impression que si le sujet est connu, on se demande 'qu'y a-t-il au-delà[3] ?' ». Dans *Leap Minute*, Rachel Lumsden a fini par recouvrir le visage des fillettes, renonçant à leur identité pour une expérience plus dérangeante, où leur tête semble détachée et désaxée, où le papier peint en arrière-plan devenu motif empiète sur le canapé. Rachel Lumsden veut préserver une certaine ambiguïté dans chacune de ses œuvres – un espace où le spectateur peut entrer et se forger sa propre interprétation. Désireuse de ne pas trop définir les choses, elle laisse la peinture prendre le dessus, préférant faire confiance à des décisions prises pendant le travail, plutôt que suivre un plan rigide.

Cette démarche a été poussée à l'extrême dans ses peintures récentes, notamment dans des intérieurs menacés de désintégration par une rafale de signes abstraits. Dans *The Elder Flower* (2015, p. 51), une femme vêtue de noir se lève d'une chaise, son visage strié par la lumière du soleil. Cependant, c'est seulement sur une reproduction de l'œuvre qu'une lecture si évidente est possible. Lorsque le spectateur se trouve devant la peinture, la surface se délite presque entièrement : la lumière du soleil devient une fluorescence d'un blanc crémeux ; les ombres bleu pâle, cobalt et aubergine sillonnent la surface comme des traverses de chemin de fer, et le visage – si tant est qu'on puisse encore lui donner ce nom – n'est plus qu'un assemblage de taches blanches et taupes sur un fond bleu passé en frottis. Un seul cercle blanc relie les traits faciaux, permettant de deviner un œil, un sourcil, un menton. Cette relation symbiotique entre sujet et surface, Rachelle Lumsden la qualifie de « fission de l'atome », demandant à la peinture de « travailler au noir » en tant que sujet, tandis que le sujet lui-même explose en boucles et en spires, en motifs de couleurs et de formes variées[4]. Le point où les deux éléments sont possibles et simultanément présents confère à l'œuvre une énergie crépitante.

En fin de compte, c'est la matière qui guide Rachel Lumsden – qu'il s'agisse de cette surface orange lumineuse comme un sorbet dans *End of a Short Day* (2015, p. 49), ou de l'audacieuse atmosphère boréale dans *Return of the Huntress*. Économe et sèche dans *Think Tank* (2015, p. 21), la matière se fait rugueuse et nerveuse dans *Leap Minute*, ou ardente et spectrale dans *Red Room*. Entre les mains de l'artiste, elle saisit le spectateur à la gorge, ses myriades de couleurs imprégnant notre esprit et se connectant directement à notre cœur. Ce ne sont pas là des œuvres que l'on peut regarder de loin ou en reproduction. Il faut les expérimenter physiquement, les ressentir – et les rêver.

Notes

1   Frederik van Eeden, *The Bride of Dreams*, 1913, extrait de *States of Mind: Experiences at the Edge of Consciousness*, éd. Anna Faherty, cat. expo. (Londres : Wellcome Collection 2016) pp. 112–114.
2   Haruki Murakami, « Sommeil » in *L'éléphant s'évapore*, éd. Belfond, Paris, 2008, p. 103.
3   Entretien entre l'artiste et l'auteur le 29 novembre 2016.
4   Ibid.

En cette fin d'après-midi hivernal, le ciel est nappé de mauve et d'émeraude, et la lumière se fait douce. Son chien trottant sur ses talons, une femme revenant de la chasse descend la colline et se dirige vers un paysage urbain de bureaux, d'usines et de parkings en terrasse. Tout est très calme.

Nous nous trouvons à une certaine distance derrière cette chasseresse, quasiment au bord de la toile. Là, des coups de brosse blancs sales s'étalent entre des bandes verticales noires, qui, sous l'emprise du personnage, deviennent des arbres.

Nous sommes conscients du mode de construction de *Return of the Huntress* (2016, p. 28), un tableau récent de Rachel Lumsden. Conscients de la matérialité de la peinture avec ses épais empâtements sur de minces lavis saignants. Conscients du plaisir à manier, à malaxer la couleur et de la manière dont elle peut être amadouée et manipulée pour exprimer texture et profondeur, voire même le toucher et le son... et pourtant, nous sommes nous aussi la chasseresse, elle marche avec nous, nous marchons avec elle.

Toutes ces qualités étaient déjà présentes voilà quinze ans dans l'œuvre de Rachel Lumsden, mais comme en témoigne cette publication et l'exposition qu'elle accompagne, ses tableaux ont connu de nombreuses évolutions depuis lors, aussi bien au niveau du sujet que du traitement de la peinture.

Rachel Lumsden a quitté Londres pour venir s'établir à Saint-Gall en 2002, quatre ans seulement après avoir obtenu un master de peinture à la Royal Academy Schools. L'héritage de Francis Bacon, Lucian Freud, Frank Auerbach et d'autres peintres de l'école de Londres, mais aussi l'influence plus récente d'artistes tels que Peter Doig, Elizabeth Peyton ou Dexter Dalwood, n'ont cessé de braquer les projecteurs sur la peinture figurative en Grande-Bretagne. Ce n'est donc pas un hasard si la manière dont Rachel Lumsden aborde son médium présente de nombreux points communs avec ces artistes, et si son style détonne sur la scène artistique suisse.

Ses peintures étonnamment grandes sont au moins de la taille de l'artiste elle-même, et déterminent un rapport physique certain face à l'œuvre à la fois pour elle et pour le spectateur. Elles nous transmettent le sentiment profond de leur processus de création, mais nous font percevoir aussi la sensibilité d'une artiste au caractère de son matériau et à la manière dont il fonctionne. Les peintures de Rachel Lumsden ne peuvent être qualifiées de narratives car elles sont trop ouvertes et ambiguës pour permettre une lecture claire ; elles évoquent plutôt des atmosphères chargées et débordantes d'énergie. Les sujets choisis par l'artiste – associant des accessoires anodins du quotidien à un univers fantastique, des fragments autobiographiques, l'inconscient collectif – s'accordent au Zeitgeist dans le domaine de la peinture, ainsi qu'aux aspects sociaux et politiques actuels. Ils n'en demeurent pas moins extrêmement personnels. Rachel Lumsden crée des peintures qui exsudent une énergie mystérieuse, oscillant entre la surface picturale et la représentation.

Groupes d'œuvres

Jusqu'en 2010, Rachel Lumsden a choisi de peindre des séries. Ce processus lui a permis de réutiliser différents motifs ou idées sur une période de plusieurs mois pour explorer les divers aspects d'une thématique et renforcer ainsi l'impact sur les regardeurs. Le résultat est impressionnant : alors que la structure sérielle instaure un dialogue graduel avec le sujet, les œuvres prises individuellement sont si denses qu'elles fonctionnent comme un film dont le déroulement serait condensé en une image forte et unique.

La série la plus ancienne examinée ici se concentre sur un objet clairement défini, évoquant certains aspects du passé de l'artiste. Dans *Ancestral Inheritance* (1998, Fig. A, p. 127), chacune des peintures représente un meuble ayant appartenu jadis à sa grand-mère. Si la représentation des objets surdimensionnés rappelle les sensations de rétrécissement d'Alice dans l'environnement du Pays des merveilles, la présence menaçante de l'obscurité sous les meubles – à la fois palpitante et inquiétante – fait écho à Roald Dahl ou Edgar Allen Poe.

La série à laquelle Rachel Lumsden s'est ensuite attaquée, *Arc Light* (2001, Fig. K p. 129), se concentre cette fois sur une seule pièce du mobilier, un abat-jour suranné. Dans chacune de ces œuvres, le fond aussi sombre que lugubre sert de repoussoir au caractère fantaisiste de l'objet, mais c'est la longueur démesurée des coulures qui transforme la simple relation arrière-plan/figure dans le tableau en une interprétation sinistre des objets usuels de la vie quotidienne. Ce qui a toujours fasciné Rachel Lumsden, c'est la manière dont des objets banals pouvaient revêtir une dimension psychologique aussi puissante qu'un portrait humain. Phénomène révélateur, Rachel Lumsden n'a presque jamais peint les visages de ses personnages en détail, préférant exprimer les caractères, les atmosphères et les relations au travers de postures ou de mouvements plutôt que d'expressions faciales.

Le jeu des contrastes entre lumière et obscurité est l'autre aspect qui caractérise l'œuvre de Rachel Lumsden. Il se manifeste déjà dans *Arc Light*. Si l'éclairage est symbolisé dans cette série par une source de lumière artificielle, dans les peintures suivantes, il s'agit de la lumière du jour, que l'on voit souvent pénétrer par la fenêtre dans un intérieur lugubre, les rayons du soleil venant accentuer l'ombre des objets ou renforcer le caractère dramatique de ciels qui s'assombrissent ou sont balayés par les vents. Certains aspects de sa pratique picturale testés au cours de cette série ont été réévalués et développés depuis, de manières variées par l'artiste.

La série *Homeland Security* (2003, Fig. B,C, p. 127) prolonge les investigations de l'artiste dans les trivialités de la vie domestique, en relation notamment avec la culture et les traditions de son pays, la Grande-Bretagne. Le choix du thème de l'omniprésent couvre-théière est directement lié à son arrivée en Suisse, au moment des attentats du 11 septembre 2001 et de la guerre en Afghanistan. À la fois perturbée par la propagande négative dirigée contre l'Angleterre pour le rôle qu'elle a joué lors de ces événements, et consciente de s'être établie dans un nouveau pays, Rachel Lumsden a choisi le couvre-théière comme archétypique du mauvais goût britannique. La peinture est recouverte de couvre-théières qui, peints de manière à remplir la toile, évoquent des tanks en manœuvre.

Dans la série suivante, *Dashboard Talisman* (2005, Fig. M p. 129), Rachel Lumsden va plus loin encore en jouant de l'ambivalence qui résulte de l'élévation d'un petit objet insignifiant au rang de sujet pictural monumental. Le fait d'avoir choisi comme sujet de ses grands formats, de petits animaux en peluche que les gens suspendent aux rétroviseurs de leur voiture, a quelque chose de résolument excentrique. Cependant, le voyeurisme de l'artiste qui se penche au-dessus du capot de chaque véhicule pour répertorier ces vulgaires mascottes s'inscrit dans une perspective davantage axée sur le point de vue et sur le tabou de l'ingérance dans le domaine privé que sur la reproduction fidèle des fétiches des conducteurs.

L'intérêt de Rachel Lumsden pour les structures naturelles et mécaniques se manifeste à l'évidence comme un fil rouge au travers de sa pratique, surtout dernièrement, dans une œuvre in situ monumentale qu'elle a réalisée pour le BZA, une école d'ingénieurs en robotique et mécatronique du canton de Thurgovie. Une structure noire réticulaire, évoquant des circuits et des nœuds, recouvre un motif de losanges richement colorés, qui rappelle la série des *Silent Inhabitants* (2006, Fig. D,E, p. 127). Ces peintures juxtaposent des microcellules et des cartes mères à des fleurs, des oiseaux et des insectes, devenus des parasites pour survivre dans un nouvel environnement. Cette série introduit une caractéristique majeure de la pratique de Rachel Lumsden, qui réapparaîtra dans des peintures ultérieures : sa capacité à créer une atmosphère sans avoir recours à la narration. Dans l'œuvre *Kriechstrom* (2006), par exemple, elle a passé une brosse à ongles sur la toile pour créer des lignes irrégulières et arachnéennes qui ressemblent à un diagramme de flux électrique, et confèrent en même temps à la peinture une sensation de mouvement dans l'urgence et l'équivalent visuel à un bruit blanc.

Le malaise demeure la tonalité générale d'un ensemble de peintures intitulées *Bird Wars* (2007–2008, Fig. F,G, p. 128), qui recourent, ici encore, à des oiseaux et des animaux pour remplacer la figure humaine et ses émotions. En dépit de leur composition plus conventionnelle, fondée sur une association d'arbres, de personnages et d'oiseaux, ces œuvres échappent à une lecture directe. Elles reposent plutôt sur des souvenirs disparates, des personnages dérangeants des contes pour enfants, des illustrations de livres et des gravures du XVIIe siècle, jusqu'aux satires et caricatures sociocritiques d'Hogarth et de Goya, ainsi qu'aux jeux électroniques.

L'empiètement du passé

Rachel Lumsden s'est toujours référée à l'histoire de l'art, et l'artiste n'hésite pas à s'approprier un sujet ou une manière d'utiliser la couleur : « J'aime les paysages automnaux de Corot chargés d'atmosphère, mais je suis aussi fascinée par la peinture de Malcolm Morley, qui est totalement à l'opposé de ma propre démarche.[1] » Dans une peinture de petit format intitulée *Morley's Deckchair* (2015, p. 85), elle rend hommage aux évocations de personnages dans des décors familiers, chers à l'artiste britannique. De part ses références à l'iconographie historique telle que les costumes baroques ou l'une des machines volantes d'Otto Lilienthal dans *Bird Wars*, ou encore les monuments publics dans *12 O'Clock High* (2012, Fig. J, p. 129) et *Mr Wolf* (2012, p. 52), Lumsden condense le passé et le présent, et synthétise l'historique, le politique et le social. L'histoire britannique reste une toile de fond récurrente de l'œuvre, comme dans la salle de contrôle de la Seconde guerre mondiale de *When Push Comes to Shove* (2012, Fig. L, p. 129), où les opérateurs peuvent faire penser à des croupiers.

Cet empiètement du passé sur le présent se manifeste essentiellement dans l'atmosphère qui règne au sein des intérieurs de Rachel Lumsden. Les meubles démodés qui apparaissent dans bon nombre de ceux-ci – guéridon, lampe, ornements divers – traduisent le confinement des salons démodés qui font partie, tout au moins en Grande-Bretagne, d'une strate bien particulière de la société contemporaine. L'intérêt permanent que Rachel Lumsden voue à ce genre, solidement ancré dans la peinture britannique, s'est vu peut-être renforcé par le fait que l'artiste a vécu longtemps en dehors de son pays : « Les peintures de Walter Sickert de la fin du XIXe siècle font partie des œuvres qui ont durablement influencé mon travail. Ses salons bourgeois plutôt mornes, de même que ses descriptions du côté crasseux de la vie londonienne nourrissent mes propres intérieurs[2]. » La représentation d'une pièce peut être très expressive lorsque des lampes ou des meubles prennent la place des personnages, que l'ambiguïté de l'espace alourdit l'atmosphère. Dans *Here we go Again* (2014, p. 89) par exemple, il n'est pas tout de suite évident que l'on regarde un dessus de cheminée qui se reflète dans un miroir. Fortement recadrés, les intérieurs offrent une vision fracturée, tout en enfermant le spectateur dans son introspection. Cette sensation inconfortable de ne pas devoir nécessairement se fier aux apparences se traduit dans l'œuvre de Lumsden par la présence de deux éléments : les portes, suggérant que d'autres mondes existent derrière elles, et les fenêtres, fournissant un cadre pour créer un tableau dans le tableau.

Infléchir la peinture

L'ambiguïté de la lecture s'étend jusqu'au processus de création des œuvres. Chez Rachel Lumsden, le traitement de la peinture – à la fois comme couleur et comme matériau physique – s'avère radical. La palette est simultanément criarde et sale, riche et fausse. Profondément enracinée dans la vie bourgeoise, la mélancolie se reflète dans la crasse et la toxicité d'intérieurs qui sentent le renfermé – qu'il s'agisse de la série *Ancestral Inheritance*, ou de peintures plus récentes qui exhalent la claustrophobie, telles que *Leap Minute* (2015, p. 31). Jusqu'à des œuvres comme *End of a Short Day* (2015, p. 49), qui se distingue par la luminosité de ses champs oranges, il était rare qu'une couleur s'exprime pleinement. Ce phénomène se produit le plus souvent lorsque des excroissances huileuses, qui relèvent davantage de la pure peinture que de la description, ou des flaques de térébenthine, surgissent sur la toile, prenant l'apparence de cavités profondes. Le noir joue un rôle d'une importance étonnante. Il luit à travers la superposition d'autres couleurs, ou les souille directement, tandis que des particules noires s'accrochent à des objets ou sont suspendues dans l'atmosphère. Cependant, sa présence est également ressentie comme un contraste à la lumière qui illumine l'œuvre de Rachel Lumsden, paraissant irradier de l'intérieur.

Néanmoins, même les ombres obscures projetées dans la puissante lumière du soleil se dissolvent lorsqu'on les voit de près, la surface picturale fournissant peu d'indices sur l'objet représenté, qui ne devient lisible que si on s'éloigne. Les formes sont spécialement floues dans les zones où la peinture a coagulé. C'est pour cette raison que le contenu de l'œuvre se voit encapsulé dans la relation entre la couleur et la matérialité de la substance picturale, cette dernière ayant souvent une dimension abstraite. Rachel Lumsden utilise la peinture à l'huile, qu'elle retravaille à maintes reprises avec des brosses et autres outils. La gestuelle du pinceau tout en douceur, qu'elle adopte souvent pour les zones larges, contraste avec les touches énergiques. Phénomène significatif, l'artiste ne travaille pas sur de moyens formats mais réalise régulièrement de petites peintures sur des plaques de Formica, du papier ou de la toile. Celles-ci peuvent jouer le rôle d'esquisses préparatoires pour de plus grandes peintures, mais sont également autonomes.

Bien que l'œuvre de Rachel Lumsden soit clairement figurative, le rôle de la figure humaine est ambigu, d'autant que l'artiste précise rarement les traits du visage, évitant par là-même toute référence à la narration ou à un personnage. Les figures font partie de cet humour à froid qui revient sans cesse dans l'œuvre de l'artiste, et dont elles sont l'une des caractéristiques essentielles. Tantôt elles illuminent des atmosphères parfois sinistres ou des thèmes oppressants, tantôt elles accentuent l'ironie – depuis les créatures hybrides de *Bird Wars* jusqu'à la relation triangulaire entre l'homme, la femme et le puma dans *On a Sticky Wicket* (2012, Fig. I, p. 128). L'artiste efface souvent un élément de l'œuvre pour activer autre chose, de manière à pouvoir créer un contraste : « Pour moi, la peinture consiste en divers actes de destruction qui rendent possible à une œuvre une deuxième, voire une troisième vie. En témoigne la peinture de deux fillettes, intitulée *Leap Minute*. J'ai effacé leur visage parce que même s'ils étaient convaincants, l'œuvre serait devenue un portrait plutôt qu'un mouvement entre différentes couches visuelles. Je voulais que le monde concret se dissolve en un plus grand nombre de formes ambiguës.[3]

Le rapport de Rachel Lumsden à son matériau a changé ces deux ou trois dernières années, notamment parce que l'artiste est devenue plus audacieuse, s'appuyant moins que par le passé sur des stratégies sécurisantes. Elle travaille des empâtements secs et étale de fines couches de peinture fluide pour atténuer telle ou telle zone. Mais elle verse aussi de la peinture pour couvrir la surface, « jusqu'à ce que ce soit vraiment comme de la soupe », dit-elle, et elle ajoute « jusqu'à ce que j'ai la sensation de nager dans la peinture.[4] » En l'étalant et en la déversant de manière partiellement – mais non totalement – contrôlable, l'artiste peut créer à la fois des zones sèches et d'autres plus poisseuses. C'est au travers de cette lutte – un dialogue avec la matérialité de la peinture – qu'elle ménage un espace pour que quelque chose se produise, de façon qu'elle puisse accéder à un nouveau territoire. Selon les termes de Rachel Lumsden, « la peinture est une forme sexy de la physique quantique, où chaque trace sur la toile n'est pas seulement une tache de couleur, mais aussi la représentation d'une forme. C'est cette dualité inhérente qui rend la peinture si exaltante. J'ai souvent la sensation d'être sur un chantier boueux, négociant entre l'idée et les matériaux, jusqu'à ce qu'une nappe de peinture liquide prenne une apparence figurative, suffisamment malléable pour permettre à la fois sa propre représentation et celle de quelque chose d'autre.[5]

Chez Rachel Lumsden, le désir de commencer une nouvelle œuvre est généralement déclenché par quelque chose qu'elle a vu. Elle procède intuitivement, tout en considérant l'intuition comme un savoir accumulé sur de nombreuses années. Elle l'utilise donc comme une composante essentielle de cet exercice d'équilibre qui consiste à créer un monde visuel tout en négociant avec la peinture/matière/couleur. L'imprévisibilité du médium donne également à l'artiste la liberté de provoquer l'erreur ou l'accident – « tout en ayant une certaine idée du résultat possible[6] », de se concentrer sur le processus plutôt que sur l'idée définie au départ : « Toute mon œuvre traite de la matérialité, dans la mesure où je renonce à bon nombre de mes idées pour permettre à la peinture elle-même de se développer. Chaque toile est son propre univers, comportant un ensemble de règles différentes, auxquelles je dois être capable de faire face. Je réalise de plus en plus que la peinture ne se produit que sur la toile, au moment même de son exécution. Je peux rechercher des sujets, trouver de nouvelles sources visuelles, expérimenter des compositions sur Photoshop, réaliser des esquisses. Mais tout cela n'est qu'une phase préparatoire qui s'arrête au moment où commence l'application de la peinture.[7] »

La chasseresse s'en retourne d'un pas léger, comme si elle dansait. Le chien lui donne des coups de museau dans les jambes, flairant le butin qu'elle porte en bandoulière.

À l'orée de la forêt, elle fait une brève pause, scrutant du regard la ville à la tombée de la nuit. Tout est très calme. C'est là qu'elle va disperser ses tableaux pour que d'autres les recueillent, les regardent et les analysent, et qu'une fois rassasiés, ils poursuivent leur route.

Notes

1   Extrait d'un entretien du 15 août 2015 entre l'auteur et Rachel Lumsden.

2–7   Ibid.

Un avion est parqué sur une piste d'atterrissage baignant dans une lumière zénithale, sans qu'on puisse lui attribuer une nationalité précise, les signes peints sur sa queue étant trop flous. Peut-être la scène se déroule-t-elle sous les Tropiques – outre l'arrière de l'appareil qui scintille dans la chaleur, la silhouette d'un personnage de dos, à la chevelure crépue, et la présence d'un palmier au premier plan, pourraient le laisser penser. Bien qu'une passerelle soit arrimée contre la carlingue, personne ne semble vouloir l'utiliser – spectacle étrangement figé, qui n'est pas sans évoquer de manière quelque peu inquiétante des images de détournements d'avion. Ou encore : une allée le long du mur d'enceinte de la Cité interdite à Beijing. Des ombres d'arbres – rythmant à intervalles rapprochés une voie pédestre chaulée ainsi que la base de la muraille, également peinte en blanc et sa partie supérieure d'un rouge chinois lumineux – attirent le regard vers des profondeurs indéterminées, où l'on n'aimerait guère s'aventurer à pied. Et qu'en est-il de cette vue nocturne d'un parking désert, où l'éclairage de surveillance haut perché sur sa hampe dispense une clarté irréelle ? Cette lumière éblouissante, entourée d'un halo laiteux, sert-elle à protéger les quelques véhicules présents, ou à dégager une atmosphère menaçante ?

Voilà donc trois atmosphères trouvées dans les œuvres esquissées que réalise Rachel Lumsden « çà et là ». Surtitrés *Here and there* (2016) et numérotés en tant que série, ce sont des travaux, de format A4, peints rapidement généralement d'après des photographies de scènes de la vie quotidienne. L'artiste leur a donné le nom de « *Here and there* » (expression anglaise qui signifie « çà et là, de temps à autres »), et s'en sert comme le lieu privilégié pour trouver des idées pour ses peintures de grand format, dans lesquelles elle crée des univers picturaux aux imbrications complexes. Le fait que sur ces grandes toiles, la matière picturale – qui obéit à ses propres règles – acquière une forte présence, et influe souvent par là-même sur le thème, constitue pour l'artiste une partie intégrante du message plastique : la matière colorée pénètre la toile, se répand, émerge à nouveau dans une consistance autre, les couches se superposent – un processus de création qui soumet le sujet de l'œuvre à la dynamique de la matière picturale.

Comme ils sont de petit format et plus rapidement peints, les travaux réalisés « çà et là » ont une matière plus sèche et les couches sont juxtaposées ou superposées de manière homogène. Le sujet est là, devant nous, dans toute sa fraîcheur et non sans une certaine fragilité, et seules quelques traces de brosse témoignent parfois de la mécanique picturale qui a précédé. Cependant, l'élément le plus déterminant reste sans nul doute la palette expressive et totalement lumineuse par laquelle, dans cette nouvelle série, Rachel Lumsden se démarque de ses grands formats peints dans des tonalités sombres. La « murkiness » (pour reprendre l'expression de l'artiste) qui émane de ces derniers – en d'autres termes, l'assombrissement conscient du sujet, tout comme l'obscurcissement du contexte afin de conquérir dans cette ouverture thématique la liberté décrite ci-dessus vis-à-vis de la peinture elle-même – a fait place dans les petits travaux récents à une lumière plus rigoureuse, et partant, à un degré plus élevé d'immédiateté. De même, les sources lumineuses choisies par l'artiste ont été modifiées : l'éclairage indirect, prodigué notamment par un abat-jour aux motifs surchargés dans un intérieur londonien, a été remplacé par les conditions de lumière franchement plus dures d'un espace public extérieur.

Sur le plan thématique, on peut observer le glissement d'un « intérieur » personnel et domestique vers un « extérieur » distancé plus neutre – ce dernier correspondant à un genre dans l'art, qui n'existe pas dans les classifications traditionnelles, mais qui, à la suite de la traduction d'un entretien avec l'artiste, a été jugé pertinent pour définir cet aspect de son œuvre. En effet, la peinture de Rachel Lumsden a la très grande particularité d'évoluer entre deux cultures, celles de la Grande-Bretagne et de la Suisse. C'est ainsi que les intérieurs dans l'art anglais relèvent d'une longue tradition, qui se perpétue encore durant une bonne partie du XXe siècle ; d'autre part, dans l'espace germanophone, la peinture est riche de paysages expressifs. L'artiste puise avec profit dans ces deux univers, et l'on pourrait considérer que ce sont les travaux réalisés « çà et là » sur le mode intuitif qui expriment au mieux cette dualité. Car définis en tant qu'« extérieurs », ils ne sont pas le reflet des états d'âme de l'artiste, contrairement aux peintures expressionnistes allemandes (ou suisses) classiques. De même que dans les grands « intérieurs » de Rachel Lumsden – dont l'artiste développe souvent la « murkiness » à la suite d'une confrontation aux sobres intérieurs de Walter Sickert, un peintre qu'elle considère comme une figure majeure de l'art moderne britannique du début du XXe siècle –, il s'agit ici aussi d'une analyse picturale de la complexion interne de ces mondes visuels : comment se génèrent-ils dans leur matérialité, quelles sont leurs composantes profondément originales, comment réagissent-ils mutuellement ? Et ensuite : comment la couleur peut-elle trouver un équivalent pour cette mécanique plastique interne ?

Mais de même que les représentations évoquées précédemment des « bedsits » londoniens qui font figure d'archétypes – intérieurs confinés, où chaque objet de l'univers très personnel d'une pièce faisant office de salon et de chambre à coucher a sa place bien définie –, les « extérieurs » de Rachel Lumsden ne montrent pas non plus des espaces débarrassés de toute présence humaine. On relève indéniablement des traces de ceux qui hantent aussi ces lieux, mais il ne reste au mieux que des indices pour rappeler leur existence en tant que personnes. Ils n'influent pas non plus sur l'espace en tant qu'êtres manifestement absents, comme c'est souvent le cas dans les grands « intérieurs » de l'artiste. En effet, c'est ce refus – parfois abrupt – de la narration, qui nous surprend peut-être le plus dans ses scènes quotidiennes peintes « çà et là ». Car autant ces compositions affichent leur sujet de manière directe, autant leur interprétation n'obéit qu'à ses propres lois – cadeau d'une peinture, qui puise avec plaisir à d'innombrables sources visuelles et trouve dans une appropriation insouciante des sujets une forme finale spécifique de l'abstraction picturale.

Biographie

Rachel Lumsden est née en 1968 à Newcastle upon Tyne (GB). Elle vit et travaille à Saint-Gall et Arbon (CH) et Londres (GB).

1995–1998
The Royal Academy Schools, Londres, Post Graduate Studies in Painting (MA)

1987–1991
Nottingham Trent University, Bachelor of Arts (Honours) Fine Art

Prix et récompenses

2016
Förderbeitrag Kanton Thurgau (CH)

2014
Werkbeitrag Kanton St. Gallen (CH)

2012
VisarteOst Artist-in-Residence, Cité Internationale des Arts, Paris (FR)

2011
Prix international d'art, Vorarlberg (AT)

2009
Förderpreis Stadt St. Gallen (CH)

2008
Artist-in-Residence der Stadt St. Gallen, La Fabrik, Berlin (DE)

2005
Werkbeitrag Stadt St. Gallen (CH)

2001
Prix, The Pollock-Krasner Foundation, New York (USA)

1998
CrestCo Art Prize, The Bank of England (GB), David Murray Prize (GB), Landseer Prize (GB)

Expositions personnelles

2018
Kunst(Zeug)Haus Rapperswil-Jona (CH)

2017
Fondation Fernet-Branca, Saint-Louis (FR)

Kunsthaus Centre d'art Pasquart, Biel / Bienne (CH)

2015
The Other Island, Galerie Bernard Jordan, Zurich (CH)

Straight Flush, Galerie Bleisch, Arbon (CH)

2013
Drunk in Charge of a Bicycle, Kunstraum Kreuzlingen (CH)

Six Impossible Things Before Breakfast, Kunstplattform Akku, Lucerne (CH)

2012
What's the Time, Mr. Wolf?, Galerie Schönenberger (CH)

2009
Man & Beast, Kunstraum Engländerbau, Vaduz (FL)

2008
Bird Wars, Katharinen, Saint-Gall (CH)

2006
Silent Inhabitants, Kunsthalle Arbon (CH) (2-person show)

Dashboard Talisman, Galerie Christian Röllin, Saint-Gall (CH)

2004
Misplaced, Vertigo Gallery, Londres (GB) (2-person show)

2001
Arc-light, Bridlesmith Gallery, Nottingham (GB)

Arc-light, The Spitz Gallery, Londres (GB)

1999
Foreign Body, Rivington Gallery, Londres (GB)

Expositions collectives

2017
London meets Altdorf, Haus für Kunst Uri (CH)

2016
Im Rausch – zwischen Höhenflug und Absturz, Kunstmuseum Thurgau (CH)

Werkschau Thurgau, Kunstraum Kreuzlingen (CH)

Ausgezeichnet!, Museum Bickel, Walenstadt (CH)

London Art Fair, Long & Ryle Gallery, Londres (GB)

2015
20/21 Art Fair, Long & Ryle Gallery, Londres (GB)

London Art Fair, Long & Ryle Gallery, Londres (GB)

Twopack, Erfrischungsraum, Lucerne (CH)

Grosse Regional, Kunst(Zeug)Haus Rapperswil-Jona (CH)

2013
Werkschau Thurgau, Bleisch Galerie, Arbon (CH)

Die Zweite Dekade, Kunsthalle Arbon (CH)

2012
Central Booking in Berlin, K-Salon, Berlin (DE)

La Suisse est une ville, Salles d'exposition de la Cité internationale des arts, Paris (FR)

2011
The Open West, Cheltenham (GB)

2010
Arthur#5, Kunsthalle, Toggenburg (CH)

Narrative Sequencing, CBA Gallery, New York (USA)
Let the Yangzte Flow,

Hubei Institute of Fine Art, Wuhan (CN)

2009
Heimspiel, Kunstmuseum St. Gallen (CH)

12/132 Biennial, Alte Fabrik, Rapperswil-Jona (CH)

Works on Paper, Raab Gallery, Berlin (DE)

AIR 2, Artists in Residence, Substitut, Raum für Aktuelle Kunst aus der Schweiz, Berlin (DE)

2008
Memory Happens, Christies auction, Kaiser Wilhelm Memorial, Berlin (DE)

Fünf Frauen für den Kaiser, Galerie Siguaraya, Berlin (DE)

2005
Berliner Liste, Messe für aktuelle Kunst, Berlin (DE)

2003
Reduced, Century Gallery, Londres (GB)

2000
Paint!, Vertigo Gallery, London (GB)

Publications

2016
Im Rausch–zwischen Höhenflug und Absturz, Kunstmuseum Thurgau, Verlag für moderne Kunst.

2013
Drunk in Charge of a Bicycle, Paintings and Everything in Between, Textes : Axel Jablonski, Robert Guy Wilson, Schwabe Verlag, Basel

2012
Eine Begegnung mit der Sammlung, VP Bank-Kunststiftung Texte : Brigitte Ulmer

2011
Sammlung Credit Suisse, Scheidegger & Spiess, Zurich

2010
Let the Yangzte Flow, Katalog FH Zentralschweiz, Hochschule Luzern

2008
*Rachel Lumsden, Paintings 1998–2008,*Textes : Felicity Lunn, Uwe Wieczorek, Bucher Verlag (AT)

Collections

Regierungsgebäude Kanton Thurgau (CH), Crédit Suisse Kunstsammlung, Zürich (CH) UBS Art Collection, Zurich (CH) VP Bank Kunstsammlung Vaduz (FL), Kanton St. Gallen Kunstsammlung, St. Gallen (CH), Stadt St. Gallen Kunstsammlung St. Gallen (CH), Collections privées (GB), (CH), (FL), (USA), Asia

Enseignement

Depuis 2007 Hochschule Luzern Design und Kunst / University of Lucerne for applied Arts and Sciences (CH)

116

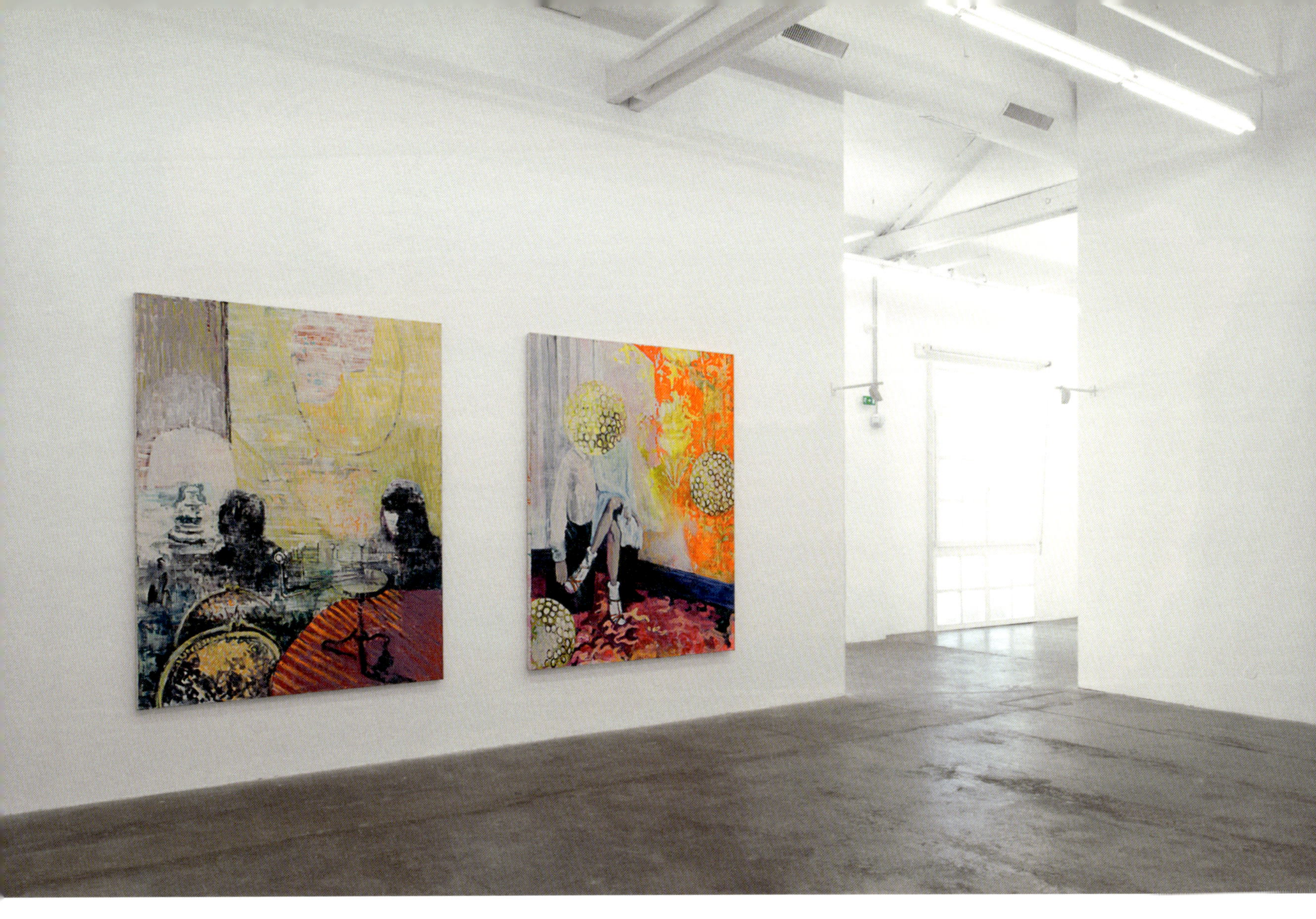

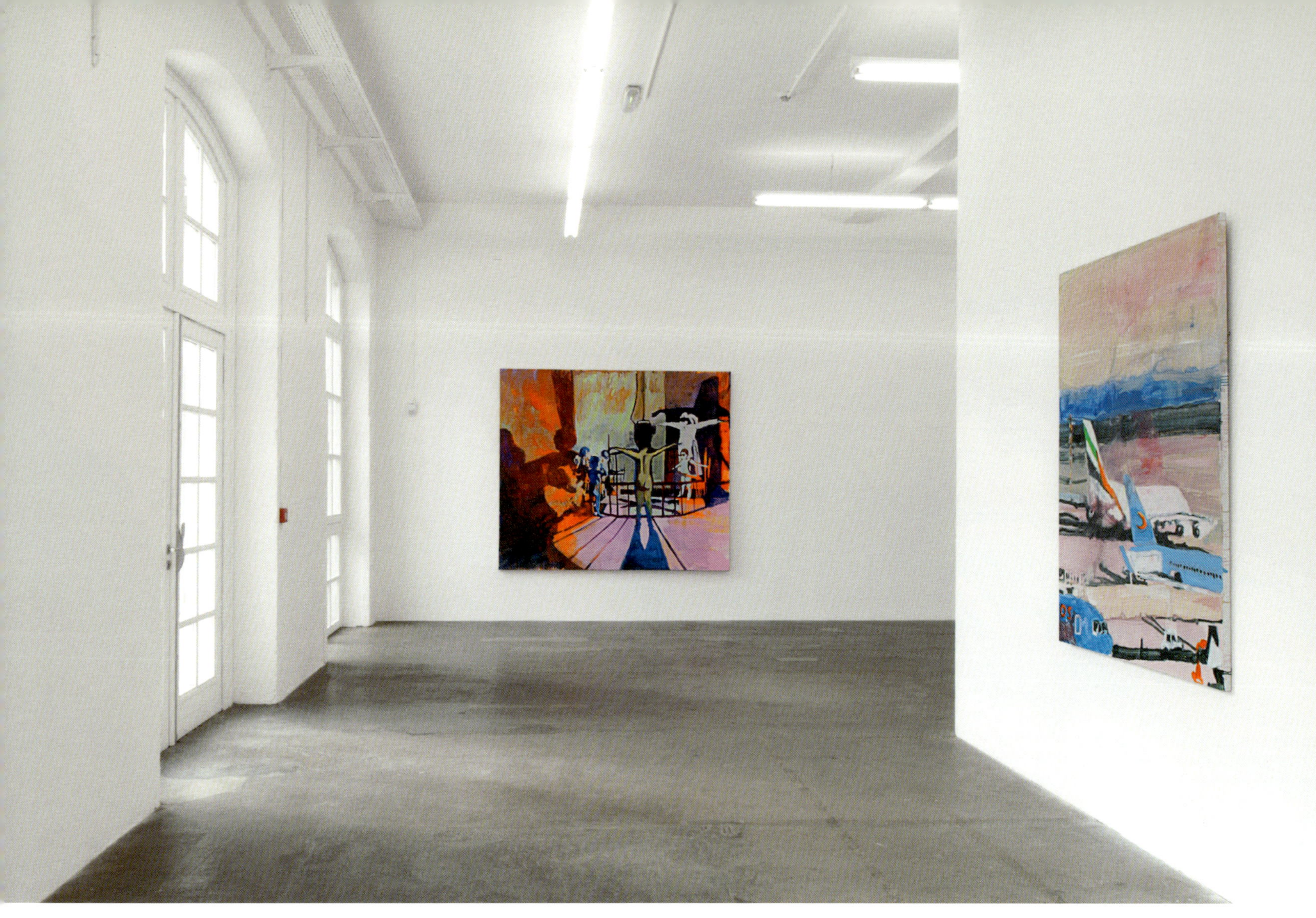

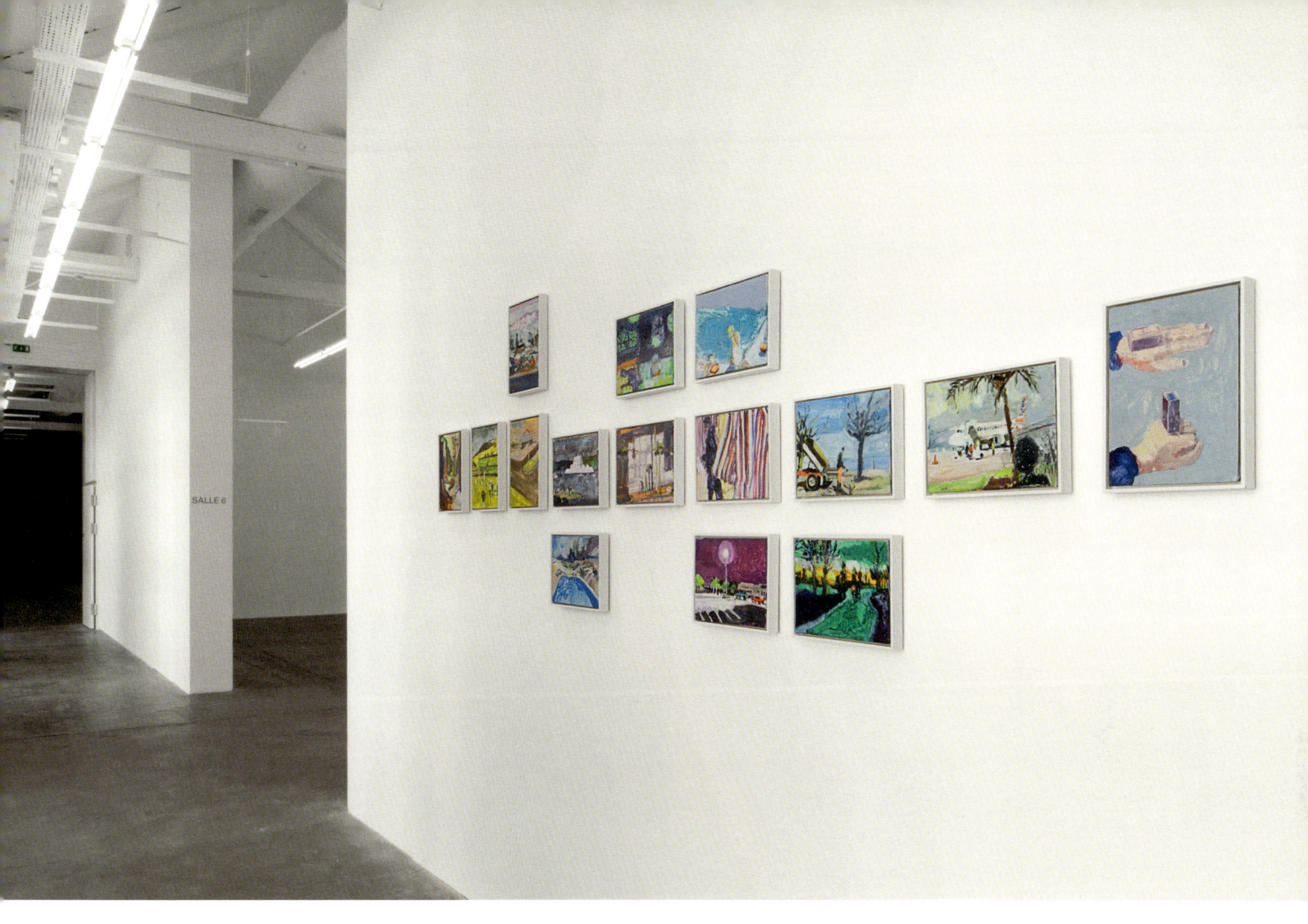

SALLE 6

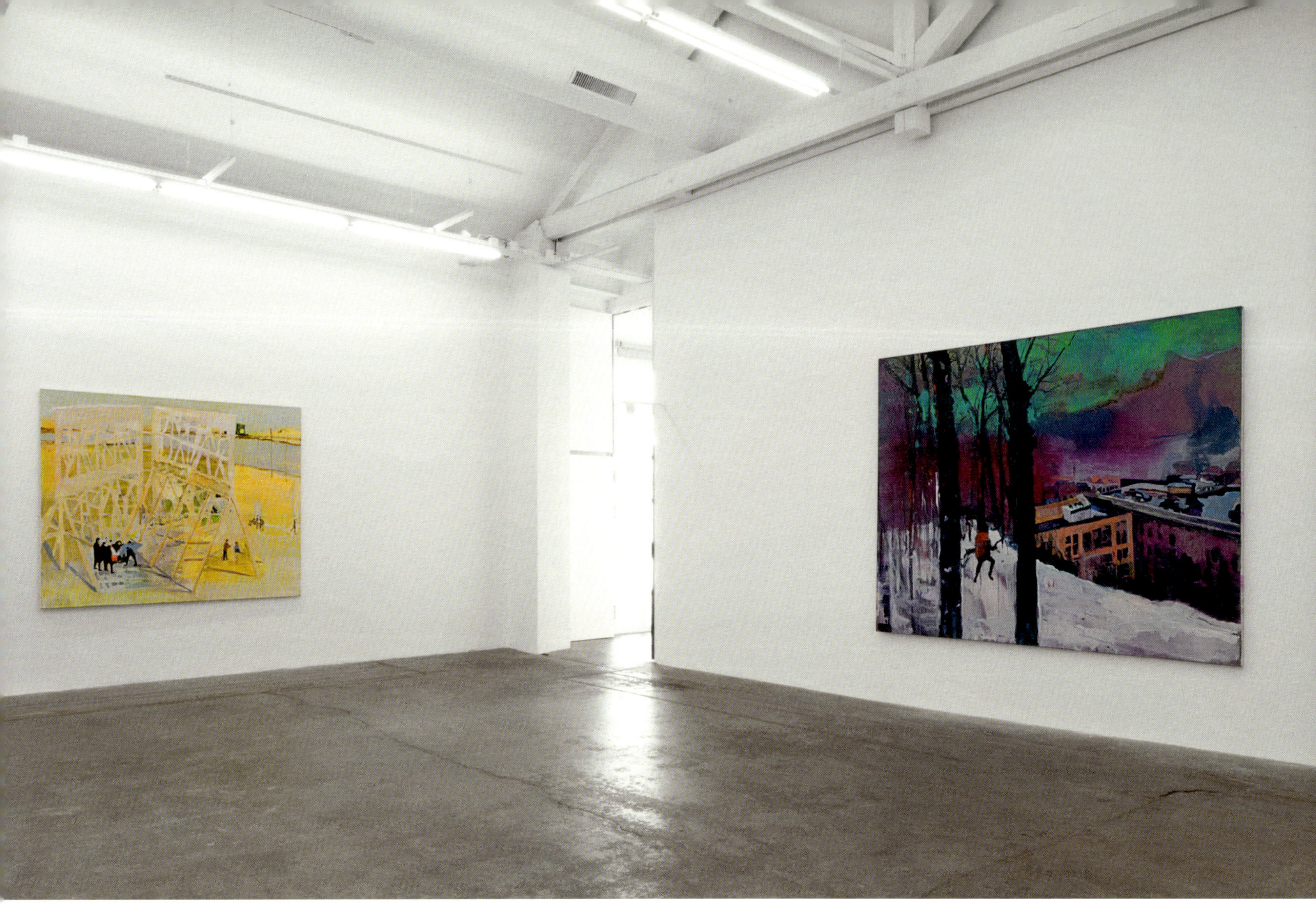

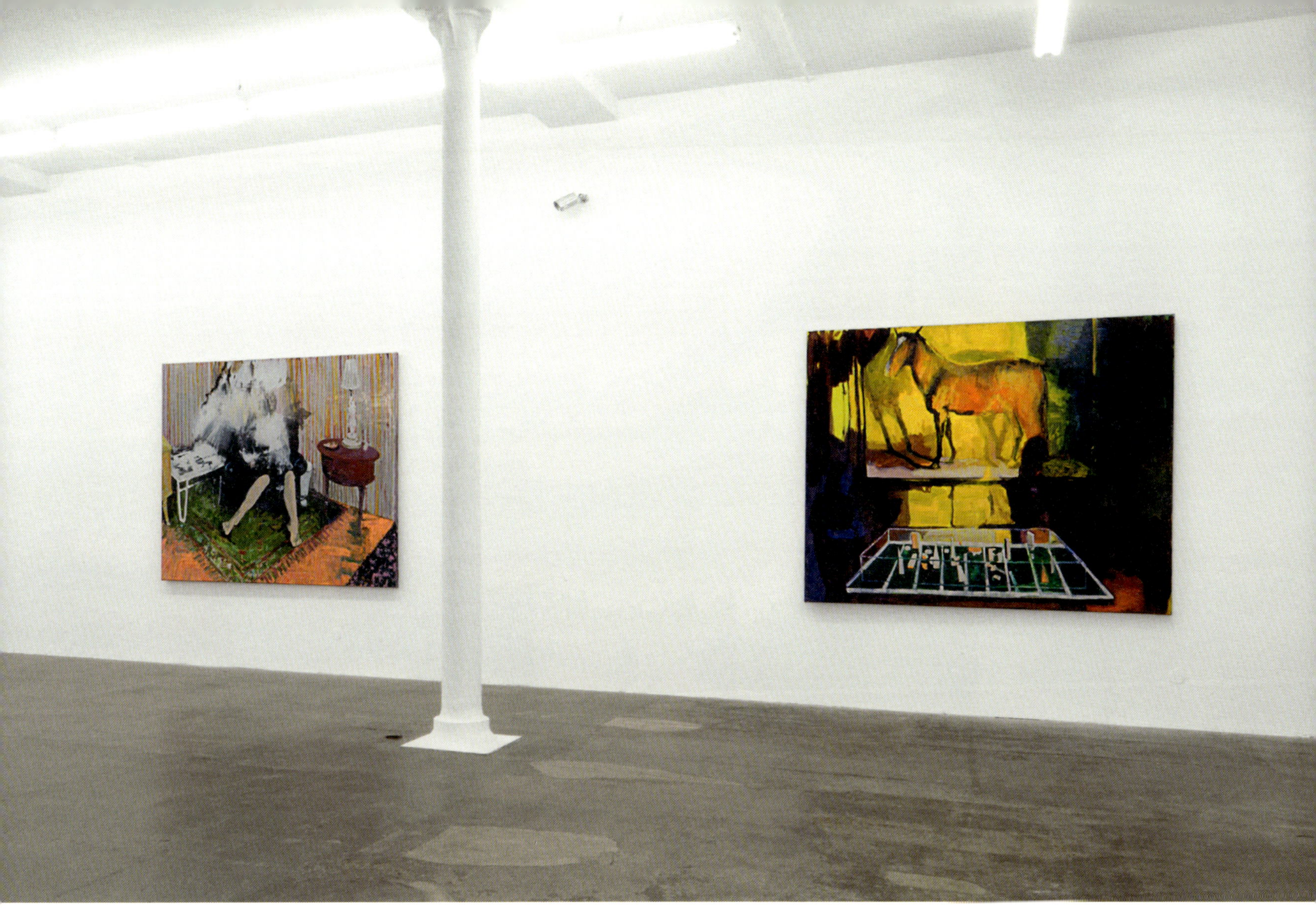

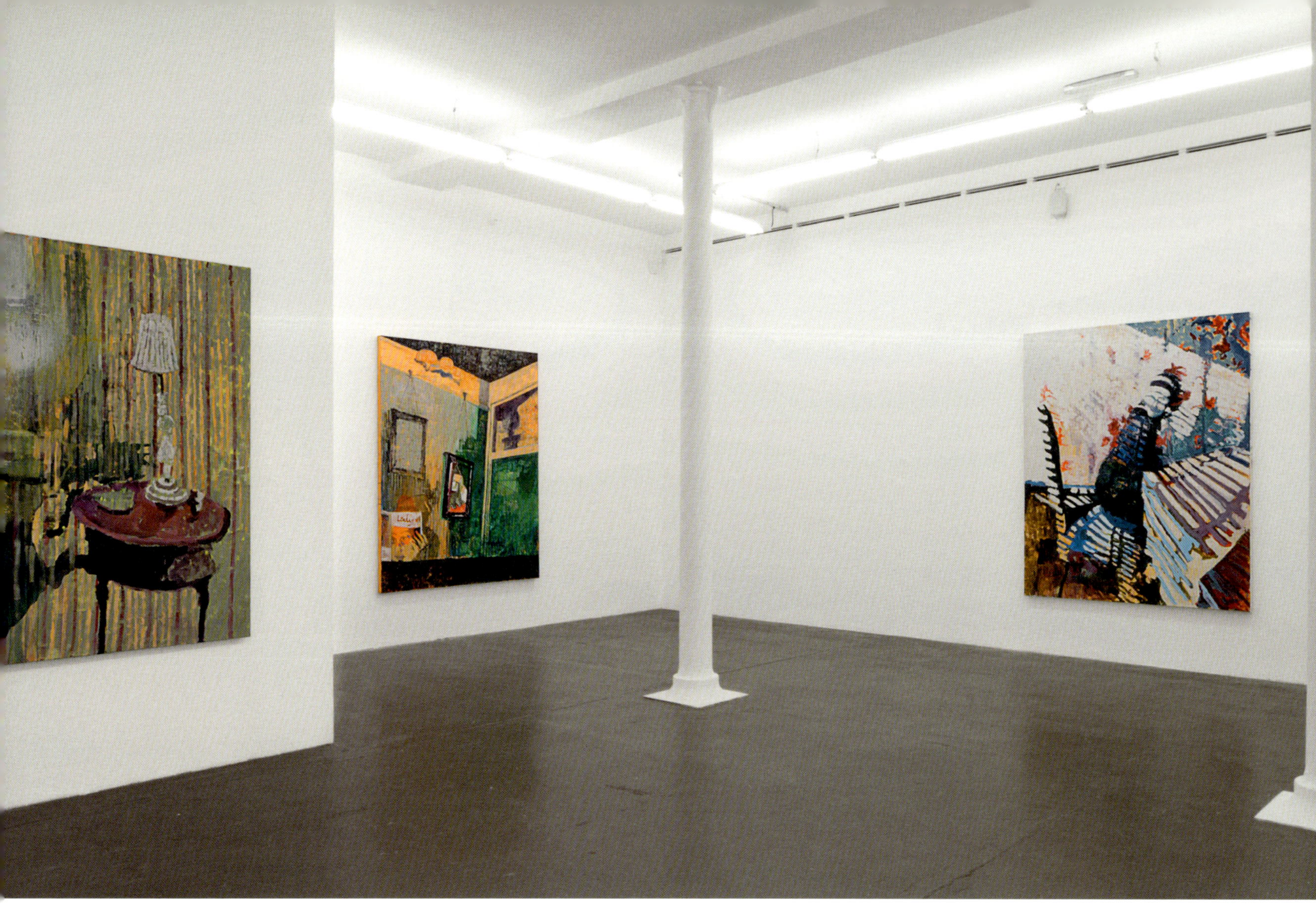

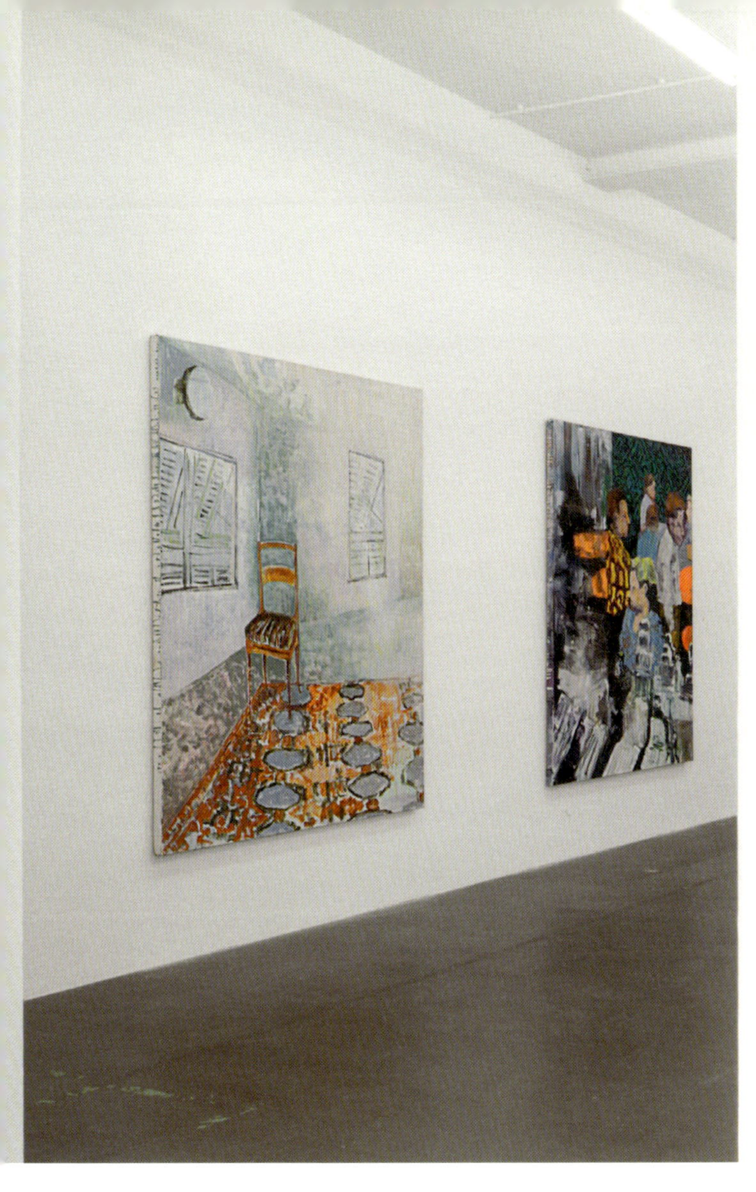
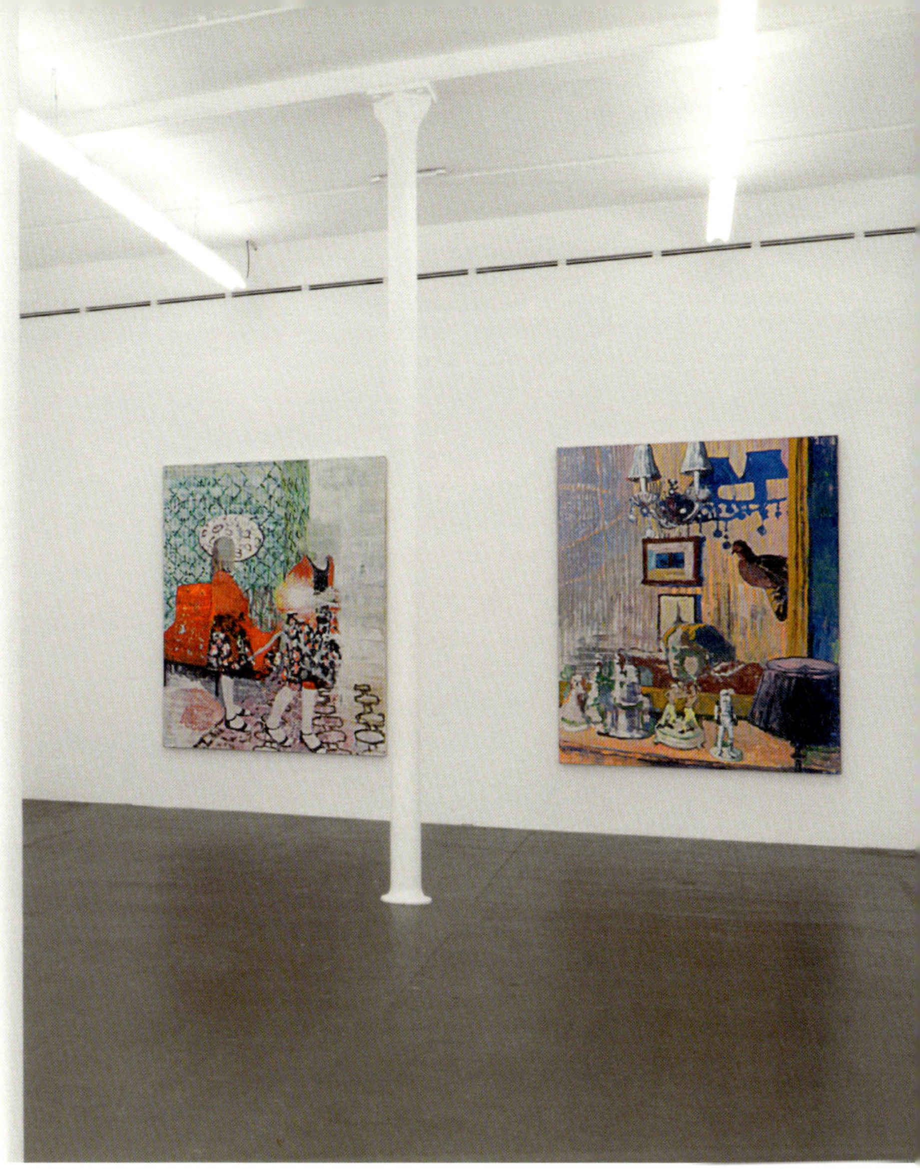

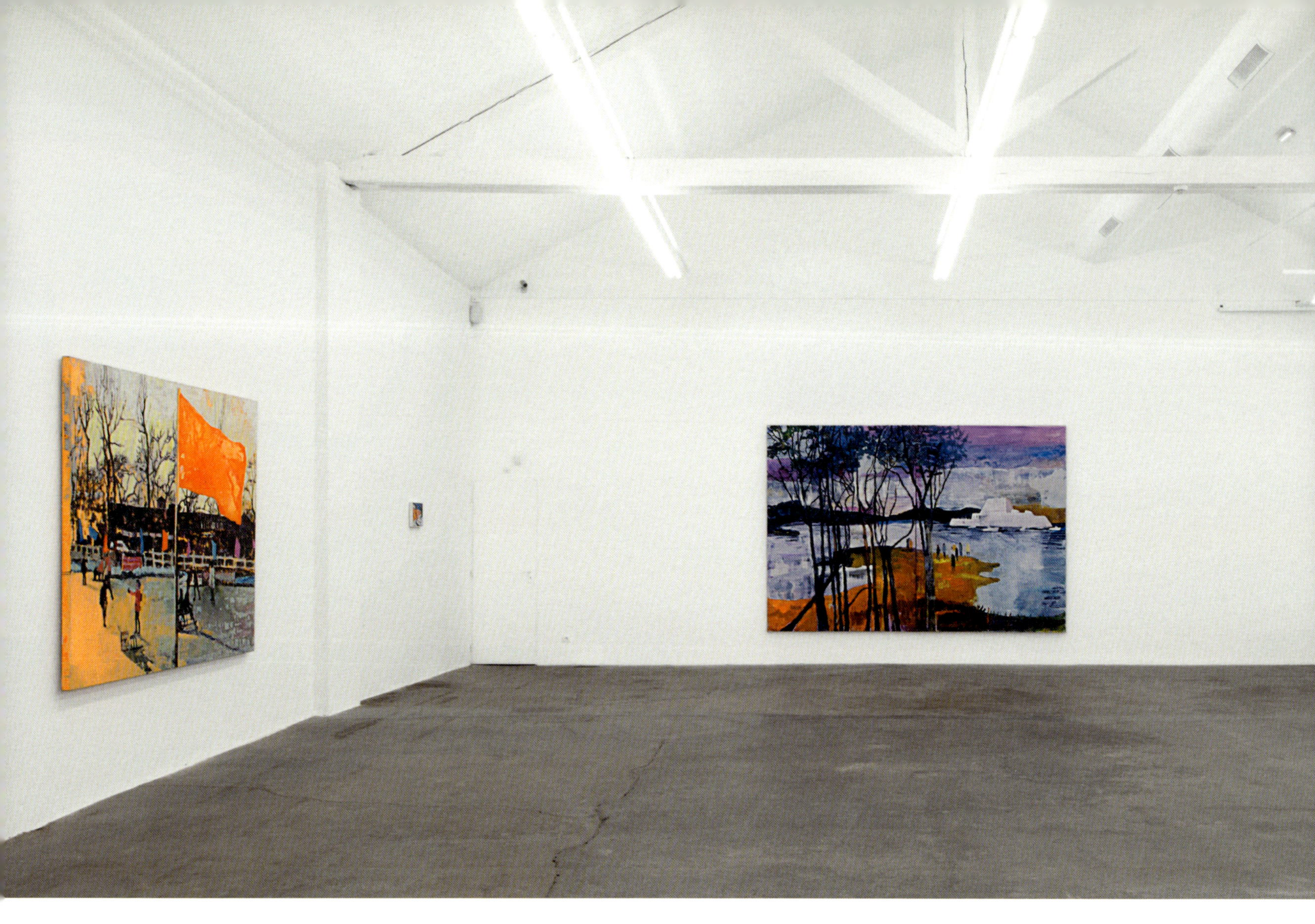

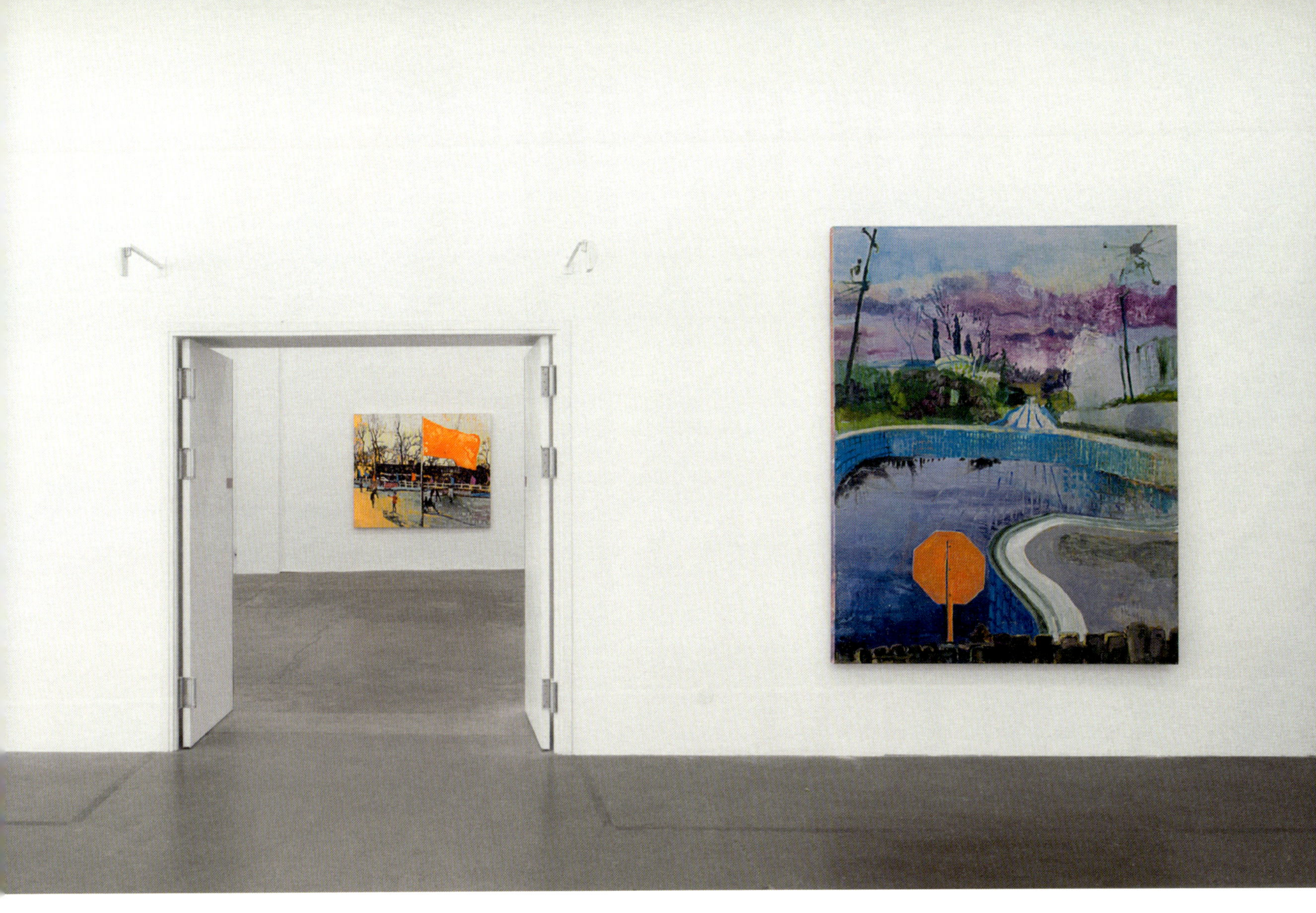

A
*The Dresser
(Ancestral Inheritance)*
1998
255 × 250 cm
oil on canvas |
Öl auf Leinwand |
huile sur toile

B
*Acid Rain
(Homeland Security)*
2003
180 × 180 cm
oil on canvas |
Öl auf Leinwand |
huile sur toile

C
*Smart Bombs
(Homeland Security)*
2003
178 × 182 cm
oil on canvas |
Öl auf Leinwand |
huile sur toile
private collection |
private Kunst-
sammlung |
collection privée

D
*Kriechstorm
(Silent Inhabitants)*
2006
170 × 180 cm
acrylic on canvas |
Acryl auf Lein-
wand | acrylique
sur toile VP
Bank Kunst-
sammlung (FL)

E
*Pulse Cluster Cobs
(Silent Inhabitants)*
2006
170 × 180 cm
acrylic on canvas |
Acryl auf Lein-
wand | acrylique
sur toile

F
*Keeping Bad
Company 1 (Bird Wars)*
2008-2009
170 × 180 cm
oil on canvas |
Öl auf Leinwand |
huile sur toile
Kunstsammlung
Crédit Suisse (CH)

G
*Keeping Bad
Company 2 (Bird Wars)*
2008-2009
170 × 180 cm
oil on canvas |
Öl auf Leinwand |
huile sur toile
Kunstsammlung
Crédit Suisse (CH)

H
Highway Gamblers
2008-2009
190 × 210 cm
oil on canvas |
Öl auf Leinwand |
huile sur toile

I
On a Sticky Wicket
2012
170 × 210 cm
oil on canvas |
Öl auf Leinwand |
huile sur toile

J
12 O'Clock High
2012
30 × 24 cm
oil on canvas |
Öl auf Leinwand |
huile sur toile

K
*Crossing Stands
(Arc Light)*
2001
180 × 198 cm
oil on canvas |
Öl auf Leinwand |
huile sur toile
private collection |
private Kunst-
sammlung | collec-
tion privée

L
*When Push
Comes to Shove*
2012
190 × 210 cm
oil on canvas |
Öl auf Leinwand |
huile sur toile

M
*Stuffed Cartoon
Creature
(Dashboard Talisman)*
2005
180 × 180 cm
acrylic on canvas |
Acryl auf Lein-
wand | acrylique
sur toile private
collection | private
Kunstsammlung |
collection privée

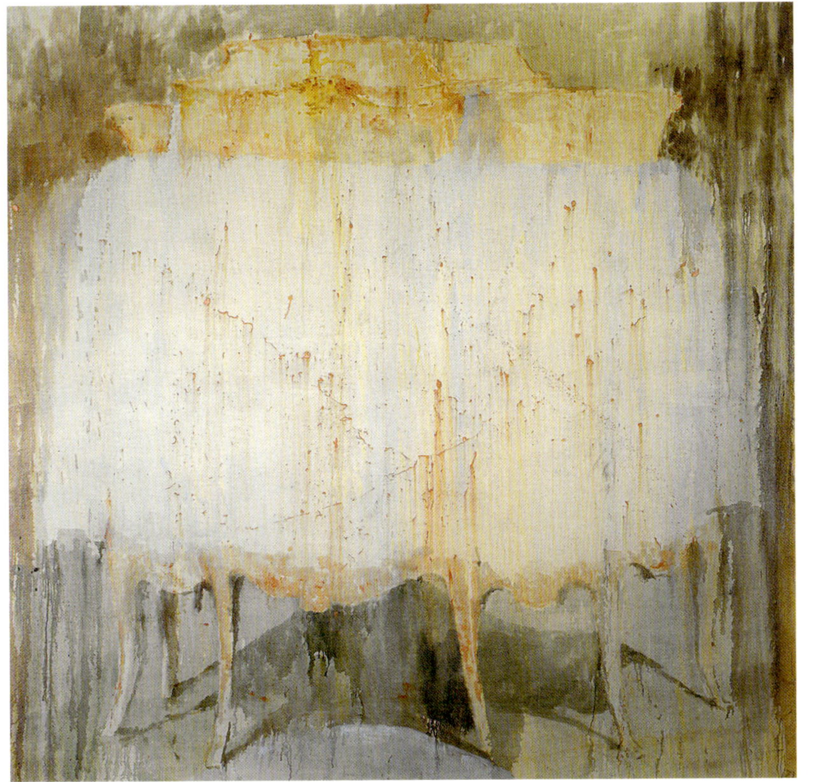

A

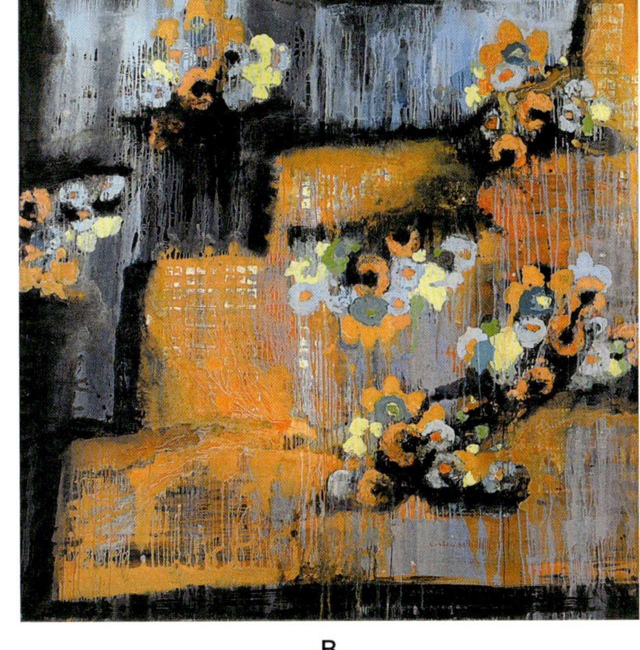

B

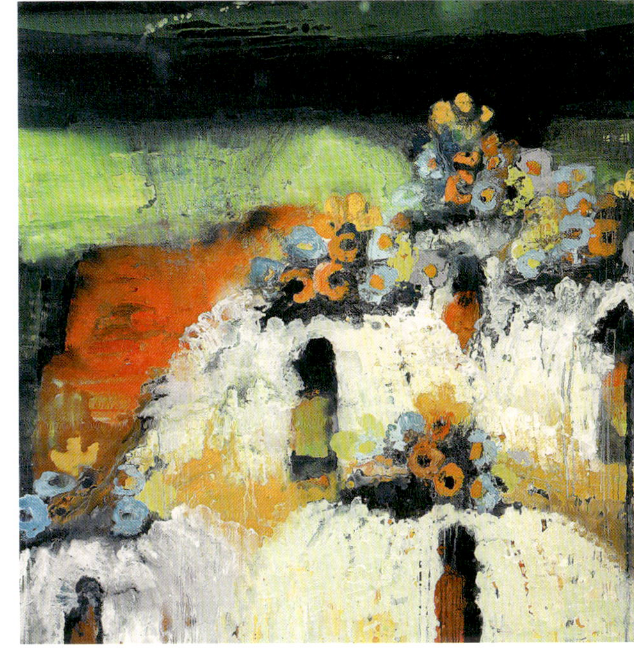

C

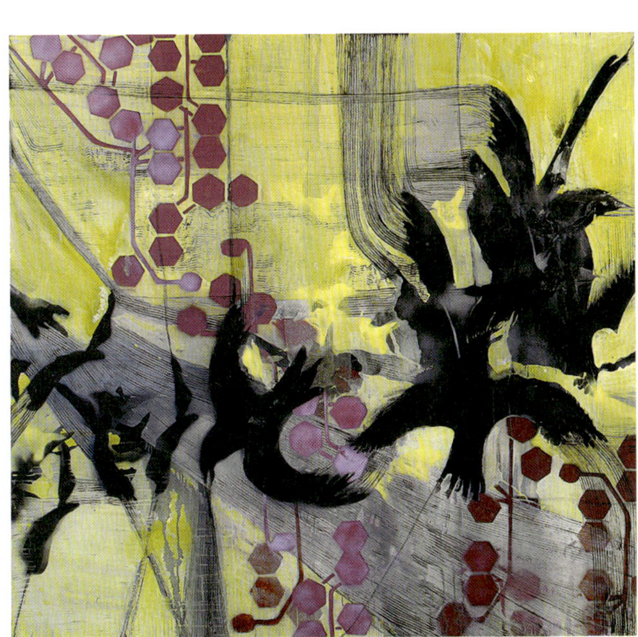

D

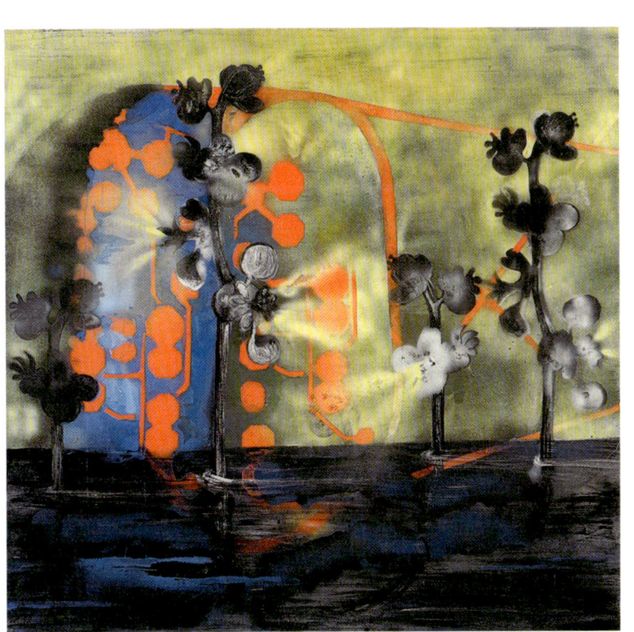

E

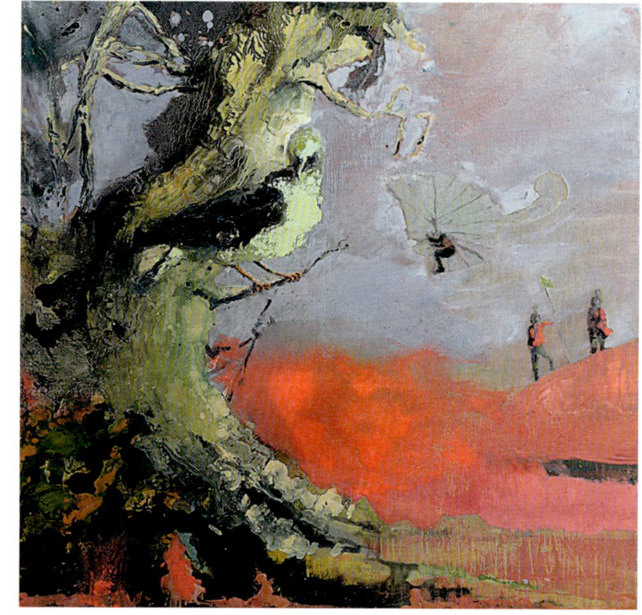

F

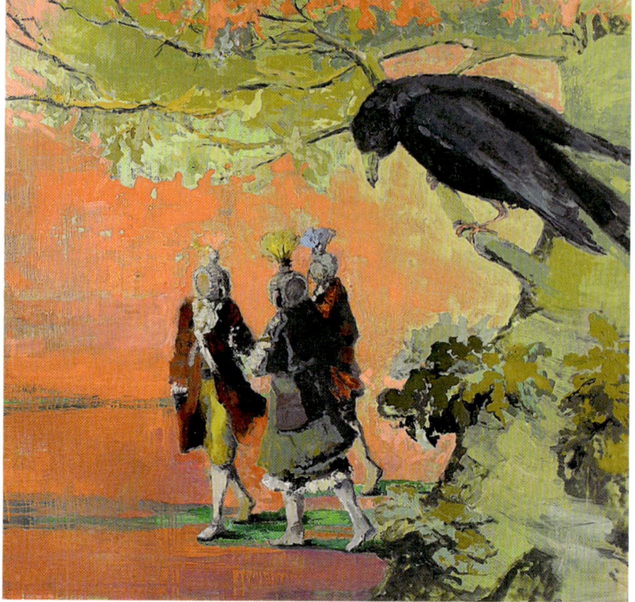

G

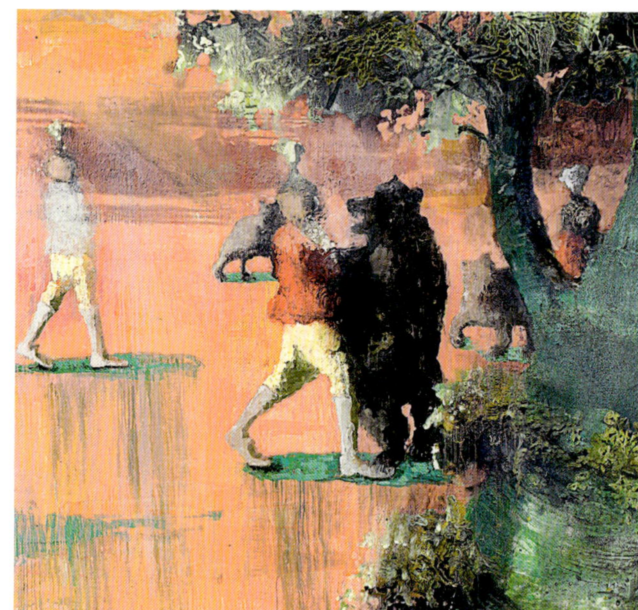

H

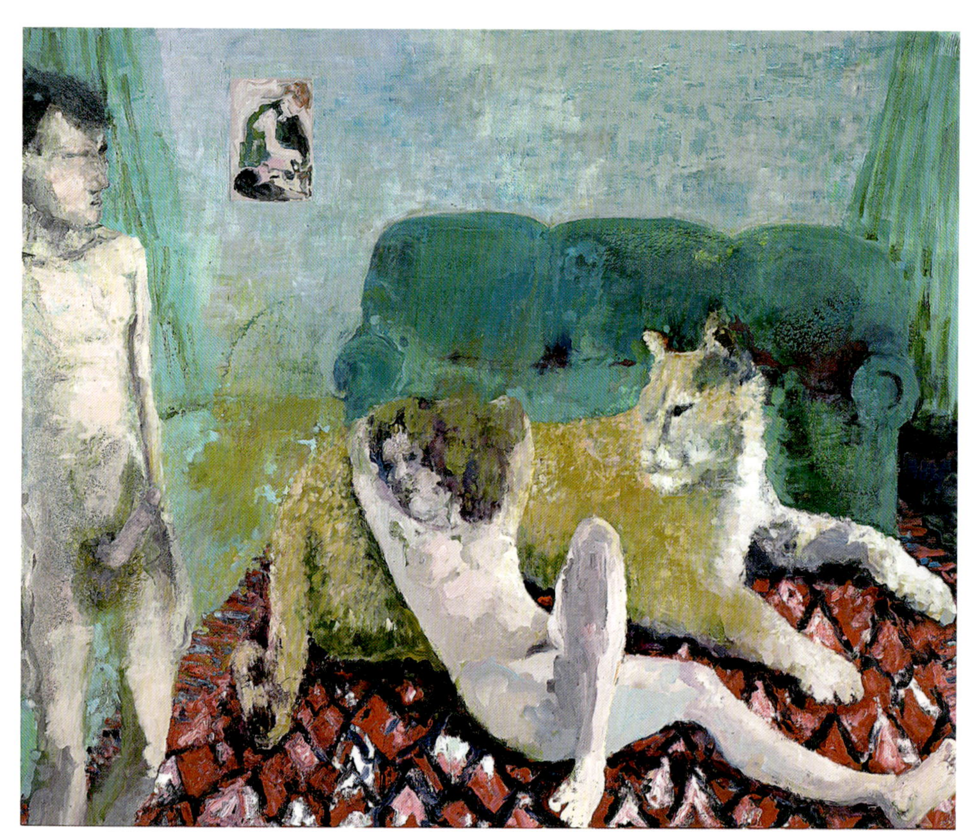

I

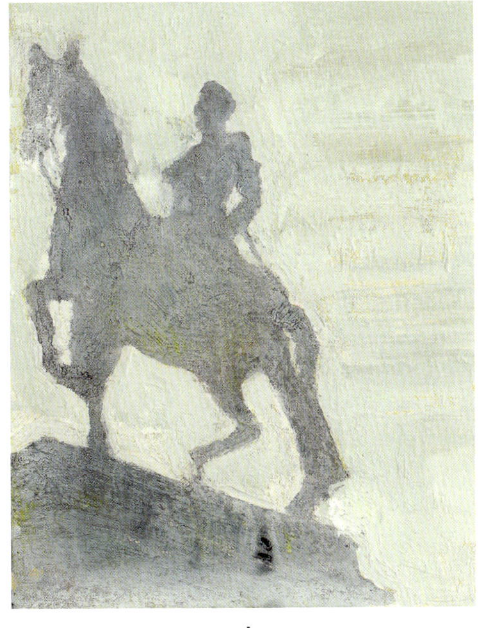

J

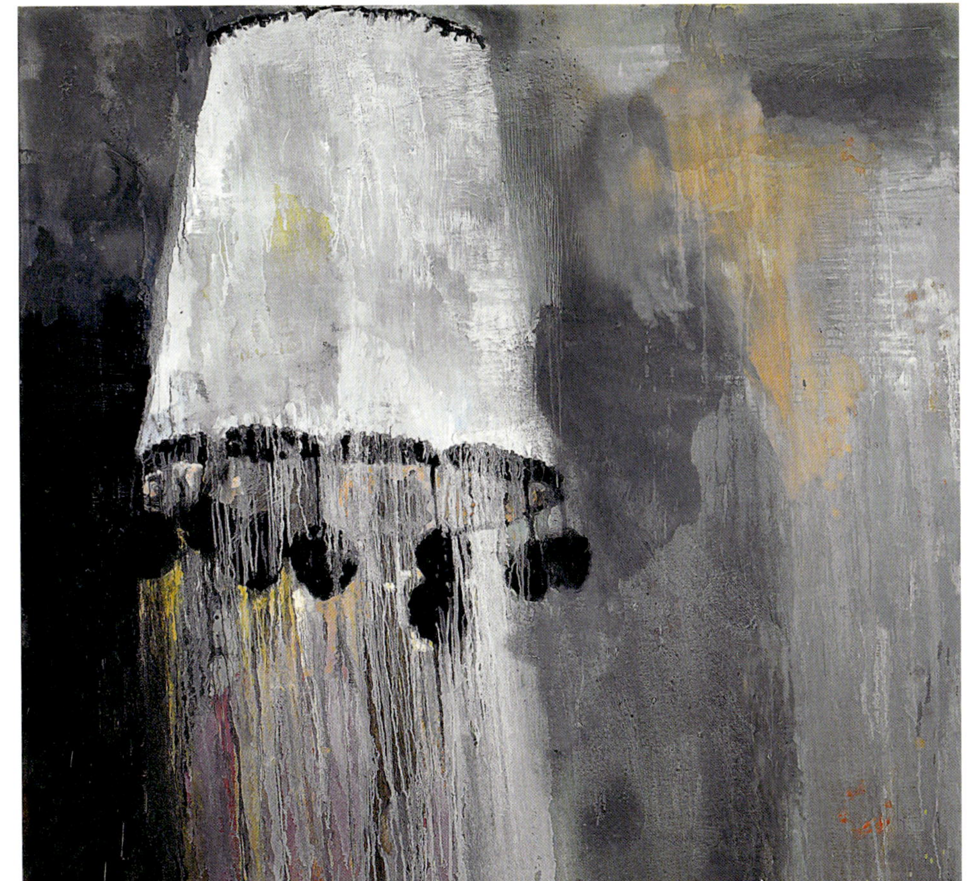

K

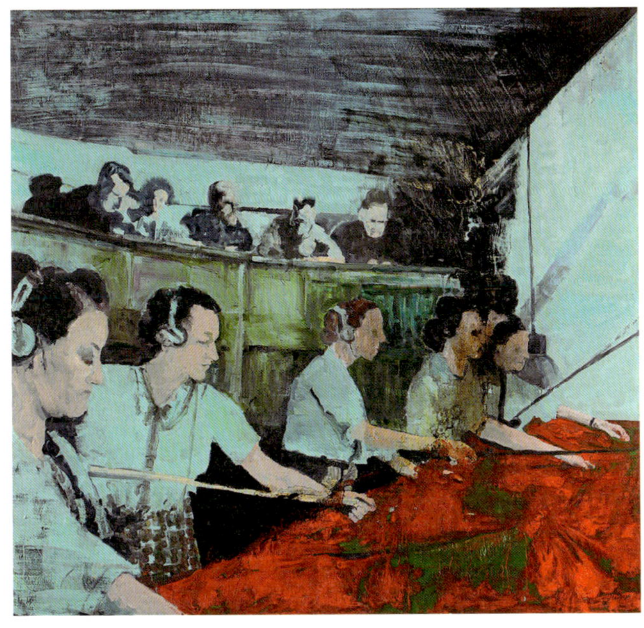

L

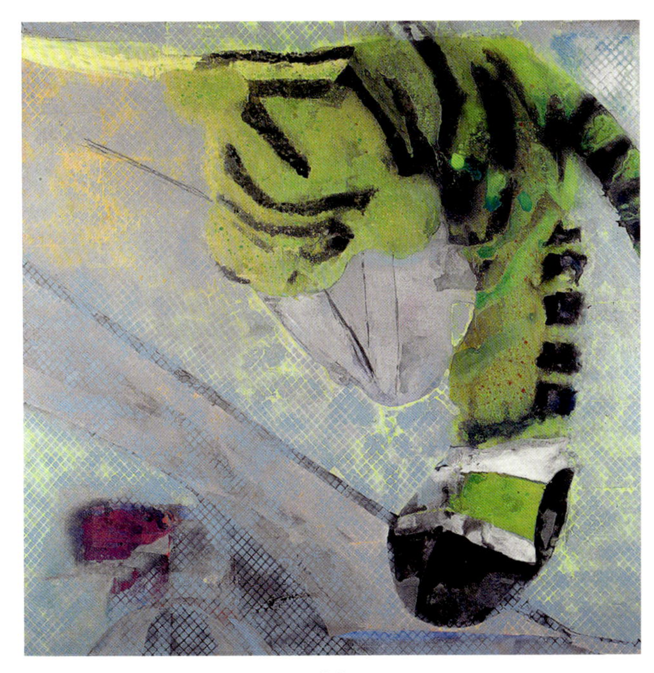

M

Colophon | Impressum | Mentions légales

This publication appears on the occasion of the exhibitions *Rachel Lumsden* at Fondation Fernet-Branca, Saint-Louis, France (19 March – 14 May 2017), the Art Centre Pasquart Biel, Switzerland (2 July to 3 September 2017) and Kunst(Zeug)Haus Rapperswil-Jona, Switzerland (November 2018 – February 2019) | Diese Publikation erscheint anlässlich der Ausstellungen *Rachel Lumsden* an der Fondation Fernet-Branca, Saint-Louis, Frankreich (19. März – 21. Mai 2017), im Kunsthaus Pasquart Biel, Schweiz (2. Juli – 3. September 2017) und am Kunst(Zeug)Haus Rapperswil-Jona, Schweiz (November 2018 – Februar 2019) | Cette publication paraît à l'occasion des expositions *Rachel Lumsden* à la Fondation Fernet-Branca, Saint-Louis, France (19 mars – 21 mai 2017), au Centre d'art Pasquart Bienne, Suisse (2 juillet – 3 septembre 2017) et au Kunst(Zeug) Haus Rapperswil-Jona, Suisse (novembre 2018 – février 2019)

Exhibition | Ausstellung | Exposition

Fondation Fernet-Branca
    2, rue du Ballon
    68300 Saint-Louis/Alsace
t   + 33 3 89 69 10 77
w   www.fondationfernet-branca.fr
m   info@fondationfernet-branca.org
Curator | Kurator | Curateur
    Pierre-Jean Sugier, Director | Direktor |
    Directeur Fondation Fernet-Branca
President of the | Präsident der | Président de la Fondation Fernet-Branca
    Jean Ueberschlag
Deputy President of the | Stellvertretender Präsident der | Président adjoint de la Fondation Fernet-Branca
    Jean-Marie Wintzenrieth
Officer for finance and patronage | Beauftragter für Finanzen und Mäzenatentum | Chargé des finances et du mécénat
    Patrick Sirdey

Kunsthaus Centre d'art Pasquart
    Seevorstadt 71 Faubourg du Lac
    CH-2502 Biel | Bienne
t   + 41 32 322 55 86
w   www.pasquart.ch
m   info@pasquart.ch
Curator | Kuratorin | Curatrice
    Felicity Lunn, Director | Direktorin |
    Directrice Kunsthaus Centre d'art Pasquart
Assistant Curator | Assistenzkurator | Commissaire d'exposition adjoint
    Damian Jurt
Technician | Technik | Technique
    Paolo Merico

Kunst(Zeug)Haus Rapperswil-Jona
    Schönbodenstrasse
    1 8640 Rapperswil-Jona
t   + 41 55 220 20 80
w   www.kunstzeughaus.ch
m   info@kunstzeughaus.ch
Curator | Kurator | Curateur
    Peter Stohler, Director | Direktor | Directeur,
    Kunst(Zeug)Haus Rapperswil-Jona

Publication | Publikation | Publication

Editor | Herausgeber | Éditeur
    Kunsthaus Centre
    d'art Pasquart Biel | Bienne
Texts | Texte | Textes
    Felicity Lunn, Charlotte Mullins,
    André Rogger
Translations | Übersetzungen | Traductions
    Jeremy Gaines (English)
    Petra Gaines, Gabriele Lechner (Deutsch)
    Françoise Senger (Français)
Proof-reading | Lektorat | Relecture
    Michaela Alex-Eibensteiner (Deutsch)
    Andrea Stettler (English/Français)
Design | Gestaltung | Conception graphique
    Thomas Bizzarri & Alain Rodriguez
    www.bizzarri-rodriguez.com
Typography | Schrift | Police de caractère
    Gerstner Programm
Lithography | Lithografie | Lithographie
    Point 11
Printing | Druck | Impression
    Escourbiac, France
Edition | Auflage | Exemplaires
    1450
Photographs | Aufnahmen | Photographies
    Stefan Rohner
    www.stefanrohner.ch
Installation views Fondation Fernet-Branca | Ausstellungsansichten Fondation Fernet-Branca | Vues d'installation Fondation Fernet-Branca
    Barbara Bühler
    www.barbarabuehler.com
Photo credits | Fotonachweis | Crédits photographiques
    Rachel Lumsden owns all reproduction rights. | Die Rechte für die Abbildungen sämtlicher Fotografien sind bei Rachel Lumsden. | Tous les droits de reproduction des photographies appartiennent à Rachel Lumsden.

Colophon | Impressum | Mentions légales

The Fondation Fernet-Branca is supported by the town of Saint-Louis, the Direction Régionale des Affaires Culturelles d'Alsace and the Région Grand Est. | Die Fondation Fernet-Branca wird unterstützt von der Stadt Saint-Louis, der Direction Régionale des Affaires Culturelles d'Alsace und der Région Grand Est. | La Fondation Fernet-Branca est soutenue par la ville de Saint-Louis, la Direction Régionale des Affaires Culturelles d'Alsace et la Région Grand Est.

The Art Centre Pasquart is supported by the City of Biel, the Canton of Bern and the Municipalities of the Region Seeland-Biel/Bienne-Jura bernois. | Das Kunsthaus Pasquart wird unterstützt von der Stadt Biel, dem Kanton Bern und den Gemeinden der Region Seeland-Biel / Bienne-Jura bernois. | Le Centre d'art Pasquart est soutenu par la ville de Bienne, le canton de Berne et les communes de la région Seeland-Biel/Bienne-Jura bernois.

The Kunst(Zeug)Haus is supported by the town of Rapperswil-Jona,Rapperswil-Jona, the Kulturförderung Kanton St. Gallen and the Avina Foundation. The Kunst(Zeug)Haus receives further regular support from the following companies: VP Bank (Schweiz) AG, LGT Bank (Schweiz) AG, Elektrizitätswerk Rapperswil-Jona, Raiffeisenbank Rapperswil-Jona and Geberit. | Das Kunst(Zeug)Haus wird unterstützt von der Stadt Rapperswil-Jona und der Kulturförderung Kantons St. Gallen sowie von der Avina Stiftung. Weitere regelmässige Unterstützung erhält des Kunst(Zeug)Haus durch folgende Firmen: VP Bank (Schweiz) AG, LGT Bank (Schweiz) AG, Elektrizitätswerk Rapperswil-Jona, Raiffeisenbank Rapperswil-Jona sowie Geberit. | Le Kunst(Zeug)Haus est soutenu par la ville de Rapperswil-Jona et le Kulturförderung Kanton St. Gallen, ainsi que par l'Avina Stiftung. Le Kunst(Zeug)Haus bénéficie également du soutien régulier des entreprises suivantes : VP Bank (Schweiz) AG, LGT Bank (Schweiz) AG, Elektrizitätswerk Rapperswil-Jona, Raiffeisenbank Rapperswil-Jona sowie Geberit.

Bibliographic information published by Die Deutsche Bibliothek

Die Deutsche Bibliothek lists this publication in the Deutsche Nationalbibliografie ; detailled bibliographic data is available in the Internet at http://dnb.ddb.de.

Bibliografische Information Der Deutschen Bibliothek

Die Deutsche Bibliothek verzeichnet diese Publikation in der Deutschen Nationalbibliografie; detaillierte bibliografische Daten sind im Internet über http://dnb.ddb.de abrufbar.

Information bibliographique publiée par Die Deutsche Bibliothek

Die Deutsche Bibliothek répertorie cette publication dans la Deutsche Nationalbibliografie; des données bibliographiques détaillées sont disponibles sur http://dnb.ddb.de.

Acknowledgment | Danksagung | Remerciements

This publication was made possible by the generous support of | Diese Publikation wurde ermöglicht durch die grosszügige Unterstützung von | Cette publication a été rendue possible grâce au soutien généreux de :

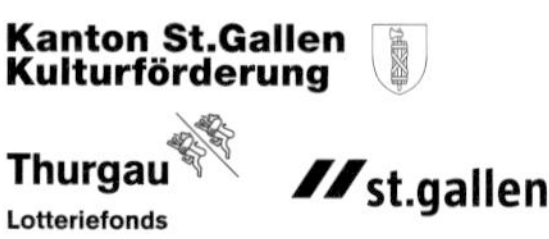

The RHW Stiftung, Vaduz (FL)

The exhibitions at Fondation Fernet-Branca and Kunsthaus Pasquart Biel were made possible by the generous support of | Die Ausstellungen an der Fondation Fernet-Branca und am Kunsthaus Pasquart Biel wurden ermöglicht durch die grosszügige Unterstützung von | Les expositions à la Fondation Fernet-Branca et au Centre d'art Pasquart Bienne ont été rendues possible grâce au soutien généreux de :

prohelvetia

The exhibition at Kunsthaus Pasquart Biel was made possible by the generous support of | Die Ausstellung am Kunsthaus Pasquart Biel wurde ermöglicht durch die grosszügige Unterstützung von | L'exposition au Centre d'art Pasquart Bienne a été rendue possible grâce au soutien généreux de :

STANLEY THOMAS JOHNSON FOUNDATION

With the generous support from the legacy of Mme M. Mottier-Lovis | Mit freundlicher Unterstützung des Legats von Mme M. Mottier-Lovis | Avec le soutien aimable du legs de Mme M. Mottier-Lovis

With special thanks to all those who have worked towards this publication | Ein grosses Dank gilt auch allen Personen, die wesentlich zu diesem Buch beigetragen haben | Un grand merci à tous ceux qui ont contribué à cette publication : Bernard Jordan, Galerie Bernard Jordan (www.galeriebernardjordan.com), Stefan Sprenger, Thomas Bizzarri & Alain Rodriguez, Felicity Lunn, Charlotte Mullins, André Rogger

ISBN: 978-3-903153-27-1
Publisher | Verlag | Éditeur
    Verlag für moderne Kunst
    www.vfmk.org
All rights reserved | Alle Rechte vorbehalten | Tous droits réservés
    © 2017 Rachel Lumsden, the authors | die Autorinnen | les auteurs, Kunsthaus Centre d'art Pasquart Biel | Bienne, Verlag für moderne Kunst
Distribution | Vertrieb | Distribution
    D, A, Europa | Europe:
    LKG, www.lkg-va.de
    CH: AVA, www.ava.ch
    UK: Cornerhouse Publications,
    www.cornerhousepublications.org
    USA: D.A.P., www.artbook.com